P9-DYZ-442

THE
STRUCTURE
OF
MIND

THE
UNIVERSITY
OF
WISCONSIN
PRESS

———

MADISON
AND
MILWAUKEE
1965

THE
STRUCTURE
OF
MIND

REINHARDT GROSSMANN

TO GUSTAV BERGMANN

PUBLISHED BY
THE UNIVERSITY OF WISCONSIN PRESS
MADISON AND MILWAUKEE
P.O. BOX 1379, MADISON, WISCONSIN 53701

COPYRIGHT © 1965 BY THE
REGENTS OF THE UNIVERSITY OF WISCONSIN

PRINTED IN THE UNITED STATES OF AMERICA
BY KINGSPORT PRESS, INC., KINGSPORT, TENNESSEE

LIBRARY OF CONGRESS CATALOG CARD NUMBER 65–13505

PREFACE

THIS BOOK avoids a number of traditional problems from the philosophy of mind. Emotions and volitions are hardly mentioned; and very little is said about imagination and memory. I am concerned in the main with only one topic: the realism-idealism controversy. This concern explains why I limited the discussion to thought and perception. It also explains why at times I had to go rather deeply into the problems of general ontology; for if my analysis is correct, the realism-idealism controversy arises from certain disagreements in general ontology.

Nor does this book deal with a number of currently fashionable topics. I say nothing on whether or not mental states are after all nothing but brain states. I do not discuss this point because I am convinced that there is nothing to be discussed. The correct answer to the question seems to me so obvious that I simply took it for granted in writing this book. The problem of our knowledge of other minds is of quite a different sort: it is, philosophically speaking, interesting and difficult. Since I do not discuss the problem, I may mention here that I consider all solutions in terms of so-called criteria for the application of expressions unsatisfactory. The one fashionable topic which I do discuss, though not under a separate heading and not in the movement's jargon, is the so-called private language argument. I am sure that the

90619

attentive reader can construct my position on this matter from the first chapter.

I would like to thank the Graduate School of Indiana University for a Faculty Summer Fellowship which helped me to complete this book. I would also like to thank Messrs. H. Veatch and R. Paul: they read part of the manuscript and made many helpful suggestions.

R. Grossmann

Bloomington, Indiana
June 1964

CONTENTS

THE
STRUCTURE
OF
MIND

INTROSPECTION

1

MENTAL ACTS are given in experience. But they are "given" in a special way. Surely, when Mr. Smith looks at a tree in front of him, he must stand where he can see it. Furthermore, except in cases of hallucination and illusion, the tree must be present when Mr. Smith sees it. Most importantly, when he sees the tree, certain causal relations obtain between his body or nervous system on the one hand, and the tree on the other. It matters little for my point what common sense or science may or may not have to say about the nature of these causal relations. Rather, what matters is that the so-called mental act of seeing must not be identified with any one or all of the previously mentioned relations. The situation must be approached from an entirely different point of view, if we wish to understand the mental act of seeing a tree. For mental acts are "given" from within. They are in some sense hidden from outside observers. Therefore they cannot possibly be observed in the very same manner in which one can observe spatial, temporal, and causal relations among perceptual objects. All this is part and parcel of saying that such acts are mental rather than perceptual things.[1]

This notion of mental acts has sometimes been criticized on the

[1] Eventually, I shall distinguish among mental, phenomenal, perceptual, and physical things.

ground that the so-called thesis of "privileged access" is but a myth. Of course, these critics do not deny that one can see a tree, imagine a mermaid, or think of Paris. But they do assert that there is nothing inherently private about one's seeing, imagining, or thinking. And since they are also inclined to agree that mental things, if there were any, would be private, they come in the end to the remarkable conclusion that there are no mental things.

Most philosophical views have their roots in common-sense beliefs. The view that there is no "privileged access" to mental acts rests on the belief that in some cases, at least, we encounter no difficulties in trying to find out whether or not another person sees a tree, imagines a mermaid, or thinks of Paris. And not only can we know in most cases whatever there is to know about another person's state of mind, we can even know it for certain. Hence there seems to be no invincible shield that prevents us forever and in principle from knowing another person's frame of mind.

On the other hand, the view that mental acts are only given in one's own experience rests on two equally common-sense beliefs —namely, that one is at times aware of one's own mental acts, and that one could not possibly be aware of the acts of other people in precisely the same manner.[2] Hence one concludes that there is a perfectly sound reason for saying that acts are private rather than public, mental rather than perceptual things.[3]

These then are the two common-sense beliefs which give rise to a philosophical argument: on the one hand the belief that one can *know* the conscious states of another person, on the other hand the belief that one can only *experience* one's own. To reject either belief, I think, invites philosophical confusion. In order to accommodate both, we must distinguish between two kinds of observation. We hold, first, that one can observe perceptual objects, their properties, and relations. In this sense of the term, one can observe the behavior, verbal or nonverbal, of other people. We hold, second, that one can observe mental acts. In this sense,

[2] Oswald Kuelpe once called this a "Binsenwahrheit."

[3] To say that mental acts, sense-impressions, sensations, feelings, and the like are "private" means, therefore, merely that they cannot be experienced by several people. It does not mean that their *properties* cannot be experienced by several people. Nor does it mean that one cannot communicate about them.

however, one can only observe what is part of one's own experience. Now we can agree that we sometimes know by observation—namely, observation of the first kind—what goes on in another person's mind. We insist, though, that one can observe one's own conscious states in an entirely different way.[4]

But even though it will be readily agreed that one can observe perceptual objects, including other people, there remains the important question as to whether or not one can in fact observe one's conscious states in a manner different from observing perceptual objects. Indeed, this seems to be one of the main issues between those who defend and those who deny the existence of mental acts. I propose to discuss this issue in the following sections.

INSPECTION OF PHENOMENAL OBJECTS

The first thing to notice is that to speak of *observation* of conscious states or conscious processes is to invite an obvious objection. For it may be said that to observe means to attend to a public object: that is, to something that could be simultaneously observed by several people. Be that as it may, it seems at any rate advisable to introduce two different terms for two things so different as observation of perceptual objects and observation of conscious states and processes. We shall therefore distinguish between *observation* and *introspection.* But introspection in turn covers a wide range of different ideas. We must therefore further distinguish between *inspection, introspection,* and *systematic introspection.* In order to explain these distinctions, let us begin with three examples of the inspection of phenomenal things.

(1) Someone is shown a certain perceptual object. He recognizes the object, he sees that it is round and that it is of a certain shade of green. Suppose now that he is instructed to describe not the perceptual object, its place and properties, but rather his visual sense-impressions in this situation. What he has been asked to do is, roughly, to forget that there is a certain perceptual object before him and to concentrate instead on his sense-impressions. If

[4] For some interesting historical remarks on this classical distinction see the excellent article by M. Chastaing, "Consciousness and Evidence," *Mind,* 65(1956):346–58.

he understands these instructions and if he has been trained to follow them, he will be inspecting certain visual sense-impressions.[5]

(2) Assume that someone imagines a mermaid and that there occurs on that occasion the mental image of a mermaid. Next, he is asked to concentrate on that image and to describe certain features of it—say, whether or not it is in color. In order to give such a description, he now inspects his mental image of a mermaid.

(3) Suppose, finally, that someone is writing an important letter. While he is writing, he feels a pain in his abdomen. After the letter is finished, having gotten worried about the persistent pain, he consults a doctor. The doctor asks him to localize the pain and to describe it. He may now realize that it is at times "stabbing," at other times "dull and throbbing." His describing the pain in detail presupposes that he inspects it carefully rather than feels it dimly while engaged in his daily chores.

These three examples allow us to make some general statements about the nature of inspection.

First. In each of the three examples, someone's *attention* was concentrated on the thing or things inspected. In this regard, there seems to be little difference between inspection on the one hand and observation on the other. For observation, too, presupposes that one attends carefully to some object or its features.

Second. The three examples were so formulated that inspection was in each case preceded by a *conscious intention* to inspect. The person was in each case, as psychologists put it, *set to inspect.*[6] It must be noted, however, that inspection can also occur without such a set.[7] A person may, for example, pay closer attention to a pain when it suddenly gets worse, and he may do so without any

---

[5] This notion of inspection corresponds roughly to the one used by C. D. Broad in *The Mind and Its Place in Nature* (New York, 1925), pp. 290–91.

[6] Concerning such intentions, compare G. E. Mueller, "Zur Analyse der Gedaechtnistaetigkeit und des Vorstellungsverlaufs," Part 1, *Zeitschrift fuer Psychologie und Physiologie der Sinnesorgane*, suppl. vol. 5(1911):64 and 71. On the notion of set see J. J. Gibson, "A Critical Review of the Concept of Set in Contemporary Experimental Psychology," *Psychological Bulletin*, 38(1941):781–817.

[7] Compare our discussion below on pages 10–11.

previous intention of inspecting his pain more closely. Here again we find a close similarity between inspection and observation. Usually, observation is preceded by a conscious intention to pay close attention to something that will happen or occur. But it can also take place without such an intention, as when one suddenly examines more closely something which one has seen all along.

Third. The intention to inspect occurred in our three examples as a consequence of a specific *task*.[8] Such a task usually has three effects: (a) it brings about a shift in mental set; (b) it also brings about a shift in conscious states: a shift, say, from perceiving a perceptual object to inspecting sense-impressions; and (c) it determines what particular things or features of things are to be inspected and described.

Fourth. In describing the first example, I added the condition that the person had to be trained to follow the instructions. This was necessitated by the fact that some inspective conscious states are notoriously hard to induce and even harder to maintain. In ordinary life, we perceive, imagine, and feel things rather than scrutinize sense-impressions, images, and pains. And even if inspection occurs in ordinary life, it lasts only a relatively short time. What we find most often, even in controlled experimental situations, is a rapid shift back and forth between inspective and noninspective conscious states.

Fifth. What was inspected in the three examples was not, say, one's *seeing* a perceptual object or *imagining* a mermaid, but rather such things as sense-impressions, images, and feelings. The objects of inspection were what I shall call *phenomenal objects* rather than mental acts or perceptual objects.[9]

The three examples, I think, leave no doubt that one can in fact inspect phenomenal objects. But does this fact alone suffice to

[8] Concerning the importance of tasks, compare O. Kuelpe, *Grundriss der Psychologie* (Berlin, 1893); H. J. Watt, "Experimentelle Beitraege zu einer Theorie des Denkens," *Archiv fuer die gesamte Psychologie*, 4(1905):289–436; N. Ach, *Ueber die Willenstaetigkeit und das Denken* (Goettingen, 1905); and O. Selz's article in *Archiv fuer die gesamte Psychologie*, 27(1913):367–80.

[9] For a more systematic distinction between phenomenal objects or things and mental acts see below pp. 27–28.

demonstrate the possibility of introspecting conscious states and processes? A brief reflection seems to show that it does not. I first perceive a certain perceptual object, its shape, its color, etc. Then there occurs a shift from perceiving to sensing.[10] After the shift, I inspect certain sense-impressions. But to perceive a perceptual object is one thing; to scrutinize sense-impressions is something else again. This seems to show that one is not introspecting one's conscious state of perceiving a perceptual object when one inspects sense-impressions. It seems to prove that one is not even introspecting one's conscious state of perceiving when one inspects certain sense-impressions and, in addition, all kinds of kinesthetic sensations, images, feelings, and the like. Yet, according to the classical notion of introspection, one is doing just that. According to this notion, a conscious state is said to be *analyzed* into its introspective *elements,* if all the phenomenal things are listed which can be discerned after a shift from the original conscious state to one of inspection. A conscious process is said to be *analyzed,* if all the phenomenal objects are listed which can be made out during inspective intervals. In both cases, the original conscious state or process is said to *consist* of the phenomenal things listed.

We see that upon the classical notion of introspection, introspection of conscious states and processes amounts to nothing more than the inspection of phenomenal objects. To claim, as so many introspective psychologists did, that one can introspect conscious states and processes, is to claim merely that it is possible to inspect phenomenal objects after a shift from a certain conscious state or process to one of inspecting phenomenal things. There can surely be no objection to this possibility. Introspection in this sense is possible. But can there also be systematic introspection of conscious processes? Consider the following three examples.

(1) Assume that the subject of a psychological experiment has been trained to search for a certain associated word whenever he

[10] The distinction between perceptual acts and acts of sensing is explained below, pp. 28–38. 'Perception' is used generically; its species are seeing, hearing, feeling, smelling, and tasting.

is presented with a particular stimulus word. Perceiving the stimulus word, searching for the appropriate associated word, and uttering the latter, constitute what might be called the *natural* conscious process in this situation.[11] Subsequently, the subject is instructed to describe what goes on in his mind while he is searching for the associated word. He is to report, in other words, on his phenomenal things. If these instructions are properly understood and if the subject has been trained to follow them, he will be set to inspect upon the occurrence of the next stimulus word. At first, though, he will search for the associated word. But then, as the effect of his instructions, a shift in conscious states will occur and he will inspect phenomenal things. After a brief moment, the subject will again turn to the task of finding the associated word. And so on. This method will now have some or all of the following effects on the natural conscious process of finding the associated word: (a) certain natural conscious states either will not occur at all, or (b) they will occur later than usual, or (c) they will not be noticed as clearly as usual.[12] This shows how a set to inspect can interfere with a natural conscious process; and since systematic introspection cannot be carried out without such a set, it shows how difficult it may be to introspect natural conscious states systematically.

(2) Suppose, for the second example, that the subject frequently catches himself having particular thoughts when presented with a certain stimulus word. He is therefore instructed to watch carefully on later trials to see whether or not this particular stimulus word evokes those thoughts. The next time the word occurs, he finds himself in a very peculiar situation. It seems entirely up to him whether or not to think those thoughts. And irrespective of what he finally does, he cannot help viewing whatever he does as being somehow influenced by a factor which does not normally belong to the situation.

---

[11] A natural conscious state can be described as one that is neither brought about nor influenced by a set to introspect. Compare G. E. Mueller, "Zur Analyse der Gedaechtnistaetigkeit und des Vorstellungsverlaufs," p. 73.

[12] *Ibid.*, pp. 73–74.

(3) Or assume that the subject under study considers several ways of going about searching for the associated word, before he is presented with the first stimulus word, but after he has been instructed to introspect. When the first stimulus word appears, he follows one of the contemplated methods, even though he would not have chosen this particular one without the instruction to introspect. As a result of the set to introspect, there occurs a conscious process different from the one which would normally occur.

It is clear from the first example that a set to introspect interrupts a natural conscious process by introspective intervals. It is also obvious from the other two examples that it may lead to conscious processes different from those which would occur without a set. This kind of influence led many psychologists to the conclusion that the *systematic* introspection of natural conscious processes is all but impossible.[13] However, introspection, or something very similar to introspection, can also occur without such a set. This explains why I distinguished between introspection and systematic introspection. We must now briefly consider introspection which is not induced by a set to inspect.

On some occasions of remembering, we notice suddenly that we have a more or less vivid memory image. In these cases, there occurs a sudden *unintended* shift in conscious states. Such an unintended shift also occurs when we catch ourselves daydreaming or thinking of Paris. A number of psychologists held that a trustworthy description of introspective elements can only be furnished if the subject experiences such a sudden unintended shift without any previous intention to introspect. They argued that only on these occasions can one be sure that the natural conscious process introspected is not influenced or disturbed by a

[13] Compare N. Ach, *Ueber die Willenstaetigkeit und das Denken,* p. 22; A. Messer, "Experimentellpsychologische Untersuchungen ueber das Denken," *Archiv fuer die gesamte Psychologie,* 8(1906):19; G. E. Mueller and F. Schumann, "Experimentelle Beitraege zur Untersuchung des Gedaechtnisses," *Zeitschrift fuer Psychologie,* 45(1889):306; H. Ebbinghaus, *Grundzuege der Psychologie* (Leipzig, 1905), vol. 1, p. 67.

set to inspect.[14] Be that as it may, it is quite true that one can catch oneself daydreaming or thinking of Paris. It is also true that one can catch oneself behaving in certain ways. But just as there has been a tendency to misconstrue the classical view on introspection, so there is a tendency to misunderstand what some psychologists meant when they spoke of introspection in connection with catching oneself in a certain conscious state.

In recent years, Ryle has been most explicit on this point. He holds, if I understand him correctly, that even if catching oneself were a criterion of introspection, seeing and hearing could not be conscious states or conscious processes or mental acts; for no one can catch himself seeing or hearing something. And he holds also that it is most certainly not that kind of criterion to begin with; for "in the same way that I can catch myself daydreaming, I can catch myself scratching." [15]

This last assertion is undoubtedly true: one can catch oneself scratching as well as daydreaming. This shows that it is certainly not always the case that what I catch myself having or doing must be some kind of mental phenomenon. But then, those who spoke of catching oneself in connection with introspection never thought that they were employing that kind of a criterion. They merely used the phrase in order to indicate that there occurs a sudden unintended shift from one conscious state or process to another. In this sense, it applies equally well whether one catches oneself daydreaming or scratching. For even if one catches oneself scratching, there does occur such a sudden and unintended shift in conscious states.

As to Ryle's contention that seeing and hearing are neither conscious processes nor conscious states nor mental acts, several things need to be pointed out.

[14] See F. Galton, *Inquiries into Human Faculty and Its Development* (London, 1883), p. 120; G. E. Mueller, "Zur Analyse der Gedaechtnistaetigkeit und des Vorstellungsverlaufs," p. 69; and J. I. Volkelt's article in *Zeitschrift fuer Philosophie und philosophische Kritik*, 90(1887):12.

[15] G. Ryle, *The Concept of Mind* (London, 1949), p. 166. See also his *Dilemmas* (Cambridge, 1954), p. 102.

First, looking at the matter from a purely linguistic point of view, it is by no means true that we always use 'to see' in such a way that it is entirely unreasonable to say we are referring to something that might also be called a conscious state or mental act.[16]

Secondly, Ryle makes much of his classification of 'to see' (and 'to hear') as a so-called achievement verb. He insists that it is not used to signify that a process is going on, but rather that something has been achieved or accomplished.[17] And from this he somehow concludes that seeing something is not a mental phenomenon or mental act. Now I think that we can agree with Ryle that the relevant use of 'to see' does not indicate that a *process* is going on. But does this mean that seeing something is not a mental act? Consider an example. I dropped a coin and I am looking for it. I get down on my hands and knees. I see all kinds of things: the cracks in the floor, dust that has settled in the cracks, a needle that must have been dropped by someone else, etc. But while I see all these things, I have not stopped looking for the coin. Finally, I see it behind the leg of a table. Am I now to say that I had no visual experience of any kind, as Ryle apparently wishes us to believe, when I suddenly saw the coin? It seems obvious that I must have had such an experience; for otherwise, how could I say that I saw all kinds of things at first but not the coin, and that I suddenly saw it behind the leg of a table? True enough, I did not have this experience while I was looking for the coin. In this sense seeing a coin is not a conscious process that goes on *while* I am looking for the coin. But mental acts are not processes anyhow.[18]

Thirdly, there is the question as to whether or not one can catch

[16] Compare, for instance, F. N. Sibley, "Seeking, Scrutinizing, and Seeing," *Mind*, 64(1955):455–78.

[17] In this respect, Ryle has precursors among philosophers who defended the mental act. T. Lipps, for example, compares a mental act to the "Einschnappen einer Klinge"; he says that seeing something after one has looked for it is like arriving at the finish line after having moved toward it. See his *Bewusstsein und Gegenstand, Pyschologische Untersuchungen* (Leipzig, 1907), vol. 1.

[18] Lipps, for instance, also remarks that certain processes can be more or less excellent, more or less successful, but that a mental act does not admit of such degrees.

oneself seeing (or hearing) something. Ryle is of course right in saying that we do not use 'to see' in this way. But again, far from proving that there are therefore no mental acts of seeing (or hearing), this fact only indicates that mental acts are not mental processes.[19] That we do not speak of catching ourselves, say, seeing a painting seems to be due to the fact that to speak of catching oneself means partly that one is at fault or responsible for what one catches oneself doing. One can catch oneself staring, eavesdropping, or daydreaming; for these expressions refer to conscious processes and circumstances that are controllable and hence preventable. But one cannot help seeing something; for a mental act of seeing something is not a mental process that goes on for some time and that could be stopped after it has been going on. A mental act of seeing either occurs or it does not occur. But one cannot cut it short after it has occurred.[20]

I have now described some of the features of the classical view on introspection. We saw that one can undoubtedly *inspect* phenomenal things: that is, sense-impressions, sensations, images, feelings, and the like. We also saw that one can therefore introspect conscious states and processes. But we found that there are a number of reasons for saying that one cannot *systematically introspect* natural conscious processes without disturbing them in some fashion. Most introspective psychologists were well aware of these limitations of their method. One of the conclusions they drew was, as we remarked, that only an unintended shift to an introspective conscious state would guarantee reliable introspective reports. In this connection, we discussed briefly Ryle's view on the notion of catching oneself and his contention that there are no acts of seeing and hearing. In conclusion I should like to point out that much of the criticism directed against the program of the classical introspectionists fails to appreciate the distinctions we drew between inspection, introspection, and systematic introspec-

[19] Frege expresses this point by saying that a judgment is an act of judging just as a leap is an act of leaping.

[20] Compare R. J. Hirst, *The Problems of Perception* (London, 1959), pp. 129–30; R. M. Chisholm, *Perceiving* (New York, 1957), p. 166; and Lipps, *Bewusstsein und Gegenstand*, pp. 25–26.

tion. Only if one fails to make these distinctions will one be tempted to deny the possibility of any kind of introspection. If they are made, however, it becomes much easier to understand why introspective psychologists did so admirably in some fields of inquiry and so poorly in others.

AWARENESS OF MENTAL ACTS

Under the general heading of introspection I have so far discussed a method that involves the inspection of phenomenal objects. But since there are also mental acts of which we are aware, it may be suggested that we can inspect not only phenomenal things but also mental acts. We must therefore attempt to answer the following two related questions. How are we aware of mental acts? Can we inspect mental acts?

There is a well-known argument purporting to show that one cannot be aware of mental acts.[21] It runs like this. Suppose that a mental act A occurs. Now any awareness of this act would have to consist of another act B. But if B were to occur, then we would have to be aware of it in turn. This means that still a further act C would have to occur. And so on. Hence any awareness of A would involve an infinite number of further acts: B, C, D, etc. But such an infinite series of acts in fact never occurs. Hence there can be no awareness of the act A.

This argument rests on two assumptions: (a) that if one can be aware of any act, one must be aware of every act that occurs; and (b) that if one can be aware of an act, such an awareness must consist of a further act. Its conclusion can therefore be avoided, if at least one of these two assumptions is rejected. This is precisely what we shall do. But before we go on, it will be instructive to outline Brentano's view on the matter, for he, too, rejects one and accepts the other of the assumptions, while arriving at a position entirely different from ours.

[21] Compare, for example, Plato's *Theatetus*, 200 B–C; Aristotle's *De Anima*, III, 2, 425 b, 10–20; Franz Brentano, *Psychologie vom empirischen Standpunkt* (Leipzig, 1874), vol. 1, pp. 159–60; E. Husserl, *Logische Untersuchungen*, 2nd ed. (Halle, 1913), vol. 2, p. 702; and J. Bergmann's article in *Archiv fuer systematische Philosophie*, 2(1896):306 ff.

Brentano argues that there are no "unconscious" acts: that is, that we are aware of every act when it occurs.[22] Thus he accepts (*a*). But he rejects (*b*) by saying that there is never a second act of awareness, when one is aware of a mental act.[23] It is obvious that this view avoids the conclusion of the argument outlined above. But it is also apparent that Brentano must explain how awareness of acts is possible without there being separate acts of awareness. Consider, then, Brentano's own example. Suppose there occurs a mental act of hearing a tone. Since Brentano accepts (*a*), he holds that one is aware of this act. But since he rejects (*b*), he cannot hold that one is aware of it through another act of awareness. He asserts that the awareness is contained in the act of hearing itself. Every act, according to him, has two "objects"—namely, a primary object and a secondary object. In our example, the primary object of the act of hearing is the tone; its secondary object is the act of hearing itself. This is called the "eigentuemliche Verflechtung" of an act with its own awareness.[24]

In order to contrast this view with ours, we must first make a distinction between *mental states* and *conscious states*.[25] A (momentary) mental state consists of an act of awareness or, as I shall also say, an act of experience.[26] A (momentary) conscious state consists of all the things which are the intentions or objects of a mental state. Certain things belong to one's conscious state at a given moment by virtue of the fact that they are objects of an act of awareness which comprises one's mental state at that moment. Two examples will shed further light on this distinction and complete the description of our view.

Consider first a case of perception. In this situation, I submit, the conscious state contains an act of perceiving. This act is thus *experienced*. The corresponding mental state, however, consists of

[22] Brentano, *Psychologie*, vol. 1, pp. 131–59; also A. Marty, *Untersuchungen zur Grundlegung der allgemeinen Grammatik und Sprachphilosophie* (Halle, 1908), vol. 1, p. 423n.

[23] Brentano, *Psychologie*, vol. 1, pp. 166–67, 173–74, 202.

[24] *Ibid.*, pp. 169–70.

[25] Compare Gustav Bergmann, "Acts," in *Logic and Reality* (Madison, 1964).

[26] I distinguish between these acts and, for example, acts of perception, acts of memory, thoughts, and others.

an act of awareness (experience). Through the latter, one is aware that one perceives something, though not of what one perceives. The perceptual object is intended not by the awareness, but by the perceptual act. Whenever there occurs an act of perceiving, one is aware of it, because it is part of one's conscious state.[27] But one is not at that very same moment also aware of one's awareness, because the act of awareness belongs to one's mental rather than conscious state.

Consider, second, a case of sensing. In this situation, the conscious state contains a sense-impression. The corresponding mental state, however, consists of an act of awareness.[28] Through the latter one is aware of (experiences) the sense-impression. Hence one is always aware of the sense-impressions which are parts of one's conscious state. But one is not at the very same moment aware of one's act of sensing, because the latter belongs to one's mental state.

The most important points can be summarized in this way: (1) Every act other than an awareness is conscious; for one is aware of it when it occurs; [29] (2) however, awarenesses, including acts of sensing, may be not conscious when they occur, for one may not be aware of them because they belong to one's mental rather than conscious states; [30] (3) if one is aware of an act, it is always through an act of awareness.

Our view avoids the infinite regress outlined above by rejecting assumption (a) and accepting assumption (b). Brentano, as we saw, accepts (a) and rejects (b). His way out is just the opposite from ours. But we can avoid Brentano's special dogma of the

[27] I say that acts of perceiving are *parts* of conscious states because such conscious states are not exhausted by them. There will also be sense-impressions, for instance, of which one is aware.

[28] Acts of sensing are awarenesses of sense-impressions. Other awarenesses may intend mental acts; if so, they are not called acts of sensing.

[29] One may of course prefer to speak of what is *noticed* and what is not noticed rather than of what is conscious—that is, part of one's conscious state—and what is not conscious—that is, part of one's mental state. A. Messer, for instance, prefers the first distinction and calls all mental entities conscious. See his *Empfindung und Denken* (Leipzig, 1908), pp. 81–83.

[30] Karl Stumpf in his *Erscheinungen und psychische Funktionen* (Leipzig, 1905) already points out that there may be acts of which one is not aware.

"eigentuemliche Verflechtung" of an act with its own awareness. Why did Brentano subscribe to this view? Why, in other words, did he feel he had to accept (a) and reject (b), rather than the other way around?

Perhaps Brentano could not bring himself to accept the existence of "unconscious" mental acts. It must be noted, however, that a rejection of (a) does not imply that one can never be aware of acts of awareness. It may happen, for example, that one becomes aware of perceiving something. In such a case, one is aware of an awareness, even though there is also a further act of awareness of which one is not aware because it constitutes the mental state. Hence, in rejecting (a) we do not wish to deny that one can be aware of acts of awareness. We hold though that whenever there is a conscious state, there is an act which does not belong to it, but belongs to the corresponding mental state.[31]

At any rate, it seems more likely that Brentano came to his view by rejecting assumption (b). He argued in the following way.[32] Consider an act of perceiving and call its object X. If one accepts (b), then an awareness of the act of perceiving would have to consist in a second act. But this seems to imply that one must be aware of X twice, if one is aware of the act of perceiving: once through the act of perceiving, once through the awareness through which one is aware of one's perceiving X. Experience, however, shows plainly that this is not the case; one is only "aware" of X once. Hence the awareness of an act cannot consist in a separate act of awareness. But since one is in fact aware of every act of perception, as experience also shows, such awareness must be contained in the very act of perceiving.

The force of this argument is not at all apparent. It is not at all apparent that the awareness of the perceptual act must also be an awareness of the object X. Let us call the perceptual act P. P intends the object X. But the separate act of awareness does not

[31] Compare G. Bergmann's "Acts." (Also published in *The Indian Journal of Philosophy*, 2[1960]:1–30, 96–117.)

[32] Brentano, *Psychologie*, vol. 1, pp. 166–67. See also Aristotle's *De Anima*, III, 2, 425 b, 10–15.

intend *X*, but rather *P*. There are two separate acts with two separate objects. I think that Brentano's argument contains a hidden premise—namely, that the object of an act is in some sense contained in the act; the object of an act is "immanent" in the act. Given this premise, Brentano's conclusion seems to follow; for if *X* is somehow a part of *P*, then the awareness of *P* will *ipso facto* be an awareness of *X*. But the hidden premise is in fact false, as we shall argue in detail later. The object of any act is in fact no part of the act. The relation which obtains between an act and its object is not that of a whole to one of its parts. Nor is an object in any other sense immanent in its act.

The second main question we must discuss concerns the possibility of inspecting mental acts. This question cannot, of course, arise for the classical view on introspection. It cannot arise, because according to this view there are no mental acts in addition to phenomenal things that could be inspected. But since we hold that there are acts, it makes sense to ask whether or not one can inspect them.

Here again we find a traditional argument which purports to show that mental acts cannot be inspected (or introspected). It appears in many different forms.[33] Sometimes it is said that inspection of acts is impossible, because such inspection would presuppose that a self or mental substance could split itself into two parts, so that one part inspects the other—an impossible feat.[34] Sometimes one argues that the inspection of mental acts is impossible, because it would presuppose that one can attend to several things at the same time. Formulated still differently, the argument claims to show that one cannot inspect acts, because one cannot attend to one's attending. Brentano, who thought more about these matters than most philosophers, provides us with the clearest version. Although he holds, as we saw, that one is aware of every act that occurs, he also thinks that one cannot inspect any mental act. According to him, an object of inspection must occur

[33] Compare, for example, Broad's *The Mind and its Place in Nature*, p. 311.
[34] Compare Auguste Comte, *Cours de philosophie positive*, 2nd. ed. (Paris, 1864), vol. 1, pp. 30 ff.

as the primary, never as the secondary, object of an act.[35] Remember that according to Brentano a tone, for example, is the primary object of an act of hearing, while this act is its own secondary object. As with this particular act, so with all others: an act is always its own secondary object. There are no acts of which another act could be the primary object. It follows that one cannot inspect mental acts, even though one is always aware of them.

But is it true that every object of inspection must be a primary object of an act? Does this not rather look like an *ad hoc* explanation of what has been taken for granted—namely, that mental acts cannot be inspected? If it is, then far from explaining *why* one cannot inspect mental acts, it simply restates in a different form *that* one cannot inspect them: namely, in the claim that one cannot inspect secondary objects of acts. It seems that we need a fresh start and a new approach to the problem.

What precisely does the inspection of phenomenal objects involve? The answer to this question promises to shed some light on the present problem, because it may show us how inspection differs from mere awareness or experience. Now we noted above that the object of inspection is always the object of *attention*. When one inspects a phenomenal thing, one does not merely experience it, but *attends* to it. Can one in this sense attend to one's conscious states? Consider a conscious state of perceiving. There is in this case a mental state which consists of an act of awareness. One's conscious state contains certain sense-impressions and an act of perceiving. Both the sense-impressions and the act of perceiving are merely experienced. The perceptual object which one perceives, however, is not merely experienced; it is the object of the act of perception. How would one now pay closer attention to one's conscious state? As long as one merely experiences it, one pays attention to the perceptual object which one perceives. If one turns one's attention away from the perceptual

[35] That one cannot inspect acts is taken for granted by most philosophers connected with Brentano's "school." See, for example, A. Meinong, "Ueber Gegenstaende hoeherer Ordnung," *Zeitschrift fuer Psychologie, 21* (1899): 182–272; O. Kuelpe's article in the *Goettinger gelehrte Anzeigen*, 1907, p. 603; and Messer, *Empfindung und Denken*, pp. 74–78.

object in order to pay attention to one's conscious state, one is no longer in the conscious state properly described as perceiving a perceptual object, but in a different conscious state. Hence any attempt at inspecting one's conscious state of perceiving would invariably destroy this conscious state. But what holds for this case holds for all similar ones. Therefore, there can be no inspection of conscious states. One can only experience them.[36]

If this argument is sound, and I think it is, does it not follow that one cannot inspect phenomenal objects and mental acts? For if one cannot inspect a conscious state, one cannot inspect what it contains: namely, phenomenal objects and acts. And if it follows, how can we reconcile this conclusion with our previous assertion that one can in fact inspect (at least) phenomenal things?

The answer follows from a very important distinction—namely, the distinction between constituents or parts of conscious states on the one hand and objects of conscious states on the other. When one merely experiences a phenomenal object (or a mental act), this object (or act) is a constituent or part of one's conscious state. However, when one inspects a phenomenal object (or mental act), one's conscious state does not contain this object (or act), but contains, say, an act of sensing. Through such acts of sensing which one experiences, one inspects the phenomenal object. Assume, for example, that there occurs an act of perceiving. When one perceives something, one has certain sense-impressions; one experiences them; they are part of one's conscious state.[37] But one does not inspect them. One does not attend to them, but rather to the object of the perceptual act. For inspection to take place there must first occur a shift in conscious states. After the shift, one no longer experiences an act of perceiving, but rather an act of sens-

[36] This does not mean, of course, that one could not inspect a conscious state which one remembers. But what one remembers is never what one experiences at that moment of remembering. One experiences an act of remembering, not the object of this act. When we say that one cannot inspect a conscious state, we mean of course that we cannot inspect it when we experience it. Some philosophers conclude from the kind of argument outlined above that all introspection must be *retrospection*.

[37] This is our explication of the fact that sense-impressions are "transparent" in perception, though not, of course, in inspection.

ing. The act of perceiving is supplanted by an act of sensing in one's conscious state. What one inspects, the sense-impression, is thus no longer part of one's conscious state, but its object. One no longer just experiences the sense impression which one inspects, but experiences acts of sensing through which one inspects the sense-impression.

By saying that one is aware of, senses, or experiences certain sense-impressions, one could mean two very different things. One could mean either that certain sense-impressions are experienced through an act of awareness which is one's mental state; or one could mean that they are experienced through an act of awareness which is contained in one's conscious state. It is clear that the sense-impressions are *experienced* in either case; it is the same *kind* of mental act which intends them. Hence inspection still consists of acts of awareness or experience. Only the whole situation has changed: in just plain experiencing, the sense-impression is part of one's conscious state, while in inspection, it is the object of a conscious state. When we speak of mere awareness or experience, we shall always mean that the object of awareness or experience is part of a conscious state. When it is the object of a conscious state, we shall continue to speak of inspection.[38]

We must therefore sharply distinguish among three entirely different situations. (1) While *perceiving* something, one experiences certain phenomenal things and an act of perception. These things constitute one's conscious state. The object of perception, however, is not part of one's conscious state. It is its object. (2) The sense-impressions which one experiences in perception are not objects of the conscious state, but part of it. (3) When inspecting a phenomenal object, one experiences not only certain other phenomenal things, but one also experiences an act of awareness. The object of inspection, however, is not part of one's conscious state. It is its object.

[38] Most philosophers do not distinguish between mere experience and inspection. Some think that phenomenal objects are always given as merely experienced, while others seem to hold that they are always given as inspected. Moore seems to have held the latter view. Compare his review of Messer's *Empfindung und Denken* in *Mind*, 19(1910):395–405.

Let us now return to the question as to how to reconcile the conclusion that one cannot inspect conscious states with the assertion that one can inspect phenomenal objects. The answer lies in our distinction between what is part and what is object of a conscious state. The argument to the effect that one cannot inspect phenomenal objects applies only if we take these objects to be parts of conscious states. What one merely experiences, one cannot inspect *when one merely experiences it*. But phenomenal objects can also be given to the mind other than in mere experience. They can be given as objects rather than constituents of conscious states. And if they are objects of conscious states, they can be inspected. The same consideration applies, of course, to mental acts. A mental act cannot be inspected when it is merely experienced. But it can be inspected when it is the object rather than a constituent of a conscious state. However, there is one further complication which distinguishes the inspection of phenomenal objects from the inspection of mental acts. A mental act, unlike most phenomenal things, is a momentary entity. It does not last for any appreciable length of time. Even though we can *attend* to it—that is, experience an experience of it—we cannot really inspect it, if by inspection we mean a conscious process which contains many successive mental acts. We cannot inspect it in the same sense in which we cannot inspect such a perceptual object as a flash of lightning. This fact shows that the notion of inspection has at least two important ingredients. The object of inspection is always the object of our *attention*. On the other hand, when we speak of inspection, we also ordinarily imply that the object is carefully examined or scrutinized and this in turn implies that the object lasts for some time. In regard to mental acts, we have so far only argued that one can pay attention to them, that one can in this sense inspect them. We did not wish to claim that one can also inspect acts in the sense of examining them carefully, scrutinizing them for some length of time. And we must keep this in mind when we speak of the inspection of mental acts on the following pages. But that one can inspect mental acts in our sense refutes the kind of argument we mentioned earlier: namely, the kind of argument which is based on the premise that one cannot attend to one's attending. Or perhaps it merely explains in detail just in what sense one can and in what sense one cannot attend to one's attending.

To sum up. One cannot inspect conscious states, for whenever one experiences a conscious state, one's attention is focused not on it but on its object. This means that one cannot inspect phenomenal objects and mental acts which are part of one's conscious state as long as they are merely experienced. But one can inspect these kinds of things when they are objects rather than ingredients of conscious states. One can pay attention to phenomenal objects as well as mental acts.

Several important considerations follow from this distinction between mere experience and inspection.

First. Our analysis implies that whatever occupies our attention at a given moment is always an object rather than a part of the conscious state at that moment. Such is the nature of attention. To pay attention to something means to experience a mental act the object of which is what we pay attention to. This explanation presupposes, of course, that one recognizes the existence of mental acts and the difference between a mere awareness of a conscious state and inspection or observation. Since many introspective psychologists recognized neither, they could not furnish an adequate analysis of attention. Remember, however, Brentano's characterization of inspection. Implicit in his description is a certain view on attention. According to Brentano, the object of attention is always the primary object of an act which is experienced. In this respect, his view closely resembles ours. The two views differ in that Brentano holds that every act contains an awareness of itself, while we think that this awareness constitutes a separate act. As a result of this difference, Brentano disagrees with our view that mental acts themselves can be the objects of attention.

Second. Our analysis sheds some light on a rather common view about phenomenal objects. Reid, for example, holds (*a*) that "sensations" cannot exist outside the mind, and (b) that a "sensation" and its being felt are one and the same thing.[39] Our analysis explains how one can come to hold the mistaken view (b). One may be led to assert (b), because one is not *aware* of an act of sensing when one merely experiences "sensations." There is such an act, contrary to (b), but this act constitutes one's mental state and is therefore not part of one's conscious state. In order to realize that a "sensation" and its being felt are two things and not one, one must turn to inspection rather than mere experience. In respect to assertion (a), a rather careful analysis of what it means to exist outside a mind is needed. We shall provide this analysis later. But it is obvious already that if one means by a sensation not an object of inspection, but something which is part of a conscious state, then (a) may merely assert that a part of a conscious state is not an object of this conscious state. (a) does not have to mean that sensations could not possibly be objects of conscious states and in this sense exist outside the mind.

Third. Some philosophers claim that mere experience (sensing) is infallible, while perception of course is not.[40] Others object that there is nothing infallible about sensing. I think that the distinction between mere experience and inspection helps to settle this controversy.

It seems quite clear that a person can make mistakes about the sense-impressions, images, feelings, and the like which he inspects. Philosophers who defend the infallibility of the "inner sense" could not possibly mean to defend the infallibility of introspective reports.[41] Such a defense would amount to defending a "naïve realism" in regard to introspection. Inspection is as fallible as perception. A phenomenal object no less than a perceptual object can be different from what it appears to be. In both cases,

---

[39] See Thomas Reid's *Essays on the Intellectual Powers of Man* (Boston, 1857).

[40] For some recent discussion of this issue see, for example, Chisholm, *Perceiving*, pp. 62–66; N. Malcolm, "Perception," *Philosophical Quarterly*, 3(1953):301–16; and Chastaing, "Consciousness and Evidence."

[41] This has often been pointed out. Compare, for example, K. Stumpf, *Zur Einteilung der Wissenschaften* (Leipzig, 1906), p. 5; and O. Kuelpe, *Einleitung in die Philosophie*, 3rd. ed. (1903), pp. 273 ff.

perception as well as inspection, there are ways of finding out what a thing really is. And this, if true, shows clearly that the distinction between what a thing is and what it appears to be must be made both for objects of perception and objects of inspection.[42]

However, some philosophers realize that the inspection of phenomenal things differs from the mere awareness or experience of them. Some distinguished therefore between the mere having, say, of a sense-impression and its description; and they claimed that the former is infallible, while the latter is not.[43] This distinction is certainly in the right direction. But it fails to provide for a clear distinction between conscious states which consist at least in part of phenomenal things and conscious states which also have phenomenal objects for their objects. Other philosophers distinguished between awareness on the one hand and predication on the other. They claimed that only the former is infallible.[44] This view, however, prejudges a very important issue, namely, whether or not a mere awareness may not already be propositional, that is, contain predication.[45]

It seems to me that the proper distinction is that between mere experience (of a conscious state) on the one hand and inspection, perception, memory, etc. on the other. I think that mere experience is "infallible," while neither inspection nor perception nor memory is.

Consider three paradigm cases of error. First, from a distance a tower looks round to me. When I approach it, however, I discover that it is square. I made a mistake in thinking that the tower was round, because it is really square. I discover this mistake, because I take for granted that the tower really looked round to me and that now, from a better vantage point, it looks square. I take for

[42] Compare K. Stumpf, *Erscheinungen und psychische Funktionen*, pp. 35–36; and also Josiah Royce, *Outlines of Psychology* (New York, 1903), pp. 109–110.

[43] See, for example, Kuelpe, *Philosophie der Gegenwart* (Leipzig and Berlin, 1914), pp. 22, 102 ff.

[44] Compare, for example, H. Bergmann, *Untersuchungen zum Problem der inneren Wahrnehmung* (Halle, 1908), p. 47 ff.

[45] I shall argue below that all acts are propositional.

granted in other words, that a certain conscious state *A* really occurred and that I am now in a different conscious state *B*. I do not question that I experience just these conscious states or acts of perception. Since I take these experiences for granted, I can discover my mistake.

Second, assume that I thought a moment ago that a certain one of my teeth was aching. On closer inspection, however, I find out it is really quite a different tooth that hurts. I made a mistake in thinking that the one tooth aches, because in fact it is really another that hurts. Again, I take for granted that a certain conscious state actually occurred and that I am now in a different conscious state. I do not question that I had these experiences of these conscious states. And since I do not question this, I discover my mistake.

These two examples presuppose that our memory of previous conscious states is not mistaken. In the first case, I take it that I now remember correctly that I previously thought that the tower is round. In the second case, I take it that I now remember correctly that I previously thought that this rather than that tooth aches. This shows that the discovery of these mistakes rests on correct memory. But memory is not infallible. Perhaps I did not really think that the tower was round. I just think now that I thought the tower was round. Hence I did not really make a mistake about the shape of the tower. Rather, I make a mistake now in thinking that I made that mistake. I make a mistake not about the tower, if I may put it so, but about my memory.

Obviously, this third kind of case could arise. It shows that memory, although often taken to be veridical when we discover that we made some other kind of mistake, is not infallible. But how do we discover that we made this kind of a mistake? First I remember, mistakenly to be sure, that I thought that the tower was round. Then I check this memory and conclude for whatever reasons there may be that my memory deceived me. But this presupposes that I now remember correctly, while I am checking, what I seemed to remember a while ago. And this means that although memory is fallible, its being so can only be discovered on the basis of further memories.

More importantly, it shows that the mere experience of conscious states is "infallible." For there is no way in which we could ever find out that the mere experience of a conscious state was mistaken. Nor, for that matter, could we ever find out that it was not mistaken. All our mistakes reside, as it were, in our perceptions, inspections, memories, thoughts, etc.—that is, in the acts which we experience, not in our experiencing them.[46] And we discover these mistakes by checking acts which we experience against each other: a perception against another perception, a memory against another memory, a perception against a memory, and so on.

A final word about the expression 'infallible.' When I said that the mere experience of a conscious state is infallible, I put the word in quotation marks. This was to serve as a caution signal. The so-called infallibility of our experiences of conscious states, once pointed out and properly explicated, is of little significance when we start to consider the classical problems of knowledge in general and perception in particular.[47]

Fourth and last. A phenomenal thing, as we saw, can be either a part or an object of a conscious state. One can be presented with it in two different ways: namely, by being aware of it as part of one's conscious state or by being aware of it through an act of awareness which is part of one's conscious state. Perceptual objects, on the other hand, are never part of a conscious state; they are never merely experienced. One can only be presented with them as objects of conscious states: that is, as objects of perceptual acts which are experienced. We note therefore this fundamental distinction between phenomenal and perceptual objects—namely, that the former can be merely experienced, while the latter cannot. However, phenomenal objects are also very different from mental acts. We saw that mental acts, just like phenomenal things, can be

---

[46] Truth and falsehood, properly speaking, attach to the contents of acts which we experience. Compare p. 113 below.

[47] Compare Chapter 6 below.

merely experienced as well as inspected. They can be parts as well as objects of conscious states. But mental acts differ from phenomenal things in that they always "point beyond themselves," they always intend objects. These general features enable us to distinguish between perceptual objects, phenomenal things, and mental acts.

SENSING AND PERCEIVING

We distinguished between mere experience, inspection, and perception. But this distinction is not generally made in precisely our way. Other philosophers hold rather different views on the issues so far discussed. It seems to me, though, that some of the problems we encounter in the philosophy of mind can only be solved if one starts from the distinction I mentioned. And I shall try to show this further by dealing with some selected problems of the philosophy of perception.

Some philosophers say such things as "only sense-impressions can be directly perceived." [48] Statements of this kind, however, are misleading—and this for at least two reasons. First, to speak of the direct *perception* of sense-impressions must give the mistaken impression that sense-impressions are perceived very much in the same manner in which perceptual objects are. This may then lead to the mistaken view that the same kind of mental act presents us both with sense-impressions and perceptual objects, the only difference being that this kind of act somehow presents sense-impressions directly, while presenting perceptual objects indirectly. Against this view it has often been correctly objected that there could be no sense-impressions at all, for if anything seems to be directly perceived, it is a perceptual object rather than a sense-impression. [49]

But this objection no longer applies if we distinguish between

[48] Compare, for example, George Berkeley's *Three Dialogues, Works* (Oxford, 1891), vol. 1, p. 381.

[49] Compare A. J. Ayer, *Foundation of Empirical Knowledge* (London, 1958), p. 60; John Wild's article in *Philosophy and Phenomenological Research*, 1(1940):70–71; and H. Reichenbach, *Experience and Prediction* (Chicago, 1938), p. 164.

perceptual acts and acts of sensing (awareness, experience). According to this distinction, perceptual acts always intend perceptual objects. Hence, only perceptual objects can be said to be "directly perceived." On the other hand, the only objects of acts of sensing are sense-impressions. Hence, only sense-impressions can be "directly sensed." But this makes the expression 'directly' completely redundant. One perceives or one senses, but one does not perceive either directly or indirectly; nor does one sense directly or indirectly.[50]

Secondly, to speak of the *direct* perception of sense-impressions may give the mistaken impression that all acquaintance with sense-impressions consists in mere experience. One only contrasts mere experience of sense-impressions with the perception of perceptual objects, while we insist on the further distinction between mere experience and perception on the one hand and inspection on the other. It is true, of course, that one's conscious state contains sense-impressions when one perceives something, while it could not possibly contain perceptual objects. In this sense, mere experience of a sense-impression may be said to be direct and perception to be indirect. However, one can also inspect sense-impressions; and when one inspects a sense-impression, this sense-impression is not part of one's conscious state, but rather its object. Inspection of sense-impressions is therefore in this sense as indirect as perception. This fact is often overlooked when it is asserted that acquaintance with sense-impressions is necessarily direct.

The assertion that only sense-impressions are directly perceived must therefore be interpreted to mean (*a*) that only sense-impressions (and, of course, mental acts) can be parts of conscious states, and (*b*) that only sense-impressions can be the objects of acts of sensing.

Almost all philosophers agree that perception somehow involves sense-impressions.[51] It has been said, for example, that

[50] This is not to deny, of course, that we may perceive something indirectly, say, through a mirror.

[51] Compare H. H. Price, *Perception* (New York, 1933), pp. 3, 151; and also Broad, *The Mind and Its Place in Nature*, p. 153, and *Scientific Thought* (London, 1923), p. 239.

one is sensing the sensory core of a percept when perceiving.[52] Or it has been claimed that we are not only acquainted with sense-impressions when perceiving, but that we also refer these sense-impressions to material objects.[53] There are many more versions of this view, but they all share the assumption that perception consists at least in part of the sensing of sense-impressions.[54]

It is clear that we do not challenge this assumption. Every perceptual conscious state, we hold, contains in addition to an act of perception also certain sense-impressions. But some philosophers seem to think that the sense-impressions which we experience in perception give rise to an act of believing and/or judging, and that this act of believing and/or judging is the essential ingredient of a perceptual conscious state. It should be clear by now that we do not share this view. Mental acts of believing or judging must not be confused or identified with perceptual acts.[55] A mental act of perceiving is qualitatively different from an act of believing or judging.[56] This is not to deny, of course, that a conscious *process* of examination or scrutiny may also contain acts of believing and acts of judging. But in as much as a certain conscious state is properly characterized as a perception, its basic ingredient will have to be an act of perceiving.[57]

To say that perception involves sense-impressions may mean also that one inspects sense-impressions when one perceives something.[58] If so, then it must be emphasized that a conscious state of perceiving is entirely different from a conscious state of inspect-

[52] See E. B. Titchener, *A Beginner's Psychology* (New York, 1922), pp. 114, 118.

[53] See H. H. Price, "Seeming," *Aristotelian Society Proceedings,* suppl. vol. 26(1952):230.

[54] Compare R. Firth, "Sense-Data and the Percept Theory," Part 1, *Mind,* 58(1949):434–65.

[55] We shall discuss below one reason which may be responsible for this common confusion and/or identification. It consists in the fact that perceptual acts are propositional.

[56] Compare p. 110 below.

[57] This may well be the meaning of William James's assertion that perception is one state of mind or nothing. See his *Principles of Psychology* (New York, 1896), vol. 2, p. 80; also J. Royce, *Outlines of Psychology,* pp. 109–10.

[58] This seems to have been G. E. Moore's view at one point. Compare his review of Messer's book.

ing. While perceiving, as we saw, one is aware of an act of perceiving; while inspecting, one is aware of an act of sensing (or awareness, experience). If someone should question this distinction between being aware of an act of perceiving and being aware of an act of sensing, I know of no argument that could convince him. But I do not think that any argument is required. One only needs to consult one's own experience. The two situations "feel different," as some philosophers have put it. Moreover, many philosophers admit this distinction implicitly; for they do admit that one is not "aware of one's sense-impressions when perceiving." [59] Of course, these philosophers do not mean by 'aware' what we mean by it; they do not wish to deny that sense-impressions are experienced when we perceive something. What they have in mind is rather that we do not pay attention to our sense-impressions when we perceive something. But to pay attention to sense-impressions is to inspect them. Hence these philosophers admit that one does not inspect sense-impressions while perceiving. But this admission implies our distinction between the mere experience of sense-impressions and their inspection. And it also implies the further distinction between inspection and perception.

But if we take it that the inspection of sense-impressions is so obviously different from perception, then the question arises how certain philosophers ever came to believe that perception consists of the inspection of sense-impressions. There seem to be at least two plausible reasons for this mistaken view. First, when a perceptual object is examined, there occur quite a number of different mental acts. In particular, the conscious states may shift back and forth between perceptions and inspections. If one then uses the term 'perception' to refer to this complicated conscious process, one may well come to the conclusion that perception consists, at least in part, in the inspection of sense-impressions. But this use of the term may also lead to the conclusion that perception involves not only inspection of sense-impressions, but also, say,

[59] Compare, for instance, Chisholm, *Perceiving*, pp. 159–60; and A. J. Ayer, *The Problem of Knowledge* (London, 1956), p. 114.

thinking, memory, believing, etc.—in short, all those different kinds of mental acts that can and do occur when one examines, scrutinizes, or observes a perceptual object. Needless to say, I have used 'perception' throughout in a very different way. I have used the term to refer to a momentary conscious state which contains as an essential ingredient an act of perceiving.

Secondly, every conscious state of perceiving can be intentionally supplanted by a conscious state of inspecting sense-impressions. This fact may lead to the view (a) that when perceiving, one is inspecting sense-impressions without being aware of it, and (b) that a perceptual object consists of the sense-impressions inspected. Taken literally, (a) makes very little sense. When one inspects sense-impressions, one is quite aware of it. However, (a) may mean nothing more than that one can inspect sense-impressions after a shift from perceiving to a different conscious state. Taken literally, (b) makes very little sense either. Perceptual objects just do not in any literal sense "consist" of sense-impressions. However, remembering the program of the introspective psychologist, (b) may be taken to mean nothing more than that a conscious process of examining a perceptual object can be supplanted by one of inspecting sense-impressions and that, furthermore, there will be in most cases a certain isomorphism between the object(s) of perception and the object(s) of inspection.

Some philosophers distinguish between a veridical and a phenomenal use or sense of perception words. Moreover, they identify the phenomenal sense with the mere experience (sensing) of sense-impressions. This seems to me to be a very obvious and basic mistake.

To set up an example, assume that you have an hallucination, that you see a dagger in front of you, when in reality there is no dagger or any other perceptual object in that place. For a moment, when you have this hallucination, you do not know that you have it.[60] You would therefore say that you see a dagger, and not, for

---

[60] One can of course have an hallucination without being, even for a moment, deceived by it.

example, that it seems to you that you see a dagger or that you merely think that there is a dagger in front of you. Someone else, however, would want to indicate to a third person that there is no dagger there and that you are merely having an hallucination. Be that as it may, one can now distinguish between a veridical and a phenomenal sense of the term 'to see.' [61] Using it in the first sense, it would be false to say that one sees a dagger, when one has an hallucination. Using it in the second sense, however, such a statement would be counted as true. It is clear, I think, that the so-called phenomenal sense corresponds to what we may call a reference to a conscious state.[62] When I say that I see a dagger, using 'see' phenomenally, what I mean to say is that I am in a conscious state which is characterized by a mental act of seeing a dagger. This conscious state would be the same, irrespective of whether or not there is actually a dagger in front of me. If I wish to describe only my conscious state, making no claim as to the existence or location of perceptual objects, I can do so either in a roundabout way or by using perception words with the understanding that they are used phenomenally.

But this means that perception words, used phenomenally, do not refer to acts of sensing sense-impressions. Rather, they indicate conscious states of perceiving. Why, then, do some philosophers think that the phenomenal use is identical with a reference to sensing sense-impressions? [63] Consider the following argument. (1) When I have the hallucination, I may truly say that I see a

[61] Compare Broad, *The Mind and Its Place in Nature,* p. 142. Some contemporary philosophers hold that verbs of perception (as well as some other verbs) must always be used in the veridical sense. They insist, for example, that what one *sees* must be physically there; otherwise, one does not see at all. Hence they would object that a man who sees an hallucinatory dagger is not seeing at all. I think that this view is quite obviously false. When one sees an hallucinatory dagger, there occurs an act of seeing. When one misremembers something, there occurs an act of remembering. When one makes a judgment while dreaming, there occurs an act of judging. For an excellent criticism of that widespread view see H. H. Price, "Appearing and Appearances," American Philosophical Quarterly, 1(1964):3–19; compare also G. Bergmann, "Realistic Postscript" in *Logic and Reality.*

[62] Compare Price, *Perception,* pp. 22–25.

[63] Ayer, for example, holds this view and seems to argue for it in the way outlined below. See his *The Problem of Knowledge.*

dagger, as long as I use 'to see' phenomenally. (2) The object of my conscious state, however, cannot be a dagger; for there is no dagger in front of me. (3) Yet, when I have this hallucination, my conscious state must have some kind of object. (4) This object (or objects), not being a perceptual object, must be a sense-impression. (5) Hence, when hallucinating, I must be referring to my having sense-impressions, particularly if I use 'to see' phenomenally.

The mistake in this argument occurs in step (4). (4) asserts that the object of my conscious state cannot be a perceptual object, but must be a sense-impression. But we saw that a sense-impression can only be the object of a conscious state of inspecting. Since one is not inspecting sense-impressions when one sees an hallucinatory dagger, it is simply false to say that the conscious state of seeing a dagger has a sense-impression as its object. And it is also false to say that when hallucinating one is merely experiencing sense-impressions; for there does occur, in addition to the experience of sense-impressions, an act of seeing. This shows how by confusing the phenomenal sense of 'to see' with sensing, one can come to the wrong conclusion that in hallucination one is merely having sense-impressions or inspecting sense-impressions.

But by saying that even an hallucinatory conscious state contains an act of seeing, we are confronted with a classical problem. Since sense-impressions cannot be objects of perceptual acts, and since, moreover, we assume that there is no dagger present, what kind of object does the act of seeing have? It is this question which lurks in the background of step (3) and (4) in the argument outlined above. One takes step (4), because one holds (a) that every mental act must have an object, and (b) that the only possible object for the hallucinatory conscious state can be a sense-impression. It is the thesis (b) which in the final analysis keeps the argument going. It is on the basis of (b) that one may come to the conclusion that perception words, used phenomenally, refer to the experience or inspection of sense-impressions.

We shall in fact defend the thesis that every mental act has an object. Hence we shall have to solve the problem of "nonexistent objects." For the present, though, I merely wish to emphasize, first, that even in hallucinatory situations one is not merely sensing or inspecting sense-impressions, but that there also occurs an act of perceiving, and, second, that it is therefore false to hold that the phenomenal use of perception words coincides with speaking about sensing or inspecting sense-impressions.

Some philosophers claim that the so-called appearing language makes all talk about sense-impressions superfluous. From this they draw the further conclusions that there are no such things as sense-impressions, that sense-impressions are the inventions of philosophers, and that any attempt to introduce the sense-impression terminology on the basis of the appearing language is spurious. Their critics argue that all three of these conclusions are false. The appearing language, far from showing that sense-impressions do not exist, proves rather that they do exist.[64]

Much of the controversy revolves around the question as to how such terms as 'appearance' and 'appears' are used by nonphilosophers in ordinary situations. This question must be distinguished from an entirely different one—namely, whether or not one could call sense-impressions appearances and acts of sensing appearings. The latter question obviously has an affirmative answer. Since perceptual conscious states contain sense-impressions, one could say that one is "appeared to" in certain ways when one is in a perceptual conscious state. One could go on and distinguish between mere sensing and inspection by distinguishing between being merely "appeared to" and being aware that one is being "appeared to." Just as it is possible to experience a sense-impression at one moment and to inspect it the next, so it would be possible to merely have an appearance at one moment, and to inspect the appearance at the next.

But let us turn to the first question. There are, of course, many

[64] For the general topic see Broad, *Scientific Thought*, pp. 236–37; Price's review of Ayer's *Foundation of Empirical Knowledge* in *Mind*, 50(1941):293, and his articles, "Seeming," pp. 227–28, and "Appearing and Appearances"; A. Quinton, "Seeming," *Aristotelian Society Proceedings*, suppl. vol. 26(1952):242, and "The Problem of Perception," *Mind*, 64(1955):28–51; and Chisholm, *Perceiving*, especially pp. 43–53 and 115–25.

different uses of appear words. Fortunately, we need not go into detail. Both parties to the controversy agree that the one use which matters is the one called the "noncomparative" use by Chisholm and the "predicative" use by Price.[65]

Consider an example. Assume that the sun looks oval to me as it approaches the horizon on a winter evening.[66] In our terminology, the following would be a somewhat abbreviated analysis of this situation. When I perceive the sun, I experience a certain act of perception and, among other things, an oval sense-impression. I also notice that I have this sense-impression—that is, I become aware that I experience it. Then I say, "Look at the sun; it looks oval." In terms of the appearing terminology, we could reformulate this analysis. When I perceive the sun, I experience a certain act of perception and I am also "appeared to," among other things, by an oval appearance.[67] I also notice that I have this appearance. And so on.

Upon either analysis there is, in addition to the round sun and my perception of it, a sense-impression or appearance which I do not perceive but experience, and which is not round but oval. There are thus two distinct things: the sun on the one hand and the sense-impression or appearance on the other.[68]

It is clear that those philosophers who deny the existence of sense-impressions or appearances must offer quite a different kind of analysis of the example.[69] It may be said, for example, that even though I did not believe the sun to be oval when it looked oval to me, I nevertheless had some *inclination* to believe that it is oval. According to this kind of analysis, there exists, in addition to the round sun, not an oval sense-impression, but rather an inclination to believe that the sun is oval. But this analysis is obviously

---

[65] Chisholm, *Perceiving*, pp. 50–53; Price, "Appearing and Appearances."

[66] I take this example from Price's last-mentioned article.

[67] For the sake of the argument, I assume here that the proponent of appearances acknowledges the existence of acts of perception. Most "sense-data philosophers," however, did not acknowledge the existence of acts.

[68] I assume that perceptual objects do not "consist" of sense-impressions or appearances.

[69] Price lists three such analyses. In what follows I merely repeat some of his points. See his "Appearing and Appearances."

incomplete. Even if we assume that there actually does occur such an inclination, why do I have this inclination at all? Why do I have this inclination on this particular winter evening? Why do I not have an inclination to believe that the sun is, say, square? The analysis gives no answers to these questions. But the answers are quite clear. If I have that inclination at all, I have it *because* the sun *looks* oval to me. I have it, because I sense at that particular time an oval sense-impression (or appearance).

The same objection applies to all accounts which refrain from mentioning sense-impressions. They all either fail to mention or deny the obvious fact that the property of being oval is presented to me when the sun looks oval to me. Take one more case in point. It may be said that I simply guard myself against being accused of having made a mistake when I say "the sun *looks* oval," rather than "the sun *is* oval." If I had said the latter, you could have reproached me for having made a mistake. But here the same question arises: why do I feel at this particular time that I have to be cautious? And again the obvious answer is carefully avoided in this account: I feel that I have to be cautious, because the property of the sense-impression which I experience or inspect is certainly not (or may not be) the property of the perceptual object which I see.

But granted that I am somehow presented with the property of being oval when the sun looks oval to me, must we conclude from this fact that there is something, a sense-impression or an appearance, which has this property? Chisholm thinks that 'the sun appears oval to me' does not imply 'there is something which is oval.' He claims that sense-impressions or appearances, whatever else they may be, are not "objects to a subject." According to him, one could replace the expression 'looks oval' by a single predicate, say, 'looksoval.' And this predicate has the same relation to 'looks' as 'green' has to 'color.'[70] He holds, in other words, that the act-object distinction does not apply to "appearings." In this way, we can presumably avoid a number of puzzling questions about the properties of sense-impressions, the relationship between sense-

[70] Chisholm, *Perceiving*, pp. 115–25.

impressions and perceptual objects, and the numerical identity of sense-impressions experienced by different persons. I do not think that these questions can be avoided by rejecting the act-object distinction. Nor do I think that Chisholm's view is satisfactory. It is clear that the property "looksoval" must be different from the property oval. If we further assume that it is also a *simple* property, then the property of being oval simply disappears from the situation in which something looks oval. Yet, we have insisted that this property is presented in such a situation. On the other hand, if we assume that "looksoval" is a *complex* property which "contains" the property of being oval, we can once more ask what entity it is that exemplifies this property in the situation. But be that as it may, after having claimed that there are acts of sensing as well as acts of perceiving, we must next raise a number of questions about the nature of mental acts, the nature of their objects, and the nature of the relation between acts and objects.

MENTAL ACTS

2

PHILOSOPHERS ARE generally not satisfied with the mere assertion that things *exist*. They wish to know what *kind* of thing it is that is said to exist. In the most general case, they wish to know whether a given existent is either an individual (particular), or a property (universal), or perhaps a relation. Usually, the classification offers no great difficulties—provided, of course, that one can agree that there are particulars, properties, and relations. Not so, as we shall see, in the case of mental acts. But one consideration seems to force itself on all philosophers who discuss the ontological status of mental acts.

Consider, for example, the sentence 'I see a tree' and compare it with the sentence '*A* is greater than *B*.' The first sentence seems to mention three things—namely, a person, a tree, and a mental act of seeing. But so does the second; it, too, seems to mention three things, namely *A*, *B*, and the *relation* of being greater than. This similarity between sentences about (two-term) relations and sentences about mental acts is rather striking. In fact, it is so striking that it all but forced upon philosophers the view that mental acts are in some sense relational.

But this is not the only reason for the view that mental acts are in some sense relational. To assume that mental acts involve relations to such mind-independent entities as trees and chairs, is to account for the fact that the mind can reach out and make contact with what is not mental. It would account for the apparent fact that we can know not only our own minds but also the world around us. Any other view either cannot explain this obvious fact or must deny it outright. As has often been noted, *realism,* as opposed to *idealism,* stands or falls with the relational view of mental acts. This is the second main reason for the view that mental acts are in some sense relational.

However, every realistic position based on the assumption that acts are relational runs into the problem of nonexistent objects. When we think of a mermaid or have an hallucination, our mental acts seem to have objects which do not exist. But how could an entity which does not exist possibly stand in any relation to anything whatsoever? If one considers this question unanswerable, he will have to give up the relational view of mental acts. Eventually, he must therefore embrace idealism. On the other hand, if he is unwilling to pay this price, he must find a solution of the problem of nonexistent objects. This, in substance, is the pattern of the traditional dialectics: realism versus idealism; relational mental acts on the one hand, nonrelational acts or no acts at all on the other; a solution of the problem of nonexistent objects or a rejection of its source. In this chapter, I shall trace some of the elementary steps which outline this dialectical pattern.

THE RELATIONAL VIEW

The relational view of mental acts may take the following form. Every mental act is conceived of as a relation. These relations obtain between a self or mental substance on the one hand and some kind of object on the other. The occurrence of every mental act thus involves the existence of two things: namely, the existence of a mental substance and the existence of an object. And this gives rise to two basic problems which I shall call the problem of the self and the problem of nonexistent objects.

Are there mental substances? One's answer to this question will depend on one's answer to a more general question. Are there substances? This question leads ultimately to a still different one:

Are there continuants which have natures? Whether or not there are such continuants depends on the ontological structure of the world. I shall argue in the later chapters that there are no substances with natures. If this is so, then we must reject the view that mental acts are relations between mental substances and objects.

But if there are no mental substances, what is the correct ontological assay of the mind? Many philosophers who reject mental substances also insist that one must, for philosophical purposes, offer an analysis of the so-called empirical self.[1] No matter what specific form such an account takes, mental substances will at any rate disappear under analysis. There are quite a number of possibilities. For example, it may be said that sense-impressions are spatially related to configurations of bodily feelings. Such a configuration, one holds, constitutes the core of a slice of the empirical self. According to this kind of view, there are no mental acts, but only phenomenal objects.[2] Other philosophers treat mental acts as events which are related to a self; and the self is conceived of as a bundle of bodily sensations or feelings. A third view has it that mental acts are individual things which constitute, together with other individual things, a temporary state of the empirical self.

It is clear from our previous discussion that the last view mentioned comes closest to what we shall hold. Mental acts are neither properties nor relations, but individual things.[3] A succession of certain mental acts (namely, acts of awareness) constitutes a mental process. A succession of conscious states constitutes a conscious process. Such conscious states contain in addition to all kinds of mental acts also sensations, feelings, sense-impressions, images, and the like. To this much we are already committed by what we have said.

[1] Compare C. D. Broad, *The Mind and Its Place in Nature* (New York, 1925).
[2] See, for example, I. Gallie, "Mental Facts," *Aristotelian Society Proceedings*, 37(1936–37).
[3] Compare G. E. Moore, "The Refutation of Idealism," *Mind*, 12(1903), and S. Alexander, *The Basis of Realism, British Academy Proceedings*, 1913–14, pp. 283 ff. This is the view accepted by many of Brentano's students, though not by Brentano himself.

These commitments determine our answer as to the nature of a mind or empirical self. A mind consists of a succession of mental states and their corresponding conscious states.[4] It thus contains mental acts and phenomenal things, but never perceptual objects. It consists at any given moment of something of which one is not aware at that moment—namely, a mental state; and it also consists at any given moment of things of which one is aware—namely, a conscious state. This fact might explain how some philosophers came to assert the existence of mental substances. Sometimes, as I pointed out earlier, we do not just perceive something. Rather, we are aware of perceiving it. Sometimes, we do not just experience sense-impressions, but are aware of experiencing them. In both of these cases, our conscious state contains an act of awareness. Now recall that it is always such an act of awareness which constitutes our mental state. One may therefore describe the matter in this way: on some occasions, when we are aware of perceiving something or of experiencing a sense-impression, we are aware of those kinds of acts which on other occasions constitute mental states. This fact, I think, may give rise to the notion that we are at times acquainted with a mental substance. In straightforward perception or mere experience there is no awareness of an awareness. The self, if I may so put it, transcends our conscious state. But there can occur a shift in one's conscious states such that one becomes aware of one's awarenesses. On such occasions one may be inclined to say that one is now aware of what has been behind one's conscious states all along—namely, a mental substance or self.

But I said I would outline some of the elementary steps of the realism-idealism controversy. Mental acts, I submit, are neither properties of mental substances nor relations between mental substances and objects. They are individual things which enter into making up a mind. This does not mean, though, that we have to give up the relational view of mental acts and hence succumb to idealism. Mental acts are individual things which are related to

[4] Some of these conscious states are of course memories of earlier ones.

objects; they exemplify a certain intentional relation to objects.[5] This shows that the problem of the self is quite independent of the problem of nonexistent objects. For it shows that no matter what analysis one proposes of the mind, the problem of nonexistent objects arises as soon as one admits that mental acts are related to objects.[6]

NONEXISTENT OBJECTS

Consider the three sentences (1) 'John sees a (hallucinatory) dagger,' (2) 'John thinks of the golden mountain,' and (3) 'John believes that the earth is flat.' Any view according to which mental acts are related to so-called objects must explain what the objects are in these three cases. *Prima facie*, the three situations involve the following three objects: (a) an hallucinatory dagger, (b) the golden mountain, and (c) the circumstance that the earth is flat. But we know that there is no dagger, that there is no golden mountain, and that the earth's being flat is not a fact. Hence the *prima facie* objects do not exist. What then are the objects of these three acts of seeing, thinking, and believing?

Traditionally, the proponent of relational acts gives one of two different answers.[7] According to the first, one must distinguish between two kinds of different entities in each of the three cases. In a case of perception, like (1), one must distinguish between sense-impressions and perceptual objects. In a case of thinking like (2), one must dintinguish between things and their concepts. And in a case of believing like (3), one must distinguish between facts and propositions. Furthermore, acts of perceiving do not always intend perceptual objects. In cases like (1), they intend sense-impressions. Similarly, mental acts of thinking and believing

[5] Compare Chapters 4 and 5 below.

[6] Incidentally, it also shows that the problem of the self is independent of the realism-idealism issue. Assume, for example, that there are mental substances and mental acts. The latter are most naturally considered to be attributes of the former. Now, as long as these attributes exemplify a certain relation with objects, one can, structurally speaking, avoid idealism. Compare Chapter 6 below.

[7] The two different answers which I distinguish for expository purposes here may of course be combined in various ways.

can intend not only things and facts, but also, as in cases like (2) and (3), concepts and propositions, respectively. There exists thus an object for each of these three cases, even though the *prima facie* objects do no exist.

In the last chapter, I criticized the view that sense-impressions are sometimes the objects of perceptual conscious states. Even an hallucinatory dagger is seen and not sensed or inspected. This criticism applies automatically to the present view. If the proponent of the relational mental act takes that criticism seriously, he will have to cast around for objects other than sense-impressions in cases like (1). Sense-impressions, at any rate, will not do. Or, alternatively, he will be forced to defend the absurd view that perceptual objects consist of sense-impressions, so that even veridical perception involves nothing but sense-impressions.

The view that when thinking of the golden mountain one thinks of a concept seems to rest on a distinction between things and their concepts.[8] It also rests on the idea that, say, the concept of the golden mountain may exist, even if there is no such thing as the golden mountain. If one is content with the introduction of concepts as full-fledged existents, however, one may even go one step further. One may claim that all acts of thinking intend concepts rather than things.

Let us assume that there are concepts and that these concepts are different from the things of which they are concepts. We should then also be able to distinguish between, say, thinking of the golden mountain on the one hand and thinking of the concept of the golden mountain on the other. But if we can distinguish between these two different cases, it becomes obvious that the thought of the golden mountain cannot intend the concept of the golden mountain, for if it intended the concept, it would no longer be a thought of the golden mountain. This objection, though rather plausible, is not absolutely decisive. It may be held that the thought of the golden mountain does indeed intend a concept rather than a thing. This is what it means to think of the golden

[8] Compare W.V.O. Quine's discussion of this distinction in *From a Logical Point of View* (Cambridge, 1953).

mountain. A thought of the concept, on the other hand, intends not the concept of the golden mountain, but rather a concept of this concept. Hence there is indeed a difference between thinking of the golden mountain and thinking of the concept of the golden mountain. But this difference does not consist in the fact that in the first case the thought intends a thing, while in the second case it intends a concept. Rather, it consists in the fact that the first thought intends a concept, while the second intends a concept of a concept. Nevertheless, the objection shows that there is a difficulty here which can only be overcome by further additions to the relational view of mental acts.

In regard to the third case, we said that it is certainly not a fact that the earth is flat. If so, how can an act of believing intend something which is not (the case)? If one could only believe what as a matter of fact is true, one could hold that all such mental acts intend facts.[9] But since we often believe what is not the case, the proponent of relational acts introduces propositions as existents. So-called negative facts alone will not serve his purpose.[10] For acts of believing and similar acts allow for four different cases which must be distinguished: (1) A believes S, and S is the case; (2) A believes not-S, and not-S is the case; (3) A believes S, and S is not the case; and (4) A believes not-S, and S is the case. Let us grant that there are negative facts. Then the analyses of (1) and (2) will offer no difficulties. In (1), the relational act holds between, say, A and the fact S.[11] For (2), it holds between A and the negative fact not-S. But for (3) and (4) there is no similar analysis. For (3), since S is not the case, the only entity available is not-S; for (4), since S is the case, the only available entity is S. But to say that A believes not-S or to say that A believes S will not do as the analyses of (3) and (4), respectively.

[9] Compare Bertrand Russell's lament in his Logical Atomism papers: "The Philosophy of Logical Atomism," reprinted in *Logic and Knowledge* (London, 1956).

[10] For the following, compare Edwin B. Allaire, "Negative Facts and Belief," *Philosophical Studies, 11*(1960):1–3.

[11] I assume, for the moment, that an act is a relation between a person and an object. This makes no difference as far as the point under discussion is concerned.

There is one other way out which falls short of introducing propositions. One could hold that 'A believes S' is synonymous with 'A disbelieves not-S.' Then one can analyze (3) and (4) into (3') 'A disbelieves not-S,' and (4') 'A disbelieves S.' Whether or not one accepts this way out depends on whether or not one is willing to overlook the obvious phenomenal difference between believing S and disbelieving not-S.

At any rate, one can deal with the four cases if one introduces propositions. Let P be the proposition that S is the case and Q be the proposition that S is not the case. (1) to (4) can then be analyzed into: (a) 'A believes P, and S is the case'; (b) 'A believes Q, and S is not the case'; (c) 'A believes P, and S is not the case'; and (d) 'A believes Q, and S is the case.' This analysis captures the idea that as far as believe is concerned, (1) and (3) on the one hand, and (2) and (4) on the other are indistinguishable from each other. In each pair of cases, the mind contemplates the same proposition, only the facts are different. Or, to put it differently, as purely mental phenomena, (1) and (3) are indistinguishable, and so are (2) and (4).

This, then, is the first answer. It consists in saying that in addition to ordinary things and facts, there are also certain extraordinary entities: namely, concepts and propositions. Obviously, this answer is only acceptable if much else is added. It may well be that there are concepts and propositions, but these entities may never be objects of mental acts. Or it may be that, say, a thought of the golden mountain, though it involves a concept, never intends the concept which it involves.[12] Moreover, the notion of a concept and the notion of a proposition are not altogether clear. They clearly need to be explained in greater detail. Until these and many more points have been cleared up, there remains the suspicion that concepts and propositions have been invented by philosophers in order to secure a relational view on mental acts.

The second traditional answer presupposes a terminological

---

[12] We shall in fact hold that this is the case. We shall hold that there are concepts and/or propositions. But these entities are properties of mental acts and not their intentions. Compare our discussion of mental contents below.

clarification. By 'object' one may mean an existent which is intended by a mental act. Or one could mean anything, be it an existent or not, which is intended by a mental act. If one means the latter, then it is of course a truism that there are objects which do not exist.[13] For example, the golden mountain is such an object which does not exist. But what sense does it make to say that there is something which does not exist? It is the answer to this question which characterizes the second view on nonexistent objects. Not all entities which are there *exist;* some merely *subsist.* There are, in other words, different modes of being. The golden mountain and similar nonexistent entities do not exist; they are subsistents. Hence they have some ontological status; they are not just nothing. Similarly for the circumstance that the earth is flat: this state of affairs does not exist; it is not a fact. Nevertheless, it has some ontological status. It is a state of affairs which subsists. Having in this fashion secured some kind of ontological status for nonexistent objects, one can now hold that the relational act aims at or intends in some case subsistents. Every mental act has an object; there is something which it intends. But this object may be a subsistent.[14]

Of course, concepts and propositions are often held to subsist rather than exist.[15] One may therefore think that there is no real distinction between what I called the first and the second answer; for the thought, say, of the golden mountain would, according to either view, intend a subsistent. But even though this is true, there is a basic difference between the two views. Consider the status and nature of propositions. According to the first view, any sentence, be it true or false, expresses a proposition. But a true sentence, in addition to expressing a proposition, also represents or

[13] Both Brentano and Meinong make this terminological point.

[14] I speak of subsistents and existents. But it is clear, I trust, that the same point can be made in different words. Meinong speaks of *"Quasisein"* and *"Aussersein."* Other philosophers distinguish between what is real (*wirklich*) and what is there, though not real. What matters is only that they acknowledge different modes of being.

[15] For example, Bolzano and Frege hold this view. And they hold it for identical reasons: concepts and propositions, unlike existents, are not localized in space and time.

refers to a fact. According to the second view, however, a true sentence does not both express a proposition and refer to a fact; it merely represents a fact. There is no proposition connected with it. Similarly for expressions other than whole sentences: according to the second view, a name or a predicate does not express a concept in addition to referring to a thing or a property. If there is no such thing or property, the name or predicate refers to a subsistent rather than existent.

But the second view is not free of difficulties either. For one, to say that an entity subsists is not to say that there is such an entity in the sense which is expressed by the existential quantifier of functional logic. Hence one may be tempted to introduce a new quantifier, analogous to the standard one, which represents the mode of subsistence.[16] Assume that one depicts subsistence by such a quantifier. Assume further that one accepts Russell's theory of descriptions. Consider now the sentence 'the round square is both round and square.' Upon analysis, this sentence is transformed into 'there subsists exactly one thing which is round and square, and that thing is round and square.' This sentence would be true. But this means in effect that the so-called law of contradiction does not hold for subsistent entities.[17]

Another difficulty is this: the general problem which the relational view of mental acts has to face arises from the assumption that a relation can only obtain if its two terms exist. According to the second view, however, one of these two terms may merely subsist. This second term, of course, has some ontological status. Yet it does not exist as required by the general rule for relations. And this seems to prove that the relation(s) involved in a mental act's intending something must be a very special one. It must be different from other relations in that it may obtain even though

[16] Compare J. K. Mish'alani, "Thought and Object," *The Philosophical Review*, 71(1962):185–201.

[17] Compare, for example, A. Meinong's *Ueber die Stellung der Gegenstandstheorie im System der Wissenschaften* (Leipzig, 1907), p. 62; and *Ueber Moeglichkeit und Wahrscheinlichkeit* (Leipzig, 1915), p. 278. See also Bertrand Russell's review of the *Grazer Untersuchungen zur Gegenstandstheorie* in *Mind*, 14(1905):533.

one of its terms merely subsists. If so, then there remains the task of explaining in detail what type of relation it is that can obtain between an existent and a subsistent.

Finally, any philosopher who accepts the second view, must explicate the terms 'existent' and 'subsistent' (or equivalent ones). And if his explication is to make sense at all, it must either be based on a real difference in the way in which things have being or it must be based on a real difference in the things themselves.

Now I do not wish to suggest that the relational view of mental acts must necessarily introduce such nebulous entities as concepts and propositions, or that it necessarily leads to a distinction between existents and subsistents. Quite the contrary: I shall argue that both of these alternatives are false. Nor do I hold that the problem of nonexistent objects is the only one that may force a philosopher to embrace an ontology which either comprises concepts and propositions or is split into existents and subsistents. Rather, I wish to point out that the proponent of the relational mental act faces certain problems, that there are two traditional attempts to solve these problems, and that a great number of further questions arise in the wake of these two attempts. It is not surprising, therefore, that some philosophers, deeply vexed by the problem of nonexistent objects, tried to avoid the problem altogether by rejecting the relational view. The consequences of such a move, however, are disastrous. Brentano's later philosophy may serve as an example.

BRENTANO'S IDEALISM

Brentano's treatment of mental acts has, as it were, two sides which can and must be distinguished. On the one hand, there is his ontological commitment to nominalism. This commitment alone forces him to reject the relational view of mental acts. If there are no universals, there are no properties and relations. If there are no relations, there can be no relational acts. Mental acts must be "individual things." On the other hand, we also find in Brentano many interesting discussions of the relational view of mental acts which do not directly arise from his nominalistic bias.

In these discussions, Brentano develops a theory of relations which can be explained and understood quite independently. In these discussions, he deals directly with the problem of nonexistent objects. Brentano's analysis of mental acts thus centers around two quite different and separate problems—namely, the problem of the existence of universals and the problems of nonexistent objects. I shall center my exposition and criticism of his view around these two issues. In doing so, I shall at first use freely such terms as 'property,' 'relational property,' and 'relation.' Only later shall we cast a brief glance at Brentano's nominalistic ontology.[18]

Brentano started out with the view that mental acts are relations. No doubt, he was influenced by the similarity between 'John sees a tree' and 'A is greater than B' which we mentioned earlier. But this view raises immediately the problem of nonexistent objects. Brentano tried to solve this problem by saying that objects exist immanently in the mind. The golden mountain, for example, does not exist in the world, but exists intentionally in the mind of those who think of it.

Somewhat later, Brentano became increasingly critical of this position. He first criticized the notion of an "immanent object." But he did not give up the idea that mental acts are relations. He held at this time that one must distinguish between two kinds of relations: namely, those that can obtain only if their terms exist, and those which can obtain even if one of their terms does not exist. Mental acts are of the latter kind.

This foreshadows his final view, which I wish to discuss. Consider the sentence 'Titus is taller than Caius' and the relational predicate 'taller than Caius.' If one treats 'taller than' as a relation which always holds between two existents, and if one derives the relational property taller-than-Caius from this relation, then it may happen that the property taller-than-Caius ceases to be ap-

---

[18] About Brentano's philosophical development and his systematic views see O. Kraus, *Franz Brentano, Zur Kenntnis seines Lebes und seiner Lehre* (1919); A. Werner, *Die psychologisch-erkenntnistheoretischen Grundlagen der Metaphysik Franz Brentano's* (Hildesheim, 1931); A. Kastil, *Die Philosophie Franz Brentanos* (Bern, 1951); and L. Gilson, *Méthode et metaphysique selon Franz Brentano and La psychologie descriptive selon Franz Brentano* (both Paris, 1955).

plicable to Titus, even if Titus does not change at all. For instance, such would be the case if Caius grew to be taller than Titus. This shows, according to Brentano, that the notion of a relational property must not be derived from the notion of a relation which can only obtain between two existents. On the contrary, the notion of a relational property must be taken as the more fundamental of the two. And one must also realize, according to Brentano, that the predication of a relational property does not necessarily presuppose that the corresponding relation holds between two existents. For example, in order that the relational property taller-than-Caius be predicable of Titus, it suffices to think of Caius as being of a certain height; whether or not Caius actually exists and whether he actually is of this or that height makes no difference whatsoever. If this is so, then it follows that the relational property taller-than-Caius will not cease to be predicable of Titus through any change in Caius. For what one predicates of Titus when one ascribes to him the relational property of being taller-than-Caius is nothing but the property of being taller than Caius is thought or imagined to be.[19]

Having done away with relations by putting into their place so-called relational properties, Brentano explains that mental acts are relational properties of mental substances.[20] Remember that to predicate of anything a relational property does not presuppose, in his view, that both terms of the corresponding relation exist. Hence, to say, for example, that 'thinking of the golden mountain' represents a relational property does not presuppose that the golden mountain exists. Brentano, it seems, has successfully solved the problem of nonexistent objects, while at the same time retaining the relational character of mental acts.

However, his solution raises several important questions. First, a relational property, as we ordinarily understand it, can be de-

---

[19] See Franz Brentano, *Psychologie vom empirischen Standpunkt* (Leipzig, 1874), vol. 1, pp. xxxvii–xxxviii; vol. 2, pp. 218–19, 232–33. Compare also Kastil, *Die Philosophie Franz Brentanos.*

[20] *Psychologie,* vol. 1, pp. xxiv–xxvi; vol. 2, pp. 133–36. Compare also J. N. Findlay's acceptance of this view in his book on Meinong, *Meinong's Theory of Objects* (London, 1933), pp. 39–41.

fined in terms of the corresponding relation. The notion of a relation is the fundamental one; that of a relational property is derivative. And this fact distinguishes relational from nonrelational properties. But we saw that Brentano reverses this order; he claims that the notion of a relational property is the basic one. This raises the question as to how Brentano distinguishes between relational and nonrelational properties. He answers that whenever one thinks, say, of Titus' being taller than Caius, there occur two acts of thinking: in *modus rectus,* one thinks of Titus; in *modus obliquus,* however, one thinks of Caius. In general, whenever one thinks of a relational property, there occur two acts of thinking, one in *modus rectus,* the other in *modus obliquus.* And whenever one thinks of a nonrelational property, the thinking in *modus obliquus* (in this sense) is absent.[21] This is Brentano's distinction between relational and nonrelational properties. Mental acts are called relational properties because one thinks of them in a certain way. In general, certain properties are called relational because one thinks of them differently from other properties. But this is no answer to our question as to how Brentano's so-called relational properties differ from nonrelational ones; for we wish to know what there is in or about relational properties themselves that makes them different from nonrelational ones. Brentano either confuses, in a typically idealistic fashion, an ontological question concerning the nature of relational properties with a psychological one: namely, how we think about them.[22] Or he does not confuse the two, but holds that there is only a psychological difference between relational and nonrelational properties. In either case, relational and nonrelational properties do not differ in themselves. Mental acts are simply properties. But they happen to be somewhat peculiar in that one always thinks of them in a certain way. When one calls a mental act a *relational* property, one merely draws attention to this peculiarity.

[21] See Brentano, *Psychologie,* vol. 2; and also Kastil, *Die Philosophie Franz Brentanos.*

[22] This immediately brings a further question to mind: why do we think differently of these two kinds of properties? What is there in or about these two kinds that makes us think of them in different ways?

Relational properties, according to this view, do not in any sense of the term involve relations, for there simply are none.[23]

Second. Now that we clearly see that Brentano's so-called relational properties, their name notwithstanding, do not in any sense involve relations, we must once more turn to the problem of nonexistent objects. Does the expression 'the golden mountain' name anything in Brentano's view? Does it perhaps name a subsistent or, at any rate, an entity which has some ontological status? According to Brentano, this expression has a naming-function.[24] He holds that " 'x' names a thing x" means nothing else but " 'x' is the linguistic expression of a presentation (Vorstellung) which intends x as an object." That 'the golden mountain' has a naming function thus means (a) that it expresses a certain presentation, and (b) that this presentation intends something as its object. The question as to how 'the golden mountain' can name something when there is no existent to be named, reduces, in Brentano's analysis, to the question as to how a presentation can intend something when there is no existent to be intended. But we just saw how Brentano answers this latter question in terms of so-called relational properties. To say that a mental act of presentation intends the golden mountain, is to say merely that a certain mental substance has a certain "relational" property. This property, moreover, bears no relation whatsoever to anything else. Hence, 'the golden mountain' may express this presentation, this mental act, this property of a mental substance, but it cannot name anything else. For there is nothing else, in addition to the property, that could be named in this case. In particular, the property does not intend anything which could be named by 'the golden mountain.' But this means that contrary to Brentano's claim, 'the golden mountain' has no naming-function. It does not name anything, be it an existent or a subsistent. It merely expresses a

---

[23] Note that this conclusion is not reached because of a nominalistic background. In this argument we assume that there are properties. Brentano reduces relations to properties. We shall see, though, that there are not even properties, according to Brentano's ontology.

[24] Compare R. Kamitz, "Acts and Relations in Brentano: A Reply to Prof. Grossmann," *Analysis*, 22(1962):73–78.

certain mental act, that is, a certain property of a mental substance.[25]

Nor is this the only consequence which we must draw from Brentano's analysis of mental acts as so-called relational properties. It seems that no expression whatsoever really can name anything. If we assume that every expression acquires its naming-function indirectly through expressing a mental act which intends a thing as its object, then it would follow that not even such an expression as 'the present President of the United States' can name anything.[26] For, to say that this expression names something merely means that it expresses a certain presentation and that that presentation intends a certain person. But again, to say that this presentation intends something means nothing more than that it is a so-called relational property of a mental substance. And this property is not in any sense whatsoever related to anything else. In a more general form, Brentano's analysis of mental acts has the following consequences: there are mental substances; mental acts are properties of these substances; these properties are not related to anything else; hence, there may or may not be other things in the world, but if there are, mental acts never intend them. Mental acts do not "make contact with them." Every mental substance is completely self-contained and is not related to anything else in the world.

It has been objected against this conclusion that the expression 'the golden mountain' names, according to Brentano, something which will *possibly* correspond to the presentation in question.[27] Now, it is true that Brentano speaks at one point about possible and actual correspondences to presentations.[28] But the question is whether or not this talk makes sense against the background of his view about mental acts as so-called relational properties. Assume that what he means is that the presentation expressed by 'the

[25] Compare my "Brentano's Ontology," *Analysis, 23*(1962):20–24.

[26] Brentano seems to make this assumption. Compare Kamitz, "Acts and Relations in Brentano," pp. 74–75.

[27] *Ibid.*, p. 75.

[28] Compare Franz Brentano, *Die Lehre vom richtigen Urteil* (Bern, 1956), p. 47.

golden mountain' intends a thing; only this thing is not an actual but rather a possible thing. Then there would be, in addition to actual things, a great number of possible things, and the golden mountain would be one of them. This view is very much like Meinong's.[29] Instead of speaking about possible things, Meinong talks about things which have "Aussersein."[30] Every presentation thus intends something, but the intentional relation may terminate either in an actual thing or in a possible thing. In this view, presentations are related to things, and possible things have some kind of ontological status. But this cannot possibly be Brentano's meaning. For Brentano holds, as we saw, that presentations are not related to anything. And he also criticized the view that there are, in addition to existents, certain other things which have a lesser mode of being.

Perhaps Brentano meant something else. Perhaps he meant that a presentation intends a thing when the thing exists. If it does not exist, like the golden mountain, then there is no such intentional relation. Rather, in this case, such a relation is only possible, but not actual. Hence, *if* the thing existed, then there *would* be an intentional relation. But Brentano could not have meant this either. First of all, he denies that there is ever any relation between a presentation and what it intends. Hence, there could be no such relation if the thing intended existed. Secondly, the view we just outlined was adopted by Marty, and Brentano reputedly rejected this view.[31]

Third. We may ask whether or not Brentano's act-properties are intentional.[32] Of course, if we mean by 'intentional' that these acts are related to something, then the answer is negative. It could be,

[29] I assume here that Meinong's "*Aussersein*" refers to some mode of being.

[30] Compare A. Meinong, *Ueber Gegenstandstheorie*, reprinted in *Gesammelte Abhandlungen* (Leipzig, 1913), vol. 2. He had held earlier that the golden mountain has "*Quasisein*." See also Findlay, *Meinong's Theory of Objects*, pp. 42–58.

[31] Compare Oskar Kraus's remark on page xxxv of Brentano's *Psychologie* (Leipzig, 1924), vol. 1. See also A. Marty, *Untersuchungen zur Grundlegung der allgemeinen Grammatik und Sprachphilosophie* (Halle, 1908).

[32] Compare my paper, "Acts and Relations in Brentano," *Analysis*, 21(1960):1–6.

though, that Brentano's analysis of act-statements yields so-called intentional contexts.[33] A criterion for intentionality in this sense of the term is well known.[34] It depends on the following feature a language L may or may not possess. Two expressions (of L) referring to the same thing are interchangeable in a given context (of L) *salva veritate*. This is the so-called principle of substitutivity. A context of L is said to be intentional, if and only if the principle of substitutivity does not hold for it. Otherwise it is nonintentional. L is said to be intentional, if and only if it contains at least one intentional context. Otherwise it is called nonintentional. English, for example, is considered to be intentional. To see why, consider that the two expressions 'the morning star' and 'the evening star' refer to the same thing, and that substitution of the former for the latter may lead from the true sentence 'John believes that the evening star is identical with the evening star' to the false sentence 'John believes that the evening star is identical with the morning star.'

Does the principle of substitutivity hold, say, for Brentano's act-predicate 'presentation-of-the-golden-mountain'? From Brentano's view follows, I think, that this must be one indivisible predicate for which the question of substitution cannot arise.[35] It seems to follow, in general, that every act-predicate is in this sense indivisible. For, whatever expression we choose, these expressions will not name anything. Hence they could not possibly name the same thing.[36] The question of substitutivity cannot even arise. What we may ask is whether or not two expressions express the same presentation. If they do, then they could perhaps be interchanged *salva veritate* in sentences about mental substances and their act-properties. But in this case we would no longer substitute

---

[33] Intentional contexts are discussed in great detail below in Chapter 4.

[34] Compare R. Carnap, *Meaning and Necessity*, 2nd. ed. (Chicago, 1956); and the excellent discussion in R. M. Chisholm, *Perceiving* (New York, 1957).

[35] Compare Chisholm's view, discussed above on page 37, that "senses green" is to "senses" like "green" is to "color."

[36] This contradicts Brentano's assertion that 'Founder of Logic' and 'Teacher of Alexander the Great' name the same thing. All he is really entitled to assert, if our criticism is valid, is that these two expressions express the same presentation.

within an expression for an act-property, but substitute in a sentence one indivisible expression of such a property for another.

So far, I have only dealt with Brentano's solution of the problem of nonexistent objects. This solution, we saw, forces him to accept the idealistic position that there are no relations whatsoever, and in particular, of course, no "knowing-relation," between a mental substance and anything else. A rejection of the relational view of mental acts, as Brentano's example shows, leads invariably to idealism.

In order to avoid possible misunderstandings, I shall close this chapter with a few words about Brentano's nominalism, even though this topic does not strictly belong to our present concern.

Brentano's ontology can be summarized in the following assertions. *First.* All individual things are *substances.* This means (1) that they are *continuants;* and it means (2) that they can exist *independently.*[37] According to (1), a mental substance can, for instance, cease to hear something and begin to see something, while remaining the same substance. According to (2), a substance could exist as a bare substance, that is, without any modifications. *Second. Universals* do not exist. This means (1) that there are no properties and relations in the usual sense; and (2) that Brentano's so-called relational properties are not universals.[38] Act-properties, in particular, are not universals. *Third.* There are *attributes.* But these attributes are not universals. Rather, they are (a) *wholes* which contain bare substances; (b) wholes which do not consist of a bare substance and something else; and (c) wholes which are nevertheless more than bare substances.[39] *Fourth.* What exists is either a bare substance or an attribute (containing a bare substance).[40]

[37] Compare Franz Brentano, *Kategorienlehre* (Leipzig, 1933), pp. 38, 53, 223, 229–30; *Wahrheit und Evidenz* (Leipzig, 1930), p. 82; *Versuch ueber die Erkenntnis* (Leipzig, 1925), p. 32.

[38] See Brentano, *Psychologie*, vol. 2, pp. 137, 210, 214, 230.

[39] *Ibid.,* vol. 1, p. 276; vol. 2, p. 214; vol. 3, p. 189; *Kategorienlehre*, pp. 11, 53–54, 222.

[40] *Psychologie*, vol. 2, p. 161; *Kategorienlehre*, pp. 18, 43, 48–49. Brentano's attributes are what we shall call below perfect particulars.

From this ontological assay it follows that thinking of the golden mountain is not a property of a mental substance. It is not even an attribute in Brentano's sense. The corresponding attribute is a whole which contains a mental substance and would best be expressed by 'a mental substance which thinks of the golden mountain.' Consider, then, the sentence 'I think of the golden mountain.' What is Brentano's ontological analysis? Brentano would say that there exists an attribute which contains a bare mental substance. But at this point his view is further complicated by the fact that he also holds that we are never acquainted with the bare mental substance itself. We can only be acquainted "in a general way" with an attribute that contains a bare substance.[41] In other words, we are never acquainted with the individuating element in an attribute. But if this is so, if we are never acquainted with an individual as such, why does Brentano assert that all things must be individual things? Put differently, why is Brentano a nominalist, even though he holds that we are never acquainted with individuals as such?

Brentano argues that the notion of a universal involves a contradiction. To hold that there are universals is to hold that two entities can agree in every respect. For example, to say that two spots have the same color is to say that there are two, say, shades of green, one here and one there, but that these two shades nevertheless agree in every respect, that they are identical. This is the alleged contradiction.[42] But this contradiction only arises if we assume that there must be two "greens" when two spots share the same color. And no realist is forced to make this assumption. Quite the contrary, he would insist that there is only one universal involved—namely, a particular shade of green, which is exemplified by two spots. However, I think that Brentano would at this point object that one and the same entity (universal) cannot be at two different places (spots) at the same time. Brentano's argument against universals thus really rests on the further assumption

[41] *Psychologie*, vol. 2, pp. 200, 269; vol. 3, p. 117; *Kategorienlehre*, pp. 240, 250, 270, 350n; *Vom Dasein Gottes* (Leipzig, 1929), p. 418.
[42] *Psychologie*, vol. 2, pp. 202–3, 212; *Kategorienlehre*, p. 20.

that all existents must be localized in space and/or time. It is this assumption which constitutes the ultimate source of Brentano's nominalism.[43]

Let us return to the sentence 'I think of the golden mountain.' We know that this sentence does not assert a relation between a mental substance and something else. Nor does it, as we just saw, predicate a certain act-property of a mental substance. Moreover, the mental substance mentioned in this sentence is never given to me as such.[44] Now, Brentano holds that the expression 'one who thinks of the golden mountain' refers to an existent: namely, an attribute which contains a mental substance. It is this attribute with which I am acquainted when I think of the golden mountain. It is this attribute which I refer to when I say, 'I think of the golden mountain.' But if this is so, then it seems that the only thing mentioned by this sentence is an attribute. Such a sentence would be nothing more than a common name for an attribute. Brentano adds therefore that the proper analysis of 'I think of the golden mountain' is not just the common name 'one who thinks of the golden mountain,' but rather the sentence 'one who thinks of the golden mountain exists.'[45] This is his complete analysis of our example. Every act-statement reduces to the assertion that a certain attribute, containing a mental substance, exists. To say that I see a tree is to say that the attribute one-who-sees-a-tree exists.

So much about Brentano's view on mental acts. We saw that his solution of the problem of nonexistent objects leads him to adopt idealism. We also saw that his nominalistic ontology rests on certain crucial ideas. Some of these ideas we shall discuss in the next chapter, because they are not only essential to the nominalistic position, but also arise from a certain view of the structure of mind.

[43] We shall have occasion to consider this criterion of localization below in Chapter 3.

[44] According to Brentano, all names are really common names. See his *Wahrheit und Evidenz*, p. 74; *Psychologie*, vol. 2, p. 211; *Kategorienlehre*, pp. 16–17, 33. On the notion of common name compare below pp. 63–64 and my paper in *Essays in Ontology* (The Hague, 1963).

[45] Compare, for example, *Kategorienlehre* (Leipzig, 1933), p. 325.

MANY CONTEMPORARY PHILOSOPHERS think that traditional meta-physical problems are "merely verbal." Others insist that meta-physics is in nature and intent a descriptive enterprise. I think that both views are partly correct.

Ontology, the very heart of metaphysics, is descriptive in that it attempts to list the categorial features of the world. Such a list may be either complete or incomplete. If it is incomplete, then it is unsatisfactory by philosophical standards. Many traditional meta-physical systems are unsatisfactory in this sense; their proponents do not list all the categorial features of the world. Of course, they agree that there are sticks and stones and that there are no mer-maids. But they do not agree on the categorial structure of the world. Their disagreement in this respect is no less factual or descriptive than any disagreement in science.

However, even if two ontological lists agree in what they men-tion, a different kind of disagreement can arise. The items in these lists differ from each other in philosophically important ways. For example, particulars may be said to be in space and/or time, while universals are not. A certain metaphysician may consider some of these differences to be more important or fundamental than others. If he does, he may transform these characteristic differ-ences into criteria for separate modes of existence. For example, even though his list includes universals, he may say that only particulars really exist, because they alone are localized in space and time. Another metaphysician, however, may claim that only universals really exist because they alone are timeless. But it is clear that as long as two metaphysicians agree on what there is and also on what important differences there are among the categories of things, their disagreement on what shall count as an existent and what shall count as a subsistent is in an important respect merely verbal. There are no different modes of existence. There are only different kinds of existents.

In addition to these two kinds of disagreement, there is yet a third. The ontological question of what there is cannot be divorced from the epistemological question of how we know what there is. To be sure, to ask the one is not to ask the other—we must not fall heir to the idealistic confusion between ontology and epistemology. But one question soon leads to the other: and to ask how we know what there is leads, quite naturally, to a consideration of the structure and powers of the mind.

In this chapter I shall discuss several views about the nature of universals. But since we are mainly interested in the structure of mind, I shall lay heavy stress on the problem of how the mind is presented with universals.

UNIVERSALS

There can be no doubt that one is acquainted in perception with red things rather than with redness alone or in isolation. Nor can there be any doubt that we are never acquainted with "bare things" alone, that is, with "things" which have no properties and exemplify no relations. This fact has often been used as an ontological criterion: what exists is what can be presented in perception independently of other things. Call this the independence criterion.[1]

Consider, next, a situation in which there are two green disks of

---

[1] For an excellent account of the independence criterion and its importance for the nominalism-realism issue see Edwin B. Allaire, "Existence, Independence, and Universals," *The Philosophical Review*, 69(1960):485–96; reprinted in *Essays in Ontology* (The Hague, 1963).

the same shade of green and nothing else. Any satisfactory onto-logical analysis of this situation must do justice to two facts: namely, (a) that there are two disks and not just one, and (b) that these two disks nevertheless have something in common—that is, they share the same color. We shall therefore give the following ontological description of the situation. First, each of the two disks contains a (bare) *particular*.[2] These particulars account for the numerical difference between the two disks. Second, each of the two disks also contains the *property* green or, rather, a particular shade of green. This accounts for the fact that even though the disks are numerically different, they share a common property. Third, the two particulars *exemplify* this property. This accounts for the fact that the property is "in" these two disks, that they *have* it. Hence our ontological assay yields four different entities: two particulars, one universal, and the nexus of exemplification.[3] *There are* (at least) these four entities.

It is clear that our ontological account implies a rejection of the independence criterion; for one cannot, of course, perceive bare particulars by themselves or unexemplified universals. But in re-jecting this criterion, we do not deny the fact that we never perceive particulars and universals in isolation.

What happens, if one clings to the independence criterion? What kind of ontological account can one offer if one accepts it? Obviously, one must insist that the situation contains only two existents, the two green disks; for they and only they are of the kind that can be perceived independently. But this cannot be the whole analysis. In order to complete it, one must somehow ac-count for the fact that the two disks share the same color. There are three plausible ways of doing this.

First. Starting from the two sentences 'this is green' and 'that is green,' one may hold that 'this' and 'that' (or '*a*' and '*b*') name the

---

[2] For a discussion of bare particulars, see Chapter 6 below.

[3] Some realists hold that our example involves some further ontological kinds. See, for instance, Gustav Bergmann's two articles: "Ineffability, Ontology, and Method," *The Philosophical Review*, 69(1960):18–40; and "Generality and Exist-ence," *Theoria*, 28(1962):1–26. Both articles are reprinted in Bergmann's *Logic and Reality* (Madison, 1964).

two disks. Next, one distinguishes between so-called proper names and common names. 'This' and 'that' serve as proper names, while 'green' is a common name of the two disks. According to this analysis, there are only two things involved in the situation, the two green disks. But these two things are named not only properly by 'this' and 'that,' but also commonly by 'green.' However this ontological account will not do, for there are no such things as common names. This can best be brought out, if we ask what possible meaning the copula could have if 'green' were treated as a common name of *this* and *that*.[4]

There seem to be only the following four cases. (1) It is clear that the copula cannot signify that a disk has the property of being green, for then 'green' would have to name a property of the disk rather than the whole disk with all its properties. (2) The copula cannot possibly express class-membership, for then 'green' would have to refer to the class of green things, rather than to each member of this class separately, as the common-name doctrine asserts. (3) The copula cannot stand for class inclusion, for then again 'green' would have to name a class and could not therefore be a common name. (4) Finally, there remains the possibility that the copula expresses identity. But a brief reflection shows that this interpretation conflicts with the common-name doctrine. The sign of identity, as explicated by the Russell-Leibniz definition, always occurs between two proper names—that is, between two names each of which names one and only one thing, be that thing an individual, a property, a class, or a relation. A common name, however, is supposed to refer to more than one thing. Hence the copula cannot possibly express identity.[5] Therefore none of these four possibilities will do. This puts us in a better position to see why there is a fundamental difficulty which the common-name doctrine cannot resolve. Since a common name must name several things without naming a class of things, the copula must somehow

---

[4] For a detailed analysis of the common-name doctrine, see my article in *Essays in Ontology* (The Hague, 1963). Compare also V. F. Sinisi, "Nominalism and Common Names," *The Philosophical Review*, 71(1962):230–35.

[5] And this is so, irrespective of whether or not one takes it to express a "second intention."

express a connection between a particular thing and a "group of things," if I may so put it, yet not express a connection between a particular thing and a class of things. What could this connection be? I do not think that the doctrine of common names can give a satisfactory answer to this question.[6]

Second. One could conceive of the copula as expressing a part-whole relation. 'This is green' and 'that is green' are then transformed into 'this is part of green' and 'that is part of green,' respectively. If asked what 'green' refers to here, one replies that it names a whole composed of the various green things in the world.

But this analysis is still unsatisfactory. First of all, it does not work for all properties.[7] More importantly, it provides no answer to the question of what there is in or about the two disks that shows that they both belong to the same whole. Spread out as this peculiar whole is through space and time, we obviously cannot first look at it in order to find out that this disk and that disk are among its parts.[8] Finally, if 'green' names a third entity, in addition to the two disks which are named by 'this' and 'that,' why should anyone think that this view is preferable to ours? The answer lies in a second criterion of existence. According to this criterion, what exists is what is localized in space and/or time. We have already seen that this localization criterion is the source of Brentano's nominalism. Conceived of as a whole composed of all green things, green can reasonably be held to be so localized; conceived of as a universal, it cannot. This suggests that the present analysis primarily appeals to those philosophers who reject universals because they are explicitly or implicitly guided by the localization criterion in formulating their ontologies. Be that as it may, we know that this analysis is unacceptable. This brings us to the third and last possibility.

[6] Nor do I think that the notion of a common name itself makes any sense. See my article in the *Essays in Ontology*. Compare also Gottlob Frege's criticism of this notion; for example, his review of Husserl's *Philosophie der Arithmetik* in the *Zeitschrift fuer Philosophie und philosophische Kritik*, *103*(1894):313–32.

[7] Compare W. V. O. Quine, *From a Logical Point of View* (Cambridge, 1953), pp. 72–73.

[8] Compare I. M. Bochenski, "The Problem of Universals," in *The Problem of Universals* (Notre Dame, 1956), p. 47.

Third. Conceiving of the copula once more as expressing a part-whole relationship, one could attempt to read the two sentences under consideration as 'green is part of this' and 'green is part of that,' respectively. What, on this interpretation, is the reference of 'green'?

If one took 'green' to be a proper name, it could only be the name of an entity which is both part of this and part of that. And this means that it would have to be the name of a universal. In order to avoid this realistic account, one might fall back on the **common-name** doctrine, suggesting that 'green' is a common rather than a proper name. But in this context, the suggestion makes no sense. For, assuming that 'green' is in this context a common name, what would it name commonly? Surely, it could not be the common name of both this and that; for then it would no longer make sense to say that green is a part of this and that. Nor would it make sense to say that 'green' is the common name of all green parts; for things that have common names also do or may have proper names, and what would be the proper name of this green part—that is, the green part of this? Any answer to this question merely leads back to the original problem—namely, how to account for the "sameness" in two numerically different disks. Hence, 'green' cannot be a common name according to this analysis.

At this point, a would-be nominalist has one and only one choice. He must hold that 'green' is a proper name. But if it is a proper name it must name something. What, then, is the ontological status of the referent of 'green'? If one accepts the independence criterion, the answer is obvious. 'Green' cannot name an existent, for the referent of 'green' is never perceived by itself. Hence it must name an entity which is not an existent. We may call such an entity a subsistent. Application of the independence criterion does not, then, in the final analysis, exclude universals from the ontological inventory. Any satisfactory ontological description of the world must mention universals. But if one employs the independence criterion or, for that matter, the localization criterion, one can assign to universals a lesser ontological status.

One can say that even though there are universals, these entities do not really exist: they merely subsist. However, one must not be misled by this choice of terminology. It has not been shown that universals have a mode of being different from that of other entities. All that has been shown is that universals differ from other kinds of entities. For example, universals, unlike such things as colored disks, are never perceived in isolation. And universals are not localized in space and time, as are particulars and disks. Such differences are then used to distinguish between existents and subsistents. In short, to distinguish between existents and subsistents is not to distinguish between different modes of being, but to distinguish between different kinds of entities.

After this ontological prelude, let us now inject the epistemological issue into the debate between realists and nominalists.

CONCEPTS

How are universals presented to us? Does the mind just grasp these entities? Or does it abstract them from what it can grasp? If the mind can grasp universals, is it presented with them in perception? Or is there a very special kind of mental act that acquaints us with universals? The possible questions here are legion. And so, of course, are the possible answers. We must adopt some kind of strategy in order to make sure that we catch the most important ones. Let us therefore begin our considerations with a well-known traditional view and trace some of its ramifications.

According to this view, there are certain mental acts which are called sensory intuitions (Anschauungen).[9] All objects of sensory intuitions are held to be localized in space and/or time. If there are universals, everyone agrees, these entities are not so localized. Hence, if there were universals, they could not possibly be objects of sensory intuitions. This leaves two possibilities. One may hold that there are no universals. If so, then one must also hold that the

[9] In the background, there is of course the traditional distinction between presentations (Vorstellungen) and judgments (Urteile). Presentations are further divided into sensory intuitions (Anschauungen) and general intuitions (Allgemeinvorstellungen).

mind can only be acquainted with objects of sensory intuitions. Or one may hold that in addition to objects of sensory intuition, there are universals. If so, then one must also hold that one is acquainted with universals through a different kind of mental act. I shall try to show that the first alternative must fail. Then I shall consider the remaining alternative in greater detail.[10]

As for the first alternative, a philosopher usually starts with two distinctions. He distinguishes first between wholes and their parts. Secondly, he distinguishes between separable and inseparable parts.[11] Consider, for example, a large square composed of several smaller squares. Assume that one of the latter is of a certain shade of green. This small square is called a separable part of the larger one. On the other hand, the shade of green is called an inseparable part of the small square. This ties in with a number of traditional views. For instance, a separable part is considered to be an independent existent, because it could exist independently of the whole to which it belongs. An inseparable part, however, could not exist alone or by itself. This shows a connection with the classical notions of independent and dependent existents. Furthermore, what exists dependently, according to some philosophers, does not really exist at all. It merely subsists. Only independent entities exist. This shows how the distinction between separable and inseparable parts ties in with certain forms of nominalism.[12]

According to the part-whole analysis, a whole consists of a number of connected parts. The equation $W = f(p_1, p_2)$ depicts this idea: W is the whole, p_1 and p_2 are its parts, and f is the nexus

[10] For the following discussion see also my "Sensory Intuition and the Dogma of Localization," *Inquiry*, 5(1962):238–51; reprinted in *Essays in Ontology*.

[11] The distinction goes back at least to Berkeley. It was revived by Stumpf and accepted in some form or another by most of Brentano's students. See K. Stumpf, *Ueber den Ursprung der psychologischen Raumvorstellung* (Leipzig, 1873), pp. 108 ff. Compare also E. Husserl, *Logische Untersuchungen*, 2nd ed. (Halle, 1913), vol. 2.

[12] It also shows how this distinction ties in with our previous discussion of the independence criterion. Independent parts are just those things which could be presented in perception by themselves, while dependent parts could not be so presented.

that connects the parts.[13] Let W be of a certain shade of green. It then contains this shade as a dependent part. Call this part green$_1$. What kind of entity is green$_1$? It cannot be a universal, that is, a shade of color which can be shared by several different wholes. For, according to the view under consideration, another whole of the same color would not contain green$_1$, but rather a different part, say, green$_2$. Nor is green$_1$ a bare particular. For it does not merely indicate a numerical difference between this part and another part of the same whole or between this part and a part of a different whole. Hence green$_1$ is neither a universal nor a particular. It is a special kind of ultimate entity, traditionally known as a perfect particular or particularized essence.

Perfect particulars, whether so-called or not, have played a major role in philosophy.[14] Their attraction can be easily understood. They do fulfill the condition of being localized in space and time and are therefore objects of sensory intuitions. But this is not all. They also seem to offer a way out of the dualism between fact- and thing-ontologies—for they are facts of a sort, rather than universals or bare particulars—and yet they are also supposed to be simple entities.[15] Furthermore, they also seem to offer a way out of the nominalism-realism controversy, for they are supposed to be localized in space and time as are particulars, and yet they also seem to function as universals. In short, perfect particulars seem to represent a satisfactory solution from any ontological point of view.

How does the advocate of perfect particulars propose to analyze the perception of, say, a green disk? He might say that the

[13] Compare, for example, K. Twardowski, *Zur Lehre vom Inhalt und Gegenstand der Vorstellungen* (Vienna, 1894), pp. 55–58.

[14] Compare, to mention just a few, Husserl, *Logische Untersuchungen,* vol. 2; A. Meinong, *Ueber die Erfahrungsgrundlagen unseres Wissens* (Berlin, 1906), p. 27; G. E. Moore, *Principia Ethica* (Cambridge, reprinted 1954), p. 41. H. Hochberg has recently offered an interesting explication of Moore's notion of a nonnatural property in terms of Moore's ontology of perfect particulars. See his "Moore's Ontology and Non-natural Properties," *The Review of Metaphysics,* 15(1962): 365–95; reprinted in *Essays in Ontology.*

[15] For a confrontation of thing- and fact-ontologies see Gustav Bergmann's review of P. Strawson's *Individuals,* in *The Journal of Philosophy,* 57(1960):601–22.

perception of a green disk consists in being acquainted through sensory intuition with a whole that is composed of green₁ and other perfect particulars.[16] But this will not do. For suppose that there are two green disks of the same shade of green. The proponent of perfect particulars could attempt to describe this new situation by the two sentences 'green₁ is part of this' and 'green₂ is part of that.' Sensory intuition would present us with two wholes and the two perfect particulars green₁ and green₂. But now we must remember that green₁ and green₂ are supposed to be simple rather than complex, and to be different entities as well. Hence, we have in green₁ and green₂ two different simple things. What, then, accounts for the sameness in regard to color? In terms of perfect particulars alone there is no satisfactory answer to this question. The universal green seems to be indispensable for a satisfactory description of the example.

I say *seems,* because there are at least two further versions of this ontological theme. First, the proponent of perfect particulars may claim that green₁ and green₂, though they do not participate in the universal green, at least jointly exemplify a certain relation of similarity. Because this relation obtains, there is a sameness in respect to color. It is clear, however, that this addition to the view introduces a universal in the form of the relation of similarity. Moreover, if the relation of similarity is considered to be an "external relation," then perfect particulars are mere or bare particulars in all but name. On the other hand, if this relation is conceived of as an "internal relation," then perfect particulars are universals in all but name and the problem of individuation of wholes remains to be solved in some other way.[17]

Second, the proponent of perfect particulars could introduce universals in the form of concepts in the mind. He may claim, in

[16] I simplify this view by leaving out all details not relevant to the ontological issue. For example, it does not matter for our purpose whether the perfect particular green₁ is a sense-impression or a "rudimentary perceptual thing." Nor does it matter whether or not perception involves, in addition to sensory intuition, some further act of judgment—for example, the judgment expressed by 'this (green₁) exists' or by 'green₁ is part of this.'

[17] Compare Gustav Bergmann, "Synthetic *A Priori*," in *Logic and Reality* (Madison, 1964).

other words, that everything in or about the two green disks is particular, but that there is, in addition, a universal in the mind: namely, the concept green. This concept is got through abstraction from the objects of sensory intuition. Presently, we shall return to the topic of abstraction. But I think that no matter what the nature of abstraction may be, concepts in the mind cannot possibly replace universals in things. Assume that there is the concept green in addition to the perfect particulars $green_1$ and $green_2$. That the two disks have the same color can then be accounted for by saying that both $green_1$ and $green_2$ fall under the same mental concept green. But this account raises the following question: is it or is it not entirely arbitrary under which mental concept certain wholes or perfect particulars fall? Now, if the connection between a certain perfect particular and "its" concept were entirely arbitrary and a matter of convention, then we would not be able to say whether or not a thing before us was green, unless we knew already that this particular thing was conventionally subsumed under the mental concept green. But clearly, we can and do say with complete confidence that something before our very eyes is green, even if no one has ever told us that it is to be subsumed under the mental concept green.

On the other hand, if the connection between a perfect particular and "its" concept is not in this sense arbitrary and a matter of convention, it must be explained what there is in or about a certain perfect particular that makes it fall under a certain mental concept and not under others. A perfect particular, being an individual entity, must be numerically different from one whole to another. This leaves two possibilities. Either two perfect particulars are merely numerically distinct or they also show qualitative sameness or difference. In the first case one could not possibly explain why the mental concept green should be abstracted from green things and not, say, from some green, some red, and some blue things. For all perfect particulars would then be merely numerically distinct. Nor, of course, is there any reason why only the perfect particulars in green things should fall under the concept green. If we assume, on the other hand, that perfect particulars may be qualitatively the same or different, then the question arises as to what there is in or about these perfect particulars that accounts for their qualitative sameness or difference. But this very same question, formulated for ordinary things (namely, two green disks) was to be answered in terms of perfect particulars. The problem was how two green disks can be qualitatively the same (in regard to color), though numerically distinct. According to the explanation in terms of perfect particulars, perfect particulars were supposed to account for this qualitative sameness. As it turns out, though, this merely shifts the problem from the level of ordinary things such as disks to the level of perfect particulars. For now one must explain how perfect particulars can be qualitatively the same, though numerically distinct.

We conclude therefore that the ontological analysis in terms of perfect particulars alone will not do. The proponent of perfect particulars is forced to acknowledge the existence of universals in addition to perfect particulars. If he also accepts the thesis that universals cannot be presented in sensory intuition, he will be forced to introduce mental acts of a second kind which present us with universals. Let us call this second kind of act general presentation (*Allgemeinvorstellung*). Universals are given in general presentation.

Add to the two perfect particulars green$_1$ and green$_2$ the universal green. With this addition, one can give the following account of the perception of two green disks. Each disk is a whole composed of perfect particulars. Perfect particulars exemplify universals. For example, the two perfect particulars green$_1$ and green$_2$ exemplify the same universal green. The two disks are numerically different because they contain numerically different perfect particulars.[18] Yet they have the same color, because green$_1$ and green$_2$ exemplify the same universal. In regard to perception, when one perceives that two disks are green, one is acquainted

---

[18] Individuation can thus be achieved, say, through the two perfect particulars green$_1$ and green$_2$. But one could also hold that there are spatial (and/or temporal) perfect particulars whose function it is to individuate. For example, the one disk may be said to contain the "place" p_1, while the other contains the place p_2.

through sensory intuition with two wholes consisting of perfect particulars and one is also acquainted through a different kind of mental act (namely, general presentation) with the universal green. Expressed in a well-known metaphor, perception involves two eyes: the eye of the senses which presents us with particular things and the eye of the mind which contemplates universals. Let us call this view *conceptualism*.[19]

Conceptualism has two characteristic features. First, as a consequence of the thesis that all objects of sensory intuition must be individual entities, a conceptualist holds that individual things and universals are presented in different kinds of mental acts and that each ontological kind is presented in isolation. Second, as a consequence of accepting perfect particulars, a conceptualist must hold that there are two fundamental connections between entities. Perfect particulars are connected with each other through a certain nexus which binds them into a whole. But they are also connected with universals through the nexus of exemplification or participation. These two features are intimately connected with each other. The thesis of localization leads to the view that objects of sensory intuition and universals must each be presented in isolation from the other. But if objects of sensory intuition are presented in isolation, it seems that they could not possibly be bare particulars, for how could mere numerical difference be presented in isolation? Thus the thesis that all objects of sensory intuition must be localized explains the conceptualist's aversion to bare particulars. But because of this aversion, the conceptualist introduces perfect particulars as objects of sensory intuition. This necessitates, in turn, the introduction of two fundamental connections, the part-whole nexus and the nexus of participation.

We see that the thesis of localization and the notion of perfect particulars are the two cornerstones of conceptualism. Neither survives a careful analysis.

I referred to perfect particulars by the expressions 'green$_1$' and

---

[19] As I use this term, conceptualism is thus an epistemological thesis. That there are universals and not just concepts in the mind is taken for granted. The issue is how these universals are presented to the mind.

'green₂.' But it is obvious that each of these two expressions consists of two parts: it consists of a word or phrase for a certain shade of green and it also contains an index. Both of these parts are essential. A mere index would indicate not a perfect particular, but a bare particular. And if we left out the index, we could no longer distinguish between two perfect particulars which exemplify the same shade of green. In other words, we would get a name for the universal. The same consideration holds for the more frequently used expressions 'this-green' and 'that-green,' and for all similar ones. It seems, therefore, that perfect particulars are not really simple entities, as claimed by the conceptualist. Each one of them really consists of a bare particular, as indicated by the index, and a universal, as indicated by the word or phrase. And if this is so, then all objects of sensory intuition contain universals—that is, entities which are not localized in space and time. Hence there would be no need to introduce acts of general presentation. Sensory intuition would acquaint us not only with individual entities but also simultaneously with universals.

A conceptualist could reply that perfect particulars are indeed simple; they are mere "thises." But since we cannot communicate in terms like 'this' and 'that' or 'a' and 'b,' we must first subsume objects of sensory intuition under appropriate universals. This is the only reason why we have to use expressions like 'this-green,' or 'green₁.' [20] In other words, it might be held that objects of sensory intuition are completely simple, but that communication requires that we speak about them by using complex expressions. The occurrence of 'green' in 'green₁,' therefore, does not mean that the perfect particular contains green. It is merely added in order to communicate to the reader that we are speaking about a certain perfect particular and not about another. But if the so-called

---

[20] This used to be a rather common view. It, as well as all other versions of what I here call conceptualism, rests on the idea that intuitions without concepts are blind. Compare, for example, B. Bolzano, *Wissenschaftslehre* (Leipzig, 1929), vol. 1, p. 327, and vol. 3, p. 95; H. Bergmann, *Untersuchungen*, pp. 3, 7, and 8; A. Messer, *Empfindung und Denken* (Leipzig, 1908), p. 35; and A. Marty, *Untersuchungen zur allgemeinen Grammatik und Sprachphilosophie* (Halle, 1908), vol. 1, pp. 433 ff.

perfect particular is in every case a mere "this," then it is simply what we have always called a bare particular. Objects of sensory intuition, according to this view, are really bare particulars rather than perfect particulars. And this raises the question of how we could possibly be presented with mere numerical difference in isolation. Remembering this difficulty, the conceptualist retreats to his original position: he asserts now that the addition of 'green' does not really add anything to what is already contained in the mere "this." [21] But then he has to admit once more that perfect particulars cannot be simple.

This criticism may pull the conceptualist in the opposite direction, as it were. Instead of saying that the 'green' is merely added for purposes of communication, he may hold that the index or 'this' is really superfluous. According to this view, the conceptualist can still distinguish between objects of sensory intuition and universals, for he could distinguish between a universal and its "instances"—that is, between so-called attributes and characters. [22] Perfect particulars are attributes; wholes are composed of such attributes; and individuation is achieved either through special and unique attributes (*haecceitates*) or through special spatial and temporal attributes. However, aside from the fact that this view involves certain well-known difficulties, it cannot really be accepted by the conceptualist. For attributes, even though they are simple, are not considered to be localized in space and time. They function, according to the classical distinction, as universals, for two different wholes can contain the same nonspatial and nontemporal attribute. And if attributes are not localized in space and time, they cannot be objects of sensory intuition.

The assertion that all objects of sensory intuition are simple is thus at odds with the assertion that they are perfect particulars. For if they are simple, there are only two possibilities: either they are bare particulars or they are so-called attributes. In the first case, the conceptualist would have to say that bare particulars

[21] See Bolzano, *Wissenschaftslehre*, vol. 1, pp. 258, 309–15; vol. 3, p. 408. Bolzano calls such intuitions "ueberfuellt." See also H. Bergmann, *Untersuchungen*, p. 5.

[22] Compare Gustav Bergmann, "Meaning and Ontology," *Inquiry*, 5(1962): 129 ff.; reprinted in *Logic and Realty*.

could be given in isolation. In the second case, he could no longer hold the thesis that all objects of sensory intuition are localized in space and time. Perfect particulars are supposed to be simple, and yet they must be complex. This is the basic contradiction in the conceptualist's notion of a perfect particular.[23]

Turning to the thesis of localization, the second cornerstone of conceptualism, it is clear that this thesis will fail if one can be acquainted with particulars and universals in one and the same mental act. For example, if perfect particulars are really complex entities which contain universals, and if they are presented in sensory intuition, conceptualism is false, for then sensory intuition does acquaint us with what is not localized in space and time. Why does the conceptualist deny this possibility? There are two arguments for the thesis of localization; one direct, one indirect, as it were.

The indirect argument takes the following form: (1) All objects of sensory intuition and only objects of sensory intuition are localized in space and time; (2) universals are not localized in space and time; (3) therefore, universals cannot be objects of sensory intuition. Now this argument allows for two different interpretations, depending on what is meant by 'localized in space and time.' An entity may be said to be localized (localized$_1$), if and only if it exemplifies spatial and temporal relations.[24] Most philosophers will agree that only particulars are localized in this sense. On the other hand, an entity may be said to be localized (localized$_2$), if and only if it is exemplified by a particular: that is, if and only if it is exemplified by an entity which itself is localized$_1$. Again most philosophers will agree that only universals can be localized in the second sense.[25]

The claim that all objects of sensory intuition are localized is

[23] It is also the basic contradiction contained in some substance-philosophies. Remember Brentano's view that an attribute *contains* a bare substance, that it is "more" than a bare substance, without, however, consisting of a bare substance and something else.

[24] Or if it can only be at some particular place at some particular moment.

[25] Since they are irrelevant to the present issue, I shall not consider universals which are exemplified by universals. On the issue of elementarism see, for example, H. Hochberg, "Elementarism, Independence, and Universals," *Philosophical Studies*, 12(1961):36–43; reprinted in *Essays in Ontology*.

certainly true, if what is meant is that there are no objects of sensory intuition which are not either particulars or exemplified by particulars. As the conceptualist correctly points out, one never sees, say, green in isolation, but rather green at this particular place and this particular moment—that is, one sees green *things*. Hence the first premise of the argument outlined above is true, if we interpret it to mean that all objects of sensory intuition are either localized$_1$ or localized$_2$. But upon this interpretation, the second premise turns out to be false. For universals, as we just saw, are certainly localized$_2$.[26] On the other hand, the second premise is certainly true if what is meant is that universals are not localized$_1$. But by this interpretation it is no longer obvious that the first premise is true. Or else, the conceptualist must insist that the first premise states, in terms of localization$_1$, that universals cannot be objects of sensory intuition. If so, then rather than proving that universals cannot be objects of sensory intuition, the conceptualist simply asserts this (in the first premise) by saying that such objects must be particulars. He must then argue on independent grounds for this assertion. This leads us to what I called the direct argument.

It rests on the assertion that one is always acquainted in sensory intuition with, say, this particular green here and that particular green there, but never with the universal green. Nor does one mean the universal when one speaks of this green here and that green there. Moreover, it is often held that this green here or that green there can come into being and disappear, while it makes no sense to say of the universal green that it comes into being or disappears.[27] As to the first point, there seems no denying that one can mean this particular shade of green here as opposed to another shade of green over there. What one has in mind, though, is

[26] There seems to be a common misunderstanding. Some say that there are no universals, but only particularized essences. If all they mean is that all universals are "particularized"—that is, exemplified by particulars—then they do not at all disagree with the ontological realist who holds that universals are "*in res.*"

[27] Compare, for example, A. Meinong, *Hume Studien* (Vienna, 1877) vol. 1, p. 24. However, Meinong talks here about so-called attributes rather than perfect particulars.

a particular *shade* of green which could also be exemplified by other things. What one has in mind is therefore still a universal rather than a particular. But could one not also mean not just this particular shade of green, as contrasted with other shades, but rather this shade as it appears here and now? And does not one always see any color as it appears at this particular place and this particular moment? Of course one does. But does this fact prove the conceptualist's point? I do not think so. I think that one means or sees in each case a universal rather than a perfect particular. More accurately, what one means or sees in such cases is a universal *as exemplified* by a certain particular. To say that one always sees (intuits) a color at a particular place and moment is to say that one never sees a color which is not exemplified by a particular. In regard to the second point, that "particular pieces of green" can come into being and disappear, we can defend a similar position. What happens in these cases is that a particular exemplifies or no longer exemplifies a certain universal.[28] We simply reject the distinction between "particular pieces of green" and the universal green. Or, rather, a particular piece of green is nothing but the universal green as exemplified by a particular. The perfect particular green$_1$ is a complex entity consisting of a particular which exemplifies a universal. We see, therefore, that the direct defense of the assertion that universals cannot be given in sensory intuition fails. And this means that the second cornerstone of conceptualism has been removed.

The conceptualist, we said, needs two "eyes": one of these sees the particular, the other sees the universal. But this is not all. The thoughtful conceptualist will have to acknowledge the existence of a third "eye" for predication.[29]

Let us assume that the conceptualist is right: assume that we are acquainted with perfect particulars in sensory intuition and with universals in general presentation. How does predication take

---

[28] This is not quite accurate. For a detailed analysis of change, compare Chapter 6 below.

[29] Hence the traditional distinctions between (a) presentation and (b) judgment. Presentations are divided into sensory intuitions and general presentations.

place? The problem confronting the conceptualist can be illustrated by the following example. Assume that there are again two disks. One is of a certain shade of green; the other, however, is red. According to the conceptualist, one is acquainted with two perfect particulars through sensory intuition; and one is also acquainted in general presentation with the two universals green and red. But how does one know that *this* disk rather than *that* one is green, or that *that* disk rather than *this* one is red? In our view, this question can easily be answered. Sensory intuition, we hold, does not present us merely with a particular or even a perfect particular. It presents us with a particular which exemplifies a certain universal.[30] Hence sensory intuition already acquaints us with one particular which exemplifies, say, green, and another particular which exemplifies red. We are acquainted not only with two particulars and two universals, but also with the nexus of exemplification *as holding* between a certain particular and a certain universal. Predication is already contained in the objects of sensory intuition, for these objects are complex entities (wholes).

But the conceptualist can solve the problem only if he admits that one is not only acquainted with particular things and universals, but also with a nexus of exemplification (of participation) as it obtains between particular things on the one hand and universals on the other. How could one be acquainted with such a nexus? Is there perhaps a third "eye" which presents us with exemplification in isolation, just as sensory intuition and general presentation present us with particulars and universals in isolation? Or does the "eye" which acquaints us with universals also present us with the nexus? Or finally, is the third "eye" one which acquaints us with particular things and universals *as connected* by the nexus?

The first two alternatives will not do. In either case, one would need still a further "eye." According to the first alternative, one would be presented with a particular, a universal, and the nexus of exemplification, but with each in isolation. Surely, this will not do. For how would we know that this particular rather than another

---

[30] It presents us with a *fact*. All mental acts, we shall hold, are propositional.

is, say, green? The second alternative leads to the same question. Even if we assume that the nexus is always presented together with the universal, that the universal is "unsaturated," so to speak, the problem is not solved. For even though we know, according to this view, that a universal needs to be "completed," nothing as yet tells us which particular "completes" it in a certain situation.[31] There is only one way out. The conceptualist must assume that there is a third "eye," judgment, different from both sensory intuition and general presentation, through which we are acquainted with particular and universal as connected.[32]

But this view runs counter to the whole conceptualistic scheme. For one thing, it would mean that there is at least one constituent, exemplification, which is not given in isolation. More importantly, judgment would have to present us with a whole that contains both an entity which is localized in space and time and an entity which is not so localized. Hence judgment would have to achieve what neither sensory intuition nor general presentation can yield. But why should one insist, as the conceptualist does, that neither sensory intuition nor general presentation can acquaint us with both universals and particulars, if one is forced eventually to introduce a mental act which can achieve this feat?

However, all these difficulties seem to disappear, if the conceptualist claims that exemplification is not at all "passively given" to the mind, but rather somehow introduced by the mind. But how does the mind succeed in connecting just the right objects of sensory intuitions with just the appropriate objects of general presentation? Only two answers have even a shadow of plausibility.[33]

[31] By saying that concepts are unsaturated, Frege avoids Bradley's regress. But he cannot by this means alone avoid the difficulty outlined above. Compare my paper on Frege, "Frege's Ontology," *The Philosophical Review* 70(1961):23–40; reprinted in *Essays in Ontology*.

[32] Presentations can therefore be distinguished from judgments in the following way. Presentations always intend simple entities—namely, particulars or universals; judgments always present us with complex entities which contain, among other things, the nexus of exemplification. In our view, there are therefore no presentations. All mental acts are judgments in the sense just defined.

[33] Both answers are *idealistic* in nature in that they presuppose that the nexus is not given to the mind, but somehow contributed by the mind.

First, it may be said that if a perfect particular is given in sensory intuition, the mind grasps what universal(s) it exemplifies, because the perfect particular affords some kind of clue as to how the mind must connect it with the appropriate universals. But what kind of clue could the mind possibly receive, if the objects of sensory intuition were either bare or perfect particulars? If they are bare particulars, they cannot possibly contain any clue; and if they are perfect particulars, they are supposed to be simple entities and again as simple entities they can provide no clue.

The second answer is somewhat more elaborate. Starting with the assumption that there are two "eyes," one for particulars, one for universals, the conceptualist claims that the third "eye," judgment, presents us with connections between mental acts of sensory intuition and mental acts of general presentation. In doing so, judgment indirectly establishes a connection between the objects of these two kinds of mental acts, that is, between particulars and universals.[34]

This account has certain advantages. For instance, if we assumed that mental acts themselves were perfect particulars or consisted of perfect particulars, judgment would grasp a connection between perfect particulars rather than a connection between a particular and a universal. Hence it would intend two localized entities rather than a localized and an unlocalized entity.[35] Also, in some sense, the nexus of exemplification could be said to be reducible to the part-whole nexus. For to speak of exemplification would mean to speak of the part-whole nexus between mental acts. Hence it might be claimed that this analysis does away with the nexus of exemplification or participation and rests on only one connection, the part-whole nexus. As against these advantages, however, the following difficulties arise. Judgment, the third "eye," must acquaint us with two mental acts *as connected*. This means that it must present to us the part-whole nexus as well as

[34] Compare Husserl's *Logische Untersuchungen* and Bergmann's analysis of this work in "The Ontology of Edmund Husserl," *Methodos,* 12(1960):359–92; reprinted in *Logic and Reality.*

[35] Of course, localization must here be understood in the narrower sense of localization in time only, for mental acts do not exemplify spatial relations.

perfect particulars. But this nexus cannot possibly be a perfect particular or, more generally, an individual thing. Hence the conceptualist is forced to hold that there is, in addition to sensory intuition and general presentation, a third kind of mental act which (a) does not present us with isolated entities, and (b) acquaints us with what is localized—namely, perfect particulars —together with what is not so localized—namely, the part-whole nexus.

To sum up. The problem of predication forces the conceptualist to part with the "dogma of isolation" and the "dogma of localization." It forces him to admit that there is at least one kind of mental act which presents us with entities as connected rather than isolated. And it forces him also to admit that there is at least one kind of mental act which presents us with the localized together with the unlocalized. Judgments, he must hold, intend not isolated simple entities, like presentations, but complex entities which contain predication. These complex entities are known by various names. They are called states of affairs, or facts, or propositions, or conceptual contents. Now the conceptualist's view that there are in addition to judgments mental acts of presentation rests on two notions: (a) that there are perfect particulars, and (b) that nothing that comes through the senses can be unlocalized. I tried to show that neither one of these two notions will stand up under scrutiny. There are no perfect particulars, and the assertion that every object of sensory intuition must be localized rests on a spurious argument. Hence there is no reason to assume that judgments presuppose presentations. Quite to the contrary, an analysis of the notion of perfect particulars shows that each perfect particular is a complex entity consisting of a particular which exemplifies one or more universals. But this means that even sensory intuition is already judgmental in character. Every act of sensory intuition intends a complex entity which contains predication. Hence it already intends state of affairs. If this is so, then two things follow. First, it follows that sensory intuition presents us not only with individual entities, but also with universals. Hence there is no need to postulate a separate kind of act of general presentation. Second, it follows that the conceptualist's distinction between presentations and judgments is spurious.[36] There are no mental acts of presentation. No mental act ever presents us with a bare particular or an unexemplified universal. All mental acts are propositional. Their intentions are always expressed by whole sentences rather than by single words.[37] There are not just two "eyes": sensory intuition and general presentation; nor are there merely three "eyes": sensory intuition, general presentation, and judgment. Rather, there are as many "eyes" as there are different kinds of mental acts. But all these "eyes" present us with states of affairs.

FREGE'S CONCEPTUALISM

Frege's philosophy contains all the basic ingredients of conceptualism. This, of course, is not at all surprising, for he could hardly have been completely untouched by the Kantian atmosphere of 19th-century German philosophy. Yet, he avoids all the common idealistic pitfalls save one. This one manifests itself in an important gap in his philosophical system. I wish to point out this gap.

The entities of Frege's system can be grouped in various ways. The exhaustive division of these entities into functions and objects, for instance, is well known.[38] But I do not think that this division goes to the heart of Frege's ontological commitments. Nor does it adequately reveal the structure of his philosophy. I shall therefore take this dichotomy for granted and call attention to two further ones.

First. All entities in Frege's ontological list are either *subjective* (mental) or *objective* (nonmental). For example, sense-impressions (*Empfindungen*), objects of sensory intuitions (*An-*

---

[36] This does not mean that one could not distinguish between mental acts of judging and certain other mental acts—say, acts of perceiving.

[37] When we are presented with the so-called perfect particular green₁ or this-green, we are aware of the fact that this is green. The world is the totality of facts, not of things. Every mental act presents us with such a "fact," not a "thing."

[38] Compare R. Wells, "Frege's Ontology," *The Review of Metaphysics,* 4(1953):537–73.

schauungen), and presentations (*Vorstellungen*) are all subjective entities.[39] They are the concern of psychology. Furthermore, Frege seems to hold that all of these entities are "inner pictures."[40] Objective entities, on the other hand, are either *concepts* (or, more generally, functions) or *objects*. Concepts, we are told, are in principle "unsinnlich."[41] They are distinguished from objects by being *unsaturated*.

Second. All entities in Frege's ontological list are either *real* or *not real*.[42] An entity which is not real has some ontological status; otherwise, it would not occur in the list at all. Let us therefore say that Frege distinguishes between existents and subsistents. His criterion for this distinction seems to be localization in space and/or time.[43] What merely subsists is not so localized. Yet it is not a nothing, for the mind can make contact with it.[44] Now it must be emphasized that the two divisions Frege makes do not coincide. Rather, they overlap. For example, concepts are subsistents, even though they are objective entities. Nor are all objects existents. A sense, for instance, is an object and yet a mere subsistent.[45]

These two divisions allow us to settle the question of whether or not Frege was a nominalist.[46] They also show convincingly that Frege was not in any obvious sense an idealist.[47] This is my reason

[39] Compare Gottlob Frege, *Foundations of Arithmetic* (New York, 1960), transl. by J. L. Austin, pp. 36, 58 (*Die Grundlagen der Arithmetik* [Breslau, 1884]).

[40] *Ibid.*, p. 37n.

[41] *Ibid.*, p. xxii, and p. 37n.

[42] *Ibid.*, p. 35.

[43] *Ibid.*, p. 35.

[44] *Ibid.*, p. 36; and also Frege, "The Thought: A Logical Inquiry," *Mind*, 65(1956):309–11.

[45] By a sense I mean here either the sense of a proper name or the sense of a sentence. I shall distinguish between proper names and sentences, keeping in mind that, according to Frege, sentences are also names. I shall sometimes call the sense of a sentence a proposition, rather than a thought, as Frege does.

[46] This question has been discussed in the following articles. Gustav Bergmann, "Frege's Hidden Nominalism," *The Philosophical Review*, 67(1958):437–59; E. D. Klemke, "Professor Bergmann and Frege's Hidden Nominalism," *ibid.*, 68(1959):507–14; and my article "Frege's Ontology," *ibid.*, 70(1961):23–40.

[47] R. Egidi has recently argued for an idealistic interpretation of Frege's philosophy. See her "La consistenza filosofica della logica di Frege," *Giornale Critico della Filosofia Italiana*, 16(1962):194–208; and also her "Matematica, logica e filosofia nell' opera di Gottlob Frege," *Physis*, 4(1962):5–32.

for claiming that they go to the heart of Frege's ontological commitments. Consider the ontological status of concepts. Concepts are listed in the first division as objective (nonmental) entities. This means (a) that they have some ontological status, and (b) that they are nonmental entities. If we apply the term 'nominalist' to a philosopher who either denies any ontological status to universals (concepts) or claims that they are merely mental entities, Frege must be called a realist. On the other hand, according to the second division, concepts do not exist, but merely subsist. They do not enjoy the same ontological status as certain objects which are localized in space and/or time. If we apply the term 'realist' to a philosopher who holds that universals (concepts) have the same ontological status as localized entities, Frege must be called a nominalist.

Concepts, then, are objective presentations.[48] Frege criticizes Kant for having associated both an objective and a subjective meaning with the term 'presentation' ('*Vorstellung*').[49] He himself, following Bolzano, distinguishes sharply between subjective and objective presentations and holds that there are both kinds of entities.[50] I think we shall not go wrong if we identify subjective presentations with objects of sensory intuitions and mental images. For Frege claims that they are (a) sensible (*bildhaft*) and (b) not communicable.[51] But how are so-called objective presentations given to the mind? Frege gives no detailed answer to this question. However, he does say that they are independent of sensing, sensory intuition, and acts of presentation, but not independent of reason (*Vernunft*).[52] He therefore distinguishes between at least two ways in which the mind makes contact with entities. Certain mental acts—for example, sensory intuition—

[48] There is some terminological roughness here. To say that a concept is an objective presentation is not to say that it is a mental act, but rather that it is the object of a certain act. I shall neglect this distinction for the time being.

[49] *Foundations of Arithmetic*, p. 37.

[50] Compare Bolzano, *Wissenschaftslehre* and also Jan Berg, *Bolzano's Logic* (Stockholm, 1962).

[51] *Foundations of Arithmetic*, pp. 37n, and 35.

[52] *Ibid.*, p. 36. It is clear from the context that objective entities do not depend on reason for their existence, but only for their being known.

acquaint us with inner pictures, subjective entities, while reason transcends the subjective realm and acquaints us with objective entities. For example, Frege holds that the sense-impression blue must be distinguished from the concept blue.[53] The sense-impression is given in sensory intuition and is subjective, while the concept is not subjective and presented in a different way. He claims, moreover, that the meaning of 'blue' which we can communicate is not our subjective sense-impression, but rather the objective concept.[54]

If we apply our previously introduced distinction between sensory intuition and general presentation, the "eye" of the sense and the "eye" of the mind, we can say that objective concepts are presented in general presentation. According to Frege, the mind grasps these objective entities. But general presentations, in this sense of the term, must also be distinguished from judgments and mere assumptions.

Frege introduced this distinction in the *Begriffsschrift*. The most important single notion of this work is that of a *conceptual content*.[55] In connection with this notion, Frege makes the following three important points.[56] First, he distinguishes between conceptual contents that can be judged and conceptual contents that cannot. He distinguishes, secondly, between the mere thought (assumption) of a conceptual content and a judgment. This, I take it, is a distinction between two kinds of mental acts: conceptual contents can be either merely thought of or judged (to be true or false). In making these two distinctions, Frege followed Bolzano. Bolzano had also claimed that objective propositions

---

[53] *Ibid.*, pp. 31, 36.

[54] *Ibid.*, pp. 36, 37. Frege holds not only that sense-impressions are subjective, but that they are not communicable. When contemporary philosophers talk about the privacy of sense-impressions, they often seem to confuse several different ideas. First, sense-impressions may be said to be private because one can only experience one's own. Second, they may be said to be private because they are in some sense mental entities. They are, in Frege's word, subjective. Finally, they may be said to be private because one cannot communicate about them. I think that sense-impressions are private in the first two senses, but not in the third.

[55] Compare Gottlob Frege, *Begriffsschrift* (Halle, 1879), p. iv.

[56] *Ibid.*, pp. 2, 13–15.

consist of objective concepts; and he had argued that the mere thought of a proposition is not yet a judgment.[57] Finally, Frege holds that the same content can be determined in different ways. That it is determined in two different ways is the content of a judgment. Equality of content is thus itself a conceptual content. But the relation of equality, according to Frege, is a relation between the expressions which stand for the contents, not a relation between the contents themselves.

Now the distinction between the mere thought of a conceptual content and a judgment finds its expression in the notation of the *Begriffsschrift:* Frege introduces the so-called content-stroke and the so-called judgment-stroke.[58] But I do not think that this is the only function which these two signs have.[59]

In the *Begriffsschrift,* Frege had not as yet distinguished between saturated and unsaturated constituents of conceptual contents. He had not as yet distinguished between objects and concepts. A proposition was simply a complex concept that had the characteristic of being a possible intention of a judgment. For example, he argues in the *Begriffsschrift* against the subject-predicate distinction which forms the basis for his later distinction between concepts and objects. But this means that he had not as yet realized that there was a problem as to how several concepts can be combined so as to yield a proposition rather than a mere list of concepts.[60] Or to be more precise, he had dimly seen this problem, but had tried to solve it in a different way, by claiming that the content-stroke combines the constituents of a conceptual content into a whole. In the *Begriffsschrift,* the content-stroke thus

[57] Compare Bolzano, *Wissenschaftslehre,* and also my paper on Frege.

[58] *Begriffsschrift,* pp. 1–2.

[59] A very different interpretation is given by both Egidi and Bergmann. The latter thinks that, say, '*p*,' '*-p*,' and '⊢ *p*' refer to the intention of a thought, a thought in a judgment, and a judgment, respectively. According to Bergmann's terminology, this means that '*p*' refers to an objective state of affairs, '*-p*' refers to a subjective property of a mental act, and '⊢ *p*' refers to the subjective act with its property. See Gustav Bergmann, "Alternative Ontologiche," *Giornale Critico della Filosofia Italiana,* 17(1963); reprinted in *Logic and Reality.*

[60] This problem also arises for Bolzano who holds that any proposition of the form '*a* is *f*' consists of three concepts: the concept *a,* the concept *has,* and the concept *f.*

has the additional function of creating wholes out of a number of concepts.

Also in the *Begriffsschrift*, Frege had not as yet introduced the sense-denotation distinction for names. In particular, he did not hold at that time that truth-values are denotations of sentences. This gap, I think, is somehow filled by the judgment-stroke. This does not mean, of course, that '⊢p' denotes the true in the *Begriffsschrift*. But truth and falsehood, if I may so put it, enter into the *Begriffsschrift* only through the judgment-stroke, while they later become independent objective entities.

The two important distinctions between objects and concepts and between sense and denotation were later made by Frege. He also revised his analysis of identity-statements. First comes the distinction between objects and concepts. He talks about it in the *Foundations* and defends it in detail against Kerry.[61] He argues that at least one constituent of a proposition must be unsaturated, for otherwise the constituents of a proposition would merely stand side by side, as it were, and not form a whole.[62] In effect Frege claims, correctly I believe, that the Bradleyan type of regress can only be avoided if at least one constituent of a whole does not need a connection in order to be tied to the rest of the constituents.[63] At least one constituent must be unsaturated so that it may tie saturated entities into a whole without in turn needing a further connection.[64] Objects and concepts are thus constituents of

[61] Compare "Ueber Begriff und Gegenstand," *Vierteljahrsschrift fuer wissenschaftliche Philosophie*, 16(1891):192–205 (translated as "On Concept and Object" in *Translations from the Philosophical Writings of Gottlob Frege*, 2nd ed. [Oxford, 1960]); and B. Kerry, "Ueber Anschauung und ihre psychische Verarbeitung," in a series of articles from 1885 to 1891 in the *Vierteljahrsschrift fuer wissenschaftliche Philosophie*. The distinction appears as one of three principles in *Foundations of Arithmetic*, p. xxii.

[62] For a more detailed discussion of this problem, see my Frege paper.

[63] We claim, in the spirit of Frege's distinction, that the nexus of exemplification is "unsaturated" in that it can connect, say, a particular with a universal without requiring some further link that connects it with both the particular and the universal.

[64] Of course, the nexus of falling under (a concept) would be unsaturated. But Frege thinks that he can ultimately do without this nexus by saying that concepts are unsaturated. Below we shall show how this elimination of the nexus leads to a certain problem in Frege's philosophy.

wholes. They are distinguished by the fact that the former are saturated, while the latter are unsaturated. And this means that the latter can "stick" to the former and thus form a whole without requiring a further entity to bind them together.

And this kind of unsaturatedness must be distinguished from another kind, which also plays a role in Frege's philosophy at this stage. Frege holds also that a concept can only be distinguished within a complex whole but not separated from the complex in which it occurs.[65] This, of course, is the familiar distinction between separable (independent) and inseparable (dependent) parts of a whole. That the notion of unsaturatedness does not necessarily coincide with that of inseparableness, however, can be seen from the fact that even objects form inseparable parts of wholes in the *Foundations*. For example, Frege says that one must never ask for the meaning of a word in isolation, but only in the context of a sentence.[66] This means not only that the meaning of a concept-word (a concept) is inseparable from the whole, but also that the meaning of an object-word is in this sense inseparable.[67] The reason which Frege gives for this view is rather interesting. He claims that if we look for the meaning of an expression in isolation, rather than in a whole, we are almost forced to accept as the meaning some "inner picture," that is, something subjective.[68] But the meanings of expressions are of course objective entities; and these objective entities only become visible when we consider whole sentences rather than isolated words.

I think we may interpret Frege's view in the following way. The basic unit of meaning is a whole. Hence the fundamental mental acts are thoughts and judgments. Now such wholes are of course complex entities; they have saturated and unsaturated parts. But these parts are never presented to us in isolation; hence Frege rejects the conceptualist's view that in judgment we simply com-

[65] Compare Frege "On the Foundations of Geometry," *The Philosophical Review*, 69(1960):13n.
[66] *Foundations of Arithmetic,* pp. xxii, 71, 81.
[67] *Ibid.,* pp. 72, 73.
[68] *Ibid.,* p. xxii.

bine what was previously given to us in presentations. Both objects and concepts are only presented to us as parts of wholes.

What shall we call these wholes? Obviously, they are not conceptual contents, for they contain not only concepts but also objects. We shall not call them propositions, because this term will be used to refer to senses expressed by sentences. Nor, finally, can we call them states of affairs, because we shall later talk about states of affairs in a technical sense. Let us call them circumstances. The sentence 'a is f,' for example, means the circumstance that the object a falls under the concept f. With the well-known distinction between sense and reference, we enter a third stage of Frege's philosophy, in which circumstances are replaced by propositions on the one hand and truth-values on the other.

The distinction between sense and reference is introduced by Frege in order to solve the remaining two problems from the *Begriffsschrift*: namely, the problem of identity and the problem of truth and falsehood. Frege no longer thinks that identity is a relation between expressions. He now holds that it is a relation between objects. But he also utilizes the idea, already contained in the *Begriffsschrift*, that two objects may be determined in different ways. The mode of presentation of an object now becomes associated with the expression for the object as its sense. A proper name, as Frege puts it, expresses a sense and refers to an object.[69]

Turning to whole sentences, Frege takes for granted that a sentence contains a proposition.[70] If this is taken for granted, two questions arise. First, is a proposition the sense or the reference of a sentence? Frege answers that it is its sense and hence expressed by a sentence. Second, what is the reference of a sentence? Frege argues that it is a truth-value.[71]

He thus arrives at the following view: (1) a sentence refers to the True or the False and expresses a proposition; (2) a proper name refers to an object and expresses a sense; (3) the sense of a

---

[69] "On Sense and Reference," *Translations*, p. 51 ("Ueber Sinn und Bedeutung," *Zeitschrift fuer Philosophie und philosophische Kritik, 100* [1892]:25–50).

[70] *Ibid.*, p. 62.

[71] *Ibid.*, pp. 62–64.

proper name enters into the proposition expressed by the sentence in which the proper name occurs.[72] How do concepts fit into this view? In particular, is there a sense-reference distinction for concept words? If there is, are concepts expressed or referred to by concept words?

In his published works, Frege never explicitly mentions a sense-reference distinction for concept words. Nor does he tell us quite explicitly that a concept is the sense rather than the reference of a concept word, or that it is the reference rather than the sense of such a word. He simply does not seem to make this distinction at all for concept words. The standard interpretation of this part of Frege's philosophy is therefore that concept words do not have a "double tie" to two entities as names have, but that they merely *mean* concepts.[73] They do not, as do names, *express* something and *refer* to something. However, this interpretation has been challenged by Dummett and by Jackson. They hold that Frege in fact thought of concept words as expressing a sense and having a reference.[74] I cannot go into all the arguments that speak for or against the standard interpretation. But I shall mention a few considerations that seem to speak for it, because these considerations are essential for an understanding of the gap in Frege's system which I mentioned earlier.

If Frege thought of introducing the sense-reference distinction for concept-words, what kinds of entities of his ontology would qualify for these two roles?

(1) A concept word could not possibly refer to a *property*, as distinguished from a concept, and express a concept. Nor could it express a property and refer to a concept. For Frege does not

---

[72] It should be noted that senses and referents are not mutually exclusive classes. A sense of one expression can be the referent of another. Nor are objects and senses exclusive: some senses are objects.

[73] Compare W. Marshall's review in *The Journal of Symbolic Logic*, *18* (1953):90–91, and his articles in *The Philosophical Review* (1953 and 1956).

[74] See M. Dummett's articles "Frege on Functions: A Reply," *The Philosophical Review*, *64*(1955):96–107, and "Note: Frege on Functions," *ibid.*, *68*(1956):229–30; also H. Jackson: "Frege on Sense-Functions," *Analysis*, *23*(1963):84–87.

distinguish between properties and concepts. Rather, he explains his notion of a concept and states then that the word 'property' may be used to refer to a concept.[75]

(2) A concept word could not possibly refer to a class (value range) and express a concept. For classes, according to Frege, are referred to by proper names and not by concept words. Nor could a concept word express a class, for if it expressed a class, this class would have to enter into propositions. But classes are saturated objects and hence could not yield propositions when conjoined with senses of proper names.

(3) A concept word could not refer to a concept and express a so-called concept-correlate.[76] For concept-correlates are saturated objects and hence could not function as unsaturated parts in propositions. Nor could a concept word refer to a concept-correlate and express a concept, for concept correlates are referred to by names and not by concept words.

(4) But it is possible to extend the sense-reference distinction to concept words, if we assume that concept words refer to concepts and express (different) concepts. If 'F' refers to the concept F and expresses the concept f, then f together with the saturated sense of a proper name would form a proposition. Thus the only plausible alternative to regarding concepts simply as meanings of concept words is to hold that concept words express concepts and refer to (different) concepts. According to Jackson, this is the view which Frege actually held.

But there is one consideration that speaks against this interpretation or, more generally, against any attempt to endow concept words with referents. Propositions are complex entities; they consist of saturated and unsaturated parts. But truth-values are obviously not complex entities: they have no parts. Yet, if we assume that the referent of a sentence consists of the referent of a name and the referent of a concept word, then a truth-value would have to be a complex entity. Furthermore, all true sentences supposedly

[75] "On Concept and Object," *Translations*, p. 51.
[76] For the notion of a concept-correlate see Wells's article. In my paper on Frege I mistakenly thought that concept-correlates could function as senses of concept words.

have the same referent, the True. But how could two entirely different true sentences possibly have the same referent, if this referent consists in each case of the referent of a name and the referent of a concept word? On the other hand, if we assume that the referents of words do not make up the referents of sentences, what kinds of entities do they yield? Are there in addition to truth-values complex entities, similar to propositions, which are referred to by whole sentences? If so, what kind of entity does a sentence refer to when it is false? The questions point to an obvious tension in Frege's system. He must either hold that the referents of words yield the referents of sentences or he must deny it. If he holds that they do, then it seems that he must give up the idea that sentences refer to truth values. Instead, they must refer to complex entities similar to propositions. If he denies that the referent of a sentence consists of the referents of the words which make up the sentence, he must add to propositions and truth-values further complex entities similar to propositions. In either case, there will be complex entities other than propositions which consist of saturated and unsaturated parts.

Notice, though, that this tension arises only if we assume that concept words refer to unsaturated entities. For if they do, such an unsaturated entity when conjoined to the referent of a name must yield a whole. And this whole cannot be a truth-value. If we assume, however, that concept words do not refer to anything, that they merely mean concepts which enter into propositions, the tension disappears. A proper name alone expresses a sense and refers to an object. When a concept word is added, we get a sentence. This sentence expresses a proposition which consists of the sense of a proper name and the meaning of a concept word. It refers to a truth-value, but this object has no parts. When we add the concept word to a proper name, we do not add an unsaturated part to the referent of a proper name. The referent of a sentence is thus a simple entity which does not consist of the referents of the words which occur in the sentence. Can the same be said about the referents of proper names? It seems that Frege came to the conclusion that even referents of proper names must be simple. In an unpublished paper of 1906, Frege states that while the sense of part of an expression is a part of the sense of the whole expression, the reference of part of a proper name (or of a name in general) is not part of the reference of the whole name. For example, the referent of 'Denmark' is not a part of the referent of the proper name 'the capital of Denmark'; Denmark, in other words, is not a part of Copenhagen.[77] But this means that all objects other than senses and propositions are simple entities. If concept words referred to concepts, Frege could not have held this view. For concepts, unlike objects, are unsaturated; they can be distinguished in the complexes in which they occur, but not separated from them. Hence, if concepts are referents, they must exist in complex entities. And this means that there would have to be complex objects other than senses and propositions.

I think, therefore, that Frege did not make a sense-reference distinction for concept words and that he also quite naturally thought of concepts as parts of propositions.[78] In addition to the argument which I just presented, there are several further considerations which speak for this interpretation.

Consider how Frege introduces senses of proper names.[79] He calls attention to the fact that one and the same thing may be presented in different ways; the planet Venus, for example, may be presented as the evening star or as the morning star. These different modes of presentation are then identified with the senses of proper names. Could one and the same concept be presented in different ways? If there were different modes of presentation for concepts, one could call these modes senses of concept words and one could distinguish between the concept and its presentations. For example, do the two expressions '(is) a featherless biped' and '(is) a human being' present the same concept in two different ways? According to Frege, they do not. Rather, they mean different concepts. Identity does not hold between these concepts, but

---

[77] See Dummett's "Note: Frege on Functions."

[78] If one calls every constituent of a sense a sense, then concepts are senses. Marshall, I think, comes to the same conclusion.

[79] Compare "Ueber Sinn und Bedeutung."

between the value-ranges associated with them. This shows that concepts are quite similar to senses of proper names. Different concepts may have the same value range, just as different senses present the same referent of a proper name.

Consider, next, how Frege introduces the two truth-values the True and the False.[80] As long as we are not interested in truth, it does not matter whether or not a proper name has a referent. Only if we are interested in truth do we have to proceed from a sense to a referent, from a proposition to a truth-value. Hence only the problem of truth forces us to consider referents of proper names and of sentences. For a proper name the question arises whether or not it has a referent in addition to having a sense; for a concept word, however, the question is not whether or not it means something (it always does), but whether or not the concept it means comprehends objects under itself.[81] Concepts are in this respect similar to senses of proper names: what matters in regard to truth is whether or not a sense determines a referent or whether or not a concept comprehends objects under itself.

That concepts are parts of senses (propositions) and as such themselves senses can also be seen from several passages in Frege's published works. For example, in "Ueber Begriff und Gegenstand" Frege says quite explicitly that the relation of falling under is an unsaturated sense which needs to be completed in order to yield a proposition.[82] And similar passages can be found in "Negation" and in "Gedankengefuege."[83]

Finally, because the application of the sense-reference distinction to concept words is such an obvious move, it is not surprising that passages in certain unpublished papers show that Frege himself seems to have contemplated making it. Now if we were correct in saying that he thought of concepts as unsaturated parts of propositions, we would expect him to wonder whether or not

[80] *Ibid.*, pp. 62–63.
[81] *Translations*, pp. 104–5.
[82] *Translations*, pp. 54–55.
[83] "Negation," *Translations*, pp. 131–32; "Gedankengefuege," in *Beitraege zur Philosophie des deutschen Idealismus*, vol. 3, no. 1 (1923), pp. 36–51 (on p. 39).

there also corresponds to a concept word something in the realm of reference. We would expect him to ask whether or not a concept word, in addition to expressing a concept, has a referent. Indeed, some passages from the unpublished papers seem to show that Frege's thoughts were just what we expect them to be, if our interpretation is correct.[84] However, the fact that he never published these papers and the fact that he later in his published articles speaks quite explicitly of concepts and relations as unsaturated parts of propositions indicate that he abandoned this attempt to introduce the sense-reference distinction for concept words. This is of course not surprising. For we have already seen that the introduction of this distinction for concept words would have involved some major changes in Frege's system.

To sum up. I think that Frege's later philosophy has the following features. (1) All objects other than senses and propositions are simple entities. (2) Sentences refer to truth-values and express propositions. (3) Proper names refer to objects and express senses. (4) Propositions consist of senses of proper names and of concepts. (5) Concept words do not have a sense and a reference, but mean concepts. (6) If we keep this in mind we may call concepts senses, for they together with senses of proper names make up complex senses (propositions). (7) Hence a proposition consists of a saturated sense (the sense of a proper name) and an unsaturated sense (a concept).[85]

[84] Compare, for example, the following passages cited by Dummett ("Note: Frege on Functions"): "It is altogether improbable that a proper name should be so different from the remaining part of a simple sentence that it should be important for it alone to have a Bedeutung: ... It is unthinkable that there could be a Bedeutung only in the case of proper names, and not in the remaining part of the sentence." Frege argues that when we make a relational statement we are saying that the "relation obtains between the Bedeutungen of the proper names" which we are using; this relation, he continues, "must therefore itself belong to the realm of Bedeutungen."

[85] Caton has claimed that Frege held three doctrines which are inconsistent with each other. According to Caton, Frege held (1) that the sense of every expression is an object; (2) that the senses of some expressions are unsaturated; and (3) that no object is unsaturated. According to our interpretation, there is no such inconsistency in Frege's system. When Frege asserts that the sense of an expression is an object, he is talking about proper names and sentences. When he says that a certain sense is unsaturated, he has a concept or relation in mind. The passages which

So far we have seen that Frege's objective world splits into two parts. One part contains propositions and their constituents—that is, concepts and senses of proper names. The other part contains the True, the False, and such objects as the earth and the number 2. What is the connection, if any, between these two parts? That there must be a connection at least between propositions and truth values can easily be seen. A certain proposition p, we assume with Frege, is true independently of our thinking of it or judging it to be true.[86] It must therefore be somehow co-ordinated with the True rather than the False. And this connection must be independent of mind. But what is there objectively in the world that accounts for this co-ordination rather than another? [87]

Frege explicitly rejects one possible answer. One could reply that a proposition is true (or false) by virtue of the fact that it has the property of being true (or false)—that is, by virtue of the fact that it falls under the concept true (or false). There is thus an objective connection between a proposition and its respective truth-value: namely, the nexus of exemplification which holds between the proposition and its truth-value. Whether we know it or not, a given proposition either exemplifies the property of being true or it does not. However, Frege rejects this answer; he argues that truth-values are objects rather than concepts under which propositions may fall.[88]

But he does not provide a plausible alternative to this answer. All he has to say on this point is that judgment constitutes an advance from a proposition to a truth-value.[89] This may or may not

Caton cites for his interpretation show quite clearly that this is the case. In other words, we agree with Caton that Frege held (2) and (3), but we deny that he held (1). Instead of (1), Frege held that some senses are objects (namely, the senses expressed by proper names and sentences) and that some senses (namely, concepts) are not objects. Compare Caton's "An Apparent Difficulty in Frege's Ontology," *The Philosophical Review,* 71(1962):462–75.

[86] Compare *Foundations of Arithmetic,* p. xviii; "Negation," *Translations,* p. 151.

[87] A similar question arises in regard to the connection between the sense of a proper name and its referent.

[88] "Ueber Sinn und Bedeutung," pp. 34–35 (*Translations,* p. 64).

[89] *Ibid.,* p. 35 (*Translations,* p. 65).

be so; at any rate, it does not answer the question—unless of course Frege wishes to claim, contrary to everything he says about the objectivity of truth, that a judgment simply *creates* a connection between a certain proposition and a certain truth-value. It seems, then, that Frege never bridges the gulf between propositions on the one hand and truth-values on the other. This is the important gap in Frege's system which I mentioned earlier.[90]

But is it not perfectly obvious that according to Frege there is a *relation* between a proposition and its truth-value, a relation which obtains between the sense and the reference of every expression?[91] I do not think that there can be such a relation in the case of propositions and truth-values and that therefore the gap cannot be closed in this manner. Concepts, as we saw, are always parts of propositions. They always connect with senses. What holds for concepts, holds automatically for relations. They, too, can only occur in propositions. They, too, can only connect senses, either senses of proper names or senses of sentences. But a truth-value is not a sense. Hence no relation could possibly obtain between a proposition and a truth-value, between the sense and the reference of a proper name or sentence. Frege himself points this out in a different way when he argues against the supposition that truth-values are properties of propositions.[92] When one says that there is a relation R between the proposition p and the truth-value T, one simply combines the predicate R with the two subjects p and T in order to get the combination $R(p,T)$. But this combination yields only a proposition. ". . . one reaches only a thought, never passes from sense to reference, never from a proposition to its truth-value. One moves at the same level but never advances from one level to the next."[93] This shows that if we think of a relation that holds between a proposition and a truth-value, we merely think of another proposition. It shows, further, that

[90] Compare also Bergmann's "Ontological Alternatives" in his *Logic and Reality*.
[91] Frege speaks about the relation of the proposition to the truth value. But this is at best a figure of speech as we shall see below.
[92] Compare "Ueber Sinn und Bedeutung," *Translations*, p. 64.
[93] *Ibid.*

truth-values cannot be *connected* with propositions, for they are not senses. But this means that the gap between propositions and truth-values cannot be closed by a relation.

That Frege himself felt rather uneasy about the problem of how a judgment can advance from a proposition to a certain truth-value can be seen from a revealing passage in "Ueber Sinn und Bedeutung." Frege explains in this passage that one might also say that judgments are distinctions of parts within truth-values. He adds that such distinctions occur by a return to the propositions. But he does not explain this idea any further.[94] Let us speculate that truth-values are really complex entities. Then there are two kinds of such entities, those that constitute the object the True, and those that constitute the object the False. All those entities which are the True can be distinguished from each other by a return to their propositions; similarly for all those entities which are the False. But how could one distinguish between the two *kinds* of entities that are the True and the False, respectively? A return to the proposition can be of no help, for propositions by themselves do not tell us whether they are true or false. Hence, there must be something in or about the complex referents themselves that tells us which of them are the True and which are the False. But Frege never tells us what this something could be. Nor can we even venture to guess on the basis of what he says elsewhere.

How are the objective entities of Frege's world presented to us? Consider first such objects as the moon or the number 2. There is, first of all, a subjective act of presentation (an idea). This mental act directly intends a sense—say, the sense expressed by 'the moon.' The moon itself is presented indirectly to us through this sense.[95] In the case of propositions, the situation is quite different. There exists again a subjective mental act of thinking. This mental act presents us directly with a proposition. But it does not present us with anything indirectly. If a judgment occurs, there occurs in

[94] *Ibid.*, p. 65.
[95] *Ibid.*, p. 60.

addition to the mere comprehension of a proposition an advance from the proposition to a truth-value.

Recall now the conceptualist's view. Perfect particulars and universals are presented in isolation through different kinds of mental acts. This view necessitates the introduction of judgments. What such a judgment intends is a complex entity consisting of a particular which exemplifies at least one universal.[96] We saw that the nexus of exemplification contained in this complex entity cannot be a product of mind. It must be given to the mind. Most conceptualists, though, did not realize that the nexus of exemplification is part of the furniture of the world. They claimed that a judgment simply "subsumes" a particular given in sensory intuition under a universal presented in general presentation. In doing so, the judgment was thought to "create" a connection between particular and universal. A similar mistake is contained in Frege's analysis. He does not seem to realize that there must be a nexus between a proposition and the true and that this nexus must be presented to us. According to him, a judgment simply "advances" from a proposition to a truth-value. In doing so, the judgment must "establish" what it does not find: namely, a connection between proposition and truth-value.

ABSTRACTION

It might be objected that concepts are, according to Frege, abstracted rather than presented to the mind.[97] But this objection would rest on the false notion that to say that a universal is abstracted and to say that a universal is presented are incompatible. When it is claimed that universals (or concepts) are got by means of abstraction, two quite different things may be meant. It may mean that universals are the product of a mental activity called abstraction, or it may mean that universals are presented to the mind in a certain way. In the first view, universals are mere

---

[96] In this context, as before, I talk of course about true judgments. For the distinction between true and false judgments see below pp. 113–114.

[97] Compare *Foundations of Arithmetic*, pp. 45, 57, 58, 61, 62, and 75.

entia rationes. According to the second view, they are nonmental entities. We might say that there is an ontological and a psychological doctrine of abstraction.[98]

The ontological doctrine amounts to this: (1) all nonmental entities are particular; (2) by going to work on such particular entities, the mind abstracts from them universals; (3) but these universals do not exist in the particulars, they only exist in the mind. For example, according to a view commonly attributed to Scotus, there are common natures and universals. Common natures are particular entities because they are numerically different in different things.[99] Universals are *entia rationes,* got from common natures through abstraction.

As for Frege, it is quite obvious that he does not subscribe to the ontological doctrine of abstraction. His concepts are not *entia rationes.* He emphasizes time and again that concepts are objective (nonmental) rather than subjective (mental) entities. Moreover, he says quite explicitly that to bring an object under a concept is just to recognize a relation that was already there independent of mind.[100] This indicates that he must be thinking of what I have called the psychological doctrine of abstraction when he says that concepts are abstracted.[101] Presently, we shall examine the psychological doctrine. First, though, let me show why the ontological doctrine must fail. This can be done briefly. Common natures, under whatever name they may appear, are simply the perfect particulars discussed above. A common nature must be either simple or complex. If it is a simple individual entity which differs from one thing to another, we cannot possibly abstract a universal from it. Bare particulars by themselves do not give us any clue as to what to abstract from them. On the other hand, if a

---

[98] On abstraction one should consult Meinong and Husserl: Meinong, *Hume Studien* and "Abstrahieren und Vergleichen," *Gesammelte Abhandlungen,* (Leipzig, 1914), vol. 1; Husserl, *Logische Untersuchungen,* vol. 2.

[99] Common natures, particularized essences, and the like are, I think, all perfect particulars. Hence they are really complex entities.

[100] Compare Frege's review of Husserl's *Philosophie der Arithmetik.*

[101] According to the psychological doctrine, not all concepts are abstracted. Some can be simply defined in terms of others. Compare Frege's *Foundations of Arithmetic,* p. 62.

common nature is a complex entity which does not consist entirely of bare particulars, it can provide us with such a clue. But whatever this clue may be, it must be common to certain common natures and not contained in others. It must be contained in all those common natures from which we presumably abstract the universal. But an entity which is common to several things is a universal. Hence, if abstraction from common natures is possible at all, these common natures must contain universals. Universals cannot be created by the mind through abstraction. They can only be discovered in common natures through a mental process called abstraction. This leads us to what I called the psychological doctrine of abstraction.

In one form, the psychological doctrine rests on the assumption that there are perfect particulars. According to this version, there is analytic abstraction and generalizing abstraction.[102] Suppose that you see a green disk. Analytic abstraction occurs if you *pay attention* to the perfect particular green$_1$ in this disk, abstracting it for the moment from other perfect particulars which are also contained in the disk. Generalizing abstraction takes place, if, while looking at the disk, you mean, intend, or think of the color of this disk as such—that is, if you mean, intend, or think of the universal green.[103] In short, in analytic abstraction, one *pays attention* to a perfect particular, while in generalizing abstraction one *pays attention* to a universal.[104]

Of course, in so far as the distinction between analytic and generalizing abstraction rests on the assumption that there are perfect particulars, it is not sound. As I have pointed out before, one can of course mean this particular shade of green as exemplified by this particular. In other words, one can abstract from the other properties which this particular has and *pay attention* to only one of them. But if one does, one pays attention to a universal

---

[102] Compare Messer, *Empfindung und Denken.*

[103] The universal green is of course a certain shade of green. This raises a further issue: one can only *see* certain shades of green, while one may *think* of green without thinking of any particular shade.

[104] If it is added that only perfect particulars exist as nonmental entities, we get the ontological view.

rather than a perfect particular; for one pays attention to a universal which happens to be exemplified by a certain particular. Thus the difference between analytic and generalizing abstraction cannot consist in their having different objects.

However, we can distinguish between the following two cases. You may *see* that the shade of green exemplified by this particular is the same as the shade of green exemplified by that particular. Or you may *think* that a certain shade of green is your favorite color. In the first case, you see the universal (this shade of green) exemplified here and over there; in the second case, you think of a universal, but do not think of it as exemplified by any particular object. The intentions of these two mental acts differ in a significant way. The first mental act, if I may so put it, intends a universal as exemplified by certain particulars, while the second does not. If one wished to distinguish between these two kinds of mental acts, one could say that the first kind is based on analytic abstraction, while the second kind is based on generalizing abstraction. But one must keep in mind that in either case the mental act intends a universal.

There is another traditional view which rests on some such distinction. Sensory intuition (perception), it is claimed, always presents us with universals which are exemplified by particulars. It never presents us with bare or pure universals. Space and time are forms of sensory intuition, and nothing can be presented in sensory intuition unless it is localized in space and time. Nothing can be presented in sensory intuition unless it is exemplified by a particular which is so localized. Thought, on the other hand, is not confined to what exists in space and time. Objects of thought, unlike objects of sensory intuition, do not have to be individuated. Only thought therefore presents us with what is truly universal. Only thought presents us with bare universals.[105]

[105] We can formulate this view more precisely in the following way. Assume that the intention of every mental act can be represented by a sentence. One can now divide all sentences into two groups: those that mention particulars and those that do not. For example, the two sentences 'this is green' and 'this has the same color as that' belong to the first group; the two sentences 'green is a beautiful color' and 'all green things are useful' belong to the second group. On the basis of this distinction,

We have come across a different dogma of localization. This time, however, it is neutral as far as the existential status of universals is concerned. It merely asserts that unexemplified universals can only be presented in thought. It does not claim that universals are not presented in sensory intuition. One who does not see this, however, may easily draw the wrong conclusion from this particular dogma of localization. He may call a universal which is exemplified by a particular a common nature, a particularized essence, or perfect particular. He may further reserve the term 'universal' for what I called a moment ago a pure or bare universal. Finally, he may hold that pure or bare universals are mental entities. If he takes all these steps, he may also arrive at the mistaken conclusion that universals, as he uses this term, are *entia rationes* or products of the mind.

---

one can now also distinguish between two groups of mental acts: mental acts whose intentions are expressed by sentences of the first kind and mental acts whose intentions can be presented by sentences of the second kind. Mental acts of the first group are called sensory intuitions or perceptions, while mental acts of the second group are called thoughts or judgments.

MEANING 4

LINGUISTIC EXPRESSIONS as marks and noises are part of the perceptual world. They are perceptual objects among other perceptual objects. We use such expressions according to certain rules. We write them down in a certain order and utter them in certain sequences. Moreover, we learn under what circumstances it is opportune, polite, improper, deceitful, to use just these expressions in just that order with a certain tone of voice. But their meaning is not exhausted by grammatical and social rules. Many expressions and strings of expressions are about the world. They represent things and states of affairs. And in so far as language is about the world, it does not just consist of marks and noises strung together according to grammatical and social conventions. To compare language with chess is singularly misleading. Of course, there is some resemblance. The chess pieces may be compared to the marks and noises of a language. The rules for moving these pieces may be compared to the formation rules of a language. Just as the rules for moving the pieces determine what moves are permissible, so do the formation rules determine what strings of expressions are possible—that is, well formed. Chess strategy may be compared to the similar strategy which we employ in the social game. We say certain things, not because we mean them, but because we want others to believe that we mean them. We say things in order to make people happy or unhappy, and so on. But this is as far as we can press the analogy. For language, as we said, is also about the world, while the chess pieces are not *about* anything. What is missing in the chess game is the descriptive function which the marks and noises of language have.

It is clear, then, that many linguistic expressions represent something. It is also clear that they do not do so by themselves or as mere perceptual objects. Rather, we *use* such marks and noises in order to refer to, in order to represent, in order to describe things. That one can use perceptual objects in this way rests, among other things, on the fact that one can *think* of things and circumstances, that one can *mean* things and circumstances, that one can *intend* things and circumstances, and that one can *have* things and circumstances *in mind*. No doubt these are the most remarkable powers of the mind.

Marks and noises are used to represent things and circumstances of which we think, which we mean, or which we describe. But this means that linguistic expressions are connected with thoughts as well as things and states of affairs. The connection is thus in two directions: a particular expression, for example, may *express* a thought and *represent* a state of affairs. Hence language presupposes two linguistic connections as well as a nonlinguistic one. The linguistic ones are, first, the connection between a thought and an expression and, second, the connection between a state of affairs and an expression. The nonlinguistic connection obtains between a thought and the state of affairs which it intends. In brief, certain well-formed expressions have both a "sense" and a "reference." [1] They have meaning because they express thoughts, and they have meaning because they represent things and states of affairs. Let us call this the double-tie view of meaning. For a long time it went unchallenged. Recently, though, it has been attacked by certain linguistic philosophers.

I said that a sentence may represent a state of affairs. But this does not mean that every expression which is, grammatically speaking, a sentence represents a state of affairs. Questions and

---

[1] It is clear, I hope, that this does not mean that they have a sense and a reference in precisely the way Frege outlines.

commands are obvious exceptions, and there may well be others.[2] But even if we restrict our investigation to so-called declarative sentences, there seem to be quite a few exceptions to the rule. At least all false sentences seem to be exceptions. This raises two connected questions. First, how can a thought intend a nonexistent state of affairs? Second, how can a false sentence represent a state of affairs? Clearly, these two questions are closely related. In our view, the answer is the same to both: we must distinguish between actual states of affairs (facts) and merely possible states of affairs. A false sentence represents not an actual state of affairs but a possible state of affairs. A thought expressed by a false sentence intends not an actual state of affairs but a possible state of affairs.[3] I shall use the term 'intention' to cover both kinds of states of affairs. Every declarative sentence thus represents an intention, and every thought intends an intention. Whether or not this view, as a whole, can be defended will be discussed in the next chapter. Let us try to see what alternatives to it there could be.

One could argue that a sentence does not represent anything if it is false. But since it nevertheless has a meaning in that we understand it perfectly well, we may conclude that the meaning of a false sentence resides completely in the thought which it expresses. For the thought most certainly exists, even if the sentence which expresses the thought is false. Generalizing from the case of false sentences to that of all sentences, one arrives at the view that the meaning of a sentence always resides in the thought which it expresses. Hence there is only one tie that connects a sentence with nonlinguistic entities—namely, the tie between a thought and its linguistic expression. But this view is clearly false. Language, whatever else it may be used for, is often used to describe the world. It is not just used to express our thoughts. However, this criticism applies only to the single-tie view, not to the view that there are some expressions which do not represent anything.

[2] This does not mean, however, that the representative function is entirely absent from questions and commands. The words in such questions and commands have such a function. Otherwise we would not know what the question is about or what we are supposed to do.

[3] The distinction between actual and possible states of affairs has been made in one form or another by many philosophers. Compare our discussion below.

The latter view stands halfway between the double-tie view (for sentences) and the single-tie view which we rejected.

This, then, is one part of the attack against the double-tie view of meaning: it is alleged that not all linguistic expressions represent. In its radical form, it asserts that no linguistic expression has a representative function. But there is also a second part of the attack. I said that sentences express thoughts. Some philosophers have argued, though, that thoughts are not connected with sentences. More accurately, they assumed that thoughts consist of nothing but "inner pictures," and then pointed out that there are often no such "inner pictures" connected with linguistic expressions. The meaning of a sentence, it was concluded, cannot consist of a thought. Here again we can distinguish between a radical and a moderate position. According to the radical view, no meaning of an expression consists of a thought, but always of what the expression represents. This, too, is a single-tie view; it is the mirror-image, as it were, of the single-tie view mentioned in the last paragraph. According to the moderate position, some expressions express thoughts and represent things or states of affairs, while others merely represent.

Both views, though, rest on the mistaken assumption that thoughts are mental pictures, images, and the like. Thoughts are mental acts and hence fundamentally different from all kinds of phenomenal objects. It seems that this criticism of the double-tie view relies on the so-called context-theory of meaning, according to which the meaning of an expression consists of the images, feelings, etc. which are aroused by the expression in a certain person. This type of meaning varies of course from person to person, and even for one and the same person from one occasion to another. If one thinks that thoughts consist of such internal responses, one may well come to the conclusion that linguistic expressions cannot possibly express certain *characteristic* thoughts.[4] To repeat, therefore—thoughts are neither mental pictures nor "meanings" as defined by the context-theory.

---

[4] Bolzano and Frege were correct in saying that there are thoughts which can be the common property of several thinkers. They went wrong, though, in holding that such thoughts are nonmental entities.

Sometimes the two radical views mentioned above are combined and the result is offered as an alternative to the double-tie view. The meaning of every expression, it is held, does not consist of a thought and of a reference. It cannot consist of the former, because it cannot consist of "inner pictures" or internal responses. It cannot consist of the latter, because expressions can be meaningful even if they do not represent anything. What, then, is the meaning of an expression?

Noises and marks, we observed, are combined according to certain rules. In using them one also obeys certain social conventions. Most importantly, though, they can be used to express our thoughts and to represent things and states of affairs. Thus it may be said that they are meaningful in at least four different ways. First, linguistic expressions are meaningful in that they are well formed according to the rules of grammar. Second, they are meaningful in that they contribute considerably to our social life. Third, they are meaningful in that they express our thoughts. And fourth, they are meaningful in that they represent things and states of affairs. Now if you deny that they have meaning in the latter two ways you are left with the view that meaning is a matter of grammatical and social rules alone. The meaning of an expression, it is said, resides in the rules for its use.

Of course, we are not forced to accept this theory of meaning; for we are not forced to accept the two radical views that lurk in the background. We do not have to hold that no linguistic expression has referential meaning, just because there may be some expressions which do not represent. Nor are we forced to hold that linguistic expressions do not express thoughts, because we do not think of thoughts as "mental pictures." On the contrary, the plain facts convince us that most linguistic expressions have the double function of expressing thoughts and of representing things and states of affairs in the world. We thus start out with the double-tie view. And this starting point will determine the course of our next inquiries. First we must discuss what precisely it is that is expressed by linguistic expressions: this will be the task of the present chapter. Then we must turn to the topic of referential meaning and investigate the connection between thought and intention: that will be our concern in the next chapter.

MENTAL CONTENTS

What shall we call the "meanings" expressed by words and sentences?[5] Until now, I have merely said that sentences express thoughts. But this is not precise enough. Certain sentences do not express thoughts, but perceptions or beliefs. Since the distinction between what an expression represents and what it expresses is not at all new, several traditional terms are at our disposal. For example, it has been said that words and sentences express *concepts* and *propositions,* respectively. Other philosophers think of such "meanings" as *inner pictures* or *inner words.* Still others use the term 'notion.' But none of these terms seems quite adequate for our purpose. Concepts and propositions, for instance, are often considered to be objective, nonmental entities, while the "meanings" we wish to discuss are, according to this rough dichotomy, mental things. Similar objections apply to other choices of terminology. Besides, there is the further fact that "meanings" as here understood are discussed at great length by Twardowski, Meinong, and Husserl. It would be desirable, therefore, to express a certain continuity of philosophical thought by our choice of terminology. I shall therefore follow Twardowski and Meinong and say that the "meanings" under study are *contents* of mental acts.

By saying that "meanings" are contents of mental acts as understood, for instance, by Twardowski and Meinong, I indicate an essential agreement with these philosophers as to the nature of "meanings." There are, however, three important respects in which my view differs from theirs.

First. We have already mentioned Twardowski's notion that complex things are to be analyzed into certain kinds of parts. This particular ontological analysis is quite common among the students of Brentano. As might be expected, they apply it to mental

[5] We shall see that only whole sentences express "meanings" in the sense under discussion.

acts as well. A mental act, they hold, is a whole which has two characteristic parts. One of these two parts is responsible for the qualitative differences among different kinds of mental acts. Acts of believing, for example, are distinguished from other kinds of acts by the fact that they share one and the same qualitative part. The other part of every mental act, its content, determines the specific object which is intended by an act. To different intentions of mental acts there thus correspond different contents in the acts. Now even though we agree with the general view that every mental act has a *quality* and a *content*, we must give a different ontological analysis of this fact. A mental act, it is true, is a complex thing. But this complex thing does not consist of parts in the sense in which these Brentano students think of wholes and parts. Rather, it consists of a (bare) *particular* which exemplifies two characteristic *properties*, one of which is the quality of the act, the other, its content.[6] That this rejection of the part-whole analysis is not just a terminological matter is clear, I think, from the ontological discussions of the last chapter. This, then, is the first difference between our view and some of the traditional views about mental contents. It rests ultimately on our rejection of certain forms of conceptualism and nominalism.

Second. Most act-philosophers distinguish between different kinds of mental acts. The most important of these distinctions, many hold, is that between presentations and judgments. These two kinds of acts are supposed to differ qualitatively. But they are also supposed to differ in their respective objects. Roughly speaking, a presentation intends an object, while a judgment intends a state of affairs.[7] Hence contents of presentations are expressed by words, while contents of judgments are expressed by whole sen-

[6] Compare Gustav Bergmann, "Realistic Postscript" (in *Logic and Reality* [Madison, 1964]), in which he calls these two properties dimensions of mental acts.

[7] In Meinong's words, a presentation intends an object, while a judgment intends an objective. Twardowski holds, for certain reasons, that the content of a presentation is a "mental picture," while the content of a judgment is the existence of the thing judged about. See his *Zur Lehre vom Inhalt und Gegenstand der Vorstellungen* (Vienna, 1894), p. 9.

tences. Our second disagreement concerns this distinction. We hold that all acts are *propositional*. The content of every mental act, in our view, is expressed by a whole sentence rather than a single word. This disagreement, too, rests on ontological considerations. So-called presentations, we argued in the last chapter, acquaint us neither with bare particulars nor with unexemplified universals. Instead, they present us with states of affairs; that is, with such facts as that a certain particular exemplifies a certain universal.

This view has several important consequences in regard to the nature of mental contents. But first of all, we must attempt to clarify the notion of a judgment. If one calls every mental act a judgment, if its content is expressed by a sentence, then it follows from our view that all mental acts are judgments. For example, since the content of an act of perceiving would be expressed by a sentence, say, 'this is green,' mental acts of perception would be judgments. But I do not think that this use of the term 'judgment' is a happy one. It blurs certain distinctions that can and must be made. There is, for example, the common distinction between judging that something is so and so and merely supposing that it is so and so. These two kinds of acts are phenomenally quite different; they have different qualities. But they do not necessarily differ in their contents: a certain supposition may have exactly the same content as a certain judgment; and this content is expressed by one and the same sentence. This is the reason why we cannot tell from a sentence alone whether it expresses a supposition or a judgment.[8] A similar point can be made in regard to the distinction between (visually) seeing that something is so and so and merely judging that it is so and so. Hence it seems more appropriate to use the term 'judgment' to indicate a certain kind of mental act, a kind that has a characteristic quality not shared by, say, acts of supposing and acts of seeing.

One consequence of our view can be expressed by Frege's

[8] Recall in this connection Frege's notational device which indicated whether something is merely considered or asserted (to be true).

principle never to ask for the meaning of a word in isolation but only in the context of a proposition.[9] For, if all mental acts are propositional, there is no content that could be expressed by an English word rather than a whole English sentence. And in so far as the meaning of an expression is the corresponding content of mental acts, there are no such meanings for words in isolation. It must be kept in mind, though, that Frege uses this principle against a very different background. In this context, meanings are for him objective entities rather than contents of mental acts.

Yet the traditional distinction between concepts and propositions does not completely disappear, in our view. Consider, for example, the "concept" green. Keep in mind that it is neither the property green exemplified, say, by the pen on my desk, nor is it the objective concept in Frege's sense. Assume that someone thinks of the property green. How would we express the content of his thought? Obviously, we cannot answer this question until we know what precisely he thinks about green. If he thinks, for example, that green is his favorite color, then the following sentence would express the content of his thought 'green is my favorite color.' However, he may think that there is such a property as green. In this case, the content of his thought would be expressed by the sentence 'there is such a property as green.'[10] Now one can distinguish between two different kinds of contents. Some contents are expressed by sentences of the form 'there is such a thing as A' or 'there is such a property as F.' Other contents are expressed by sentences like 'A is green,' 'green is a beautiful color,' etc. And one may then call contents of the first kind concepts and contents of the second kind propositions, keeping in mind, of course, that both concepts and propositions turn out to be properties of mental acts.[11] Notice, however, that this distinction between concepts and propositions does not rest on whether a content is expressed by a word or by a whole sentence. Both concepts and

---

[9] *Foundations of Arithmetic* (New York, 1960), p. xxii.

[10] More accurately, the sentence would read, 'There is a property f and this property is identical with green.'

[11] Compare Gustav Bergmann and H. Hochberg, "Concepts," *Philosophical Studies,* 7(1957):19–27.

propositions are in fact expressed by whole sentences. The distinction depends on what kind of sentence expresses a certain content. Whether or not one would wish to call some contents concepts and others propositions depends on whether or not one thinks that the distinction between these two kinds of contents is important enough to warrant a terminological distinction.

Another consequence of our view pertains to the explication of truth and falsehood. Philosophers agree that truth and falsehood attach to whole sentences rather than single words or phrases. In regard to mental acts, they agree that truth and falsehood can only be predicated of judgments and not of presentations. Since we hold that all mental acts are propositional, it follows that all mental acts can either be true or false.[12] But this way of talking is not quite accurate; it does not go to the heart of the matter. Properly speaking, truth and falsehood are predicated of mental contents. Let f be the content expressed by the sentence 'this is green.' If this is green, f is true. If this is not green, f is false. Truth and falsehood are properties of mental contents—that is, properties of properties. These properties can be defined.[13] A content f is true if and only if it intends a certain state of affairs and this state of affairs is an actual rather than a possible one. It is false if and only if it intends a certain state of affairs and this state of affairs is a possible rather than actual one.[14]

Contents of mental acts are properties of acts and they are expressed by sentences. Therefore truth and falsehood can also be predicated of mental acts and of sentences. A mental act may be said to be true or false, depending on whether its content is true or false. It is in this sense that we can predicate truth and falsehood of "judgments." Recall that some philosophers hold that every sentence expresses a judgment. In our view, every sentence may be said to express a mental act, though not necessarily a judgment.

[12] Except, of course, those mental acts which would be expressed by questions, commands, and the like.

[13] Compare Gustav Bergmann, "Intentionality," *Semantica* (Archivio di Filosofia, Padua 1955), also reprinted in Bergmann's *Meaning and Existence*.

[14] For the distinction between actual and possible states of affairs see below pp. 163–168.

Hence one might say that every mental act is either true or false. Furthermore, since mental contents are expressed by sentences, these sentences themselves may be said to be true or false. But to say that a certain sentence 'p' is true is not to talk about the mark or noise 'p.' To say that 'p' is true if and only if p, is to say that 'p' is true if and only if 'p' expresses the content f and this content intends the actual state of affairs p.

Third. Most act-philosophers hold that contents can be either simple or complex. For example, they hold that the presentation of a complex thing involves a complex content. Both of these complex entities are analyzed into their respective parts, and it is assumed that there is a certain isomorphism between the parts of the complex thing and the parts of the complex content. Our third disagreement concerns this distinction between simple and complex contents. It seems to us that all contents are simple. A mental content is expressed by a sentence and intends a state of affairs. Both the sentence and the state of affairs are complex things. But the mental content itself is not a complex thing.

Consider Twardowski's distinction between simple and complex mental contents.[15] A complex entity, according to Twardowski, contains two kinds of parts: material parts and formal parts. For example, a green and round thing contains (at least) the two material parts green$_1$ and round$_1$. But these material parts (together with others) form a whole. The connection or connections which obtain between the material parts and combine them into a whole, are the formal parts of the green and round thing. Consider next the isomorphism between a complex thing and "its" complex content. There seem to be two possibilities here. First, one could hold that the material parts of the thing were co-ordinated to material parts of the content, while its formal parts correspond to formal parts of the content. Second, one could hold that both the formal parts and the material parts of the thing were co-ordinated to material parts of the content. In the latter case, no parts of the thing correspond to the formal parts of the content. One might say that there is only a partial isomorphism between

[15] Twardowski, *Zur Lehre vom Inhalt und Gegenstand der Vorstellungen.*

thing and content. Both of these possible views raise important problems.[16]

According to the first possibility, formal parts of the content intend formal parts of the thing. But if we think of a complex content as consisting of simple contents and relations among these simple contents, then it follows that these relations are not contents at all. If so, how could they possibly intend anything? To put this argument differently: whatever intends anything must be a content—either a complex content or a simple one. Relations among such contents, however, are not themselves contents. Hence they cannot intend anything. In particular, they could not possibly intend the formal parts of a thing. But if these formal parts of the thing are not intended, it remains obscure how a complex content can ever intend a complex whole rather than several different material parts in isolation. Obviously, the crux of this argument consists in the assertion that relations among simple contents cannot intend anything. But this shows, I think, that the connection between content and thing is not conceived of as the logical relation that obtains between two isomorphic fields. For something to intend something else it is not enough that there be a mere isomorphism. The intentional relation between a content and what it intends is not that of one-one correspondence. Only certain kinds of entities can stand in the intentional relation to others, while just about anything can be isomorphic to anything else. If the connection between mind and world is not that of one-one correspondence, if only contents can intend something, then one must give up or at least modify the first possible view.

According to the second possible view, all parts of a thing, the formal parts as well as the material parts, are intended by material parts of the content. This view is based on the kind of consideration we just mentioned. Contents and only contents can intend. Therefore, contents and only contents can intend all parts of a complex whole. But this view raises a different problem. Assume that the complex thing under consideration consists of two material parts, p_1 and p_2, such that p_1 is to the left of p_2. The corre-

[16] Twardowski seems to vacillate between these two views.

sponding content would then contain three material parts, P_1, P_2, and P_3. P_1 and P_2 intend p_1 and p_2, respectively. P_3 intends the spatial relation which obtains between p_1 and p_2. But now a thing consisting of p_2 to the left of p_1 would also have to be intended by a content which contains P_1, P_2, and P_3. Hence there would be no difference between the two contents as far as their material parts are concerned. If we further assume that only the material parts of a content distinguish it from another content, there will be no difference whatsoever between the two contents. Yet there must be such a difference, for if the two things are different, as they clearly are, their two contents must be different. Otherwise we would not know what thing is intended by what content.[17] One way out of this difficulty is hinted at by Twardowski.[18] One could argue that to the difference in things there corresponds a difference in the way in which the material parts of the respective contents are related to each other. Even though the two contents have the same material parts, these material parts form different contents because they are combined in different ways. But this view leads us back to the first one which we considered in the last paragraph. For, in this view, the formal parts of a content determine in part what kind of thing the content intends. In order to do so, however, the formal parts themselves must in some way intend something in or about the things which are intended. And this is impossible, if only contents and not relations among contents can intend. It is impossible if the intentional relation is not a mere isomorphism but a unique nexus that obtains only between certain entities.

Since this point is of some importance, let us reformulate it in our own terminology. To speak of complex contents would mean to speak of complex properties of mental acts. Assume that there is a complex content (property) F which consists of two simple

[17] Geach raises a similar objection against one of Russell's views. However, Geach himself holds that judgments (contents) are complex and accepts a kind of view similar to our first possibility. See P. Geach, *Mental Acts* (London, 1957).

[18] Compare Twardowski, *Zur Lehre vom Inhalt und Gegenstand der Vorstellungen*, and also J. N. Findlay, *Meinong's Theory of Objects* (London, 1933), pp. 16–17.

contents (properties) f_1 and f_2. Assume that these two simple contents intend the two simple properties red and round which are contained in a complex thing. F consists of f_1 and f_2 and the logical relation represented by 'and.' The thing intended consists (at least) of the two properties red and round which are also connected by this logical relation. Now does this logical relation between f_1 and f_2 intend anything? In particular, does it intend itself as it holds between red and round? Our answer will depend on how we view the intentional relation. If we hold that only certain properties of mental acts, properties like f_1 and f_2, are intentional, then the connection between f_1 and f_2 cannot intend anything, for it is not such a property. On the other hand, if we think of the intentional relation as mere one-one correspondence, there is no reason for denying that the connection between f_1 and f_2 intends the connection between red and round.

But we have said that all mental acts are propositional. Hence there are no contents such as F which intend complex properties. Consider, then, an example which takes account of this fact. Assume that the simple contents A and F are co-ordinated to the particular a and the property f which are contained in the fact a is f. What is the content that intends this fact? Obviously, it cannot consist merely of A and F, standing side by side, so to speak. If it consisted merely of A and F, we would have a content which intended a and a content which intended f, but not a content which intended the fact that a is f. Nor could it consist of A and F and some further (simple) content X, all three of which were unconnected, so to speak. For even these three contents would merely intend three unconnected entities. There seems to be only one way out. We must assume that the contents A and F are connected in a certain way and that the fact that A and F are thus connected represents the fact that a is f. But this means that the connection between A and F must intend something, contrary to our view that only properties of mental acts can intend anything.

The assumption that mental contents can be complex properties of mental acts must therefore be given up if we wish to hold, as we shall, that the intentional nexus is not a mere isomorphism. Even the most complex sentence can only express a simple content. Meanings, as distinct from sentences and states of affairs, are unanalyzable.[19]

Mental contents intend states of affairs. Contents are properties of mental acts; states of affairs are not properties at all and hence could not possibly be properties of mental acts. One must therefore always distinguish between the content of a mental act and its intention. The proponents of contents have always argued for this distinction. They have argued that one must sharply distinguish between the content and the object of a mental act. Three such arguments are of special interest.[20] I shall call them the argument from nonexistent objects, the argument from predication, and the argument from different contents.

The argument from nonexistent objects. Twardowski gives the following version of this argument. Whoever makes a true judgment to the effect that there is no such thing as a certain object must have a presentation of this object. But if there is a presentation of this object, there must be a content which intends the object. Hence there is a content, even if the object itself does not exist.[21] From this argument it follows that one must distinguish between the content of a presentation and the object of this presentation.

Sometimes the argument appears in a different form. It is a fact that one can think of objects which do not exist. For example, one can think of the golden mountain. One can even think of the square circle. In either case, there occurs a mental act of thinking. Furthermore, the two thoughts I just mentioned are clearly different from each other. But in what could this difference consist? Obviously, these two thoughts cannot be different just because

[19] This fact, I think, may be used to explicate the idealistic notion of the unity of thought (mind).
[20] The general distinction between content and object of presentation was not only made by the Brentano students, but also, for example, by Bolzano, Zimmermann, and Noël. Compare B. Bolzano, *Wissenschaftslehre* (Leipzig, 1929), §49; R. Zimmermann, *Philosophische Propaedeutik* (Vienna, 1867), §18 and §26; and G. Noël, "Noms et concepts," *Revue philosophique, 31*(1891):471.
[21] Twardowski, *Zur Lehre vom Inhalt und Gegenstand der Vorstellungen,* p. 30.

they intend different objects, for there are no such things as the golden mountain and the square circle, and if there are no such things, such things cannot make a difference. The felt difference must therefore lie on the side of the acts, if I may so put it. It is a difference in contents. The contents expressed by 'the golden mountain' and 'the square circle' do exist, even if there is no golden mountain and no square circle. Moreover, these contents are different. And this difference explains the difference between the two thoughts.

If it is granted that there are mental contents in addition to objects, it is clear, I think, that one must keep them apart. But does the argument from nonexistent objects show that there must be contents? I do not think it does. Moore, for example, claims that "it is impossible to verify by observation the existence of any internal qualitative difference between every pair of acts which have different objects." [22] Could we convince him by the argument outlined above that he must be mistaken? [23] How could he account for the difference between the two thoughts mentioned above, without acknowledging the existence of mental contents? Now Moore also claims that there is a difference between, say, the direct apprehension of a particular blue color and the direct apprehension of a particular red color. But this difference, according to him, consists in the fact that the two acts have different objects. If we applied this view to the example under discussion, it would assert that the difference between a thought of the golden mountain and a thought of the square circle is a difference in objects. But this implies that there must be two entities, the golden mountain and the square circle, which are different and which account for the difference between the two thoughts. Does this implication agree with what we all know to be a fact, that there is no golden mountain and no square circle? If it does not agree with this fact, we cannot possibly hold that the only difference between acts

[22] See G. E. Moore's review of A. Messer's *Empfindung und Denken*, *Mind*, 19(1910):403–4.

[23] I think that Moore is wrong here: the existence of such an internal qualitative difference can be established by "observation." We do experience mental contents when we experience mental acts.

stems from their having different objects. We seem to be forced to accept the view that mental acts are different because they have different contents. We seem to be forced to acknowledge the existence of mental contents.

It must be noted, however, that the relational view seems to force one in any case to acknowledge such objects as the golden mountain and the square circle. Most proponents of mental contents accept such objects anyway.[24] To be sure, the issue is rather complicated. It is admitted that there are of course no such things as the golden mountain and the square circle. Nevertheless, it is claimed that there are these things *as* objects of acts. It is asserted that every mental act intends an object, irrespective of whether or not the object exists. In short, it is held that there are objects which do not exist. But this view, I think, is all one needs in order to hold that the difference between two acts is always a difference between their objects. However marginal the ontological status of certain objects may be, as long as they have any ontological status at all they can be used to explain the difference between different acts.

Our consideration shows two things. It shows that one does not need contents in order to explain the difference between thinking of the golden mountain and thinking of the square circle. But one can only explain this difference by granting some ontological status to the golden mountain and the square circle. It shows also that one may be forced to grant ontological status to them even if one holds that every mental act has a content.

The argument from predication. This argument consists simply in the claim that the properties of objects of mental acts are not the properties of their contents. Twardowski, for example, says that the property of being golden which one predicates of the golden mountain, even though there is no golden mountain, cannot be predicated of the corresponding content. That content is neither golden nor a mountain. A content, being part of a mental act, cannot have the properties which perceptual objects have. Hence

[24] Compare Meinong's and Twardowski's systems and our discussion of possible entities below.

content and object are two different things and must not be identified.

It is clear that Twardowski's point is well taken. If there are mental contents, these contents cannot have the same properties as their objects. However, the argument does not show that there are mental contents. It does not refute Moore's view.

The argument from different contents. It is a fact that things are what they are independently of whether or not we think of them and how we think of them. When thinking of the morning star and when thinking of the evening star, one thinks of one and the same thing. Nothing changes in this thing just because we think of it in different ways. Only our thoughts differ. If so, how can one possibly explain a difference between two acts in terms of the difference between their objects? How can the thought of the evening star differ from the thought of the morning star—as it clearly does—if these two thoughts have one and the same object? If one assumes that there are mental contents, one can explain the difference. For one can say that these two mental acts differ in their contents even though they have the same object.

This argument for mental contents rests on the assumption that the thought of the morning star and the thought of the evening star have the same object. But someone like Moore does not have to agree to this assumption at all: it could be held that these two thoughts have different objects. In the one case, the object is the evening star; in the other, it is the morning star. In this view, one needs a further distinction. For example, one could distinguish between *objects* and *ultimate objects* of mental acts. Two acts with different objects may have the same ultimate object. For example, thinking of the morning star and thinking of the evening star, we have two different objects but the same ultimate object— namely, the planet Venus. If one makes this distinction, one can account for the distinction between these two mental acts in terms of their objects instead of their contents.[25]

---

[25] Compare Frege's view that we are presented with things through the medium of senses. These senses correspond roughly to the objects; the things behind them, to the ultimate objects of acts.

To sum up: we have seen that the three arguments do not prove that there must be mental contents in addition to objects. They show at most that if there are contents, these contents must be distinguished from the objects which they intend. But they also indicate that one who denies the existence of mental contents and accepts the relational view of mental acts must hold two things. He must hold first that objects like the golden mountain or the square circle have some ontological status. And, secondly, he must hold that there is a distinction between the immediate objects of mental acts and their ultimate objects. These commitments are necessary because of the undeniable fact that two mental acts may differ even if they have the same ultimate object or have no existent objects at all.

But if these arguments do not show that there are mental contents, what argument could? There comes a point when all one can do is to appeal to experience. I think that the experience of seeing a red thing differs from the experience of seeing a blue thing in a "wholly indescribable qualitative way." [26] This difference is not a difference between objects, but is contained in my experiences. As Meinong puts it, "es ist uns anders zu Mute." This difference is a difference between mental contents.

In conclusion, let us stress the following three points. First, mental contents are not sense-impressions, feelings, images, and the like. They are properties of mental acts. When we see a green disk, we experience certain sense-impressions. These sense-impressions are part of our conscious state. But they are not to be identified with the mental content expressed by, say, 'this is a green disk,' even though this content is also part of our conscious state and hence experienced.

Second, mental contents are not to be thought of as images or pictures of their objects. There is no resemblance between a mental content and what it intends. For example, the content expressed by 'this is a green disk' is not a mental picture of a green

[26] To be more accurate: what I experience are two different mental acts with two different contents. The red thing and the blue thing are not experienced, but seen. The difference occurs not only in what I see, but also in what I experience.

thing. To experience a mental act with its content is not to experience an inner picture of the thing intended by the mental act.

Third, whenever there occurs a mental act as part of our conscious state, we do not at that moment pay attention to this act and its content. Rather, we pay attention to the thing which the mental content intends. When we experience a mental content, we pay attention to its object. Just as it will require a shift in conscious states if we wish to scrutinize a sense-impression rather than a perceptual object, so it will require a shift in conscious states if we wish to attend to the content of an act rather than to its object.

INTENTIONAL CONTEXTS

Consider the following form of the so-called principle of substitutivity (PS): Expressions can be interchanged in every context (of a language L) without changing the meaning of the context, if and only if they have the same meaning. One possible interpretation of this general principle restricts contexts to sentences; it takes the meaning of such a context to be a truth-value and interprets sameness of meaning for two expressions as sameness of reference. Upon this interpretation, PS says that two expressions can be interchanged in every context (of L) *salva veritate*, if and only if they refer to the same thing. So interpreted, PS is false for intentional contexts. Put differently, sameness of meaning in the sense of sameness of reference does not guarantee substitutivity in intentional contexts. If one wishes to retain PS for intentional contexts, one must find a different interpretation. The problem is to discover a meaning of 'meaning' for which PS holds in general—that is, for intentional and nonintentional contexts alike.

Now there is a technical use of 'meaning' which is employed in logical matters. More accurately, there is such a use of the phrase 'same meaning.' Two expressions have the same meaning, if and only if the corresponding identity-statement is analytic.[27] Whole sentences have the same meaning, if and only if they are analyti-

---

[27] By 'analytic' I mean logically true. A logical truth is either a tautology (as explicated by the truth-tables) or a universally valid sentence (as explicated by validity theory).

cally equivalent. In these terms, *PS* can be formulated as follows: two expressions can be interchanged in every context *salva veritate,* if and only if they refer to the same thing as a matter of analyticity.

It is well known that this form of *PS* holds for certain intentional contexts and does not hold for others. It holds for all modal contexts, but not for so-called belief-contexts. From now on, I shall restrict the term 'intentional contexts' to contexts of the latter kind. This is merely a terminological matter. It is suggested by the fact that all intentional contexts in this new meaning of the term mention mental acts: that is, intentional entities.

At any rate, we have found a meaning of 'meaning' which allows us to apply *PS* at least to modal contexts. To see this, consider the two sentences: (1) '9 is necessarily greater than 7' and (2) 'The number of planets is necessarily greater than 7.' (1) is true, while (2) is false, since it is not a necessary but a contingent fact that there are 9 planets. Thus we can obtain a false sentence from a true one by substituting for '9' the phrase 'the number of planets.' This shows that sameness of reference does not assure substitutivity *salva veritate* in modal contexts. However, if we require that the sameness of reference be a matter of analyticity, we can substitute in this modal context, and indeed in all modal contexts. That this condition does not suffice for intentional contexts can be seen from the following example. Consider the two sentences (1) 'Peter believes that $2 + 2 = 4$' and (2) 'Peter believes that $\int x \, dx = x^2/2 + C$.' It is clear that (1) may be true and (2) false. Yet, the two sentences '$2 + 2 = 4$' and '$\int x \, dx = x^2/2 + C$' are analytically equivalent. And this shows that analytic equivalence for sentences (and analytic identity for expressions) is not a strong enough criterion to assure substitutivity *salva veritate* in intentional contexts.

This fact may lead to a search for still a different meaning of 'meaning.' Let us call this kind of meaning *intentional meaning.* The idea is this: in order to hold on to the principle of substitutivity, one must specify a kind of meaning which will allow substitutivity *salva veritate* in intentional contexts. Sameness of reference, we have seen, is not sufficient. Nor is, as we pointed out, analytic sameness of reference. We thus need a stronger criterion of sameness of meaning. Intentional meaning is supposed to fulfill this criterion. Since Frege's time, hundreds of articles have been devoted to this problem. I propose to survey some of the more important proposals that have been made and to offer a solution which I think is satisfactory.

The problem in its modern form originates with Frege.[28] Every name, according to Frege, has a sense and a reference. It thus has referential meaning; but it also has intentional meaning, for Frege's notion of 'sense' is precisely the one we called intentional meaning. Frege holds that PS holds for all contexts, if we interpret sameness of meaning as sameness of sense. The sense of any complex name remains unchanged if we replace a constituent of this name by another expression with the same sense. A similar principle holds for the referents of sentences: a sentence does not change its truth-value if we substitute for a part of this sentence another expression with the same reference.

This latter principle does not seem to hold for intentional sentences. However, Frege can apply it even to intentional contexts because he makes the following assumption. Consider the two sentences (1) 'Peter believes that the earth is round' and (2) 'Peter believes that the earth is a planet.' Assume that (1) is true and (2) is false. According to Frege, (1) denotes the True and (2) denotes the False. On the other hand, both (a) 'the earth is round' and (b) 'the earth is a planet' denote the True. Substitution of (b) for (a), it seems, can lead from a true sentence to a false sentence, even though (a) and (b) have the same truth-value. Frege assumes, however, that dependent clauses in intentional contexts do not refer to their ordinary referents—that is, to the truth-values which they have when standing in isolation. Rather, they refer in such contexts to their ordinary senses, that is, the senses which they express when standing in isolation. Hence he can hold that our example does not violate the general principle of substitutivity for referents. (a) and (b) have the same reference

[28] Compare his "Ueber Sinn und Bedeutung."

but not the same sense. Since the referents of (1) and (2) contain the senses of (a) and (b) rather than their referents, we cannot expect that substitution of (b) for (a) will preserve the truth-value of the intentional context under consideration.

It follows from Frege's analysis of intentional contexts that sentences can be substituted for each other *salva veritate*, if and only if they have the same ordinary sense. Substitutivity *salva veritate* is thus guaranteed, if two or more sentences have the same intentional meaning. The criterion for substitutivity is therefore identity of intentional meaning. Can this criterion be formulated in terms of a certain relation between referents? We have seen that the two obvious attempts to do so must fail. Identity of reference does not guarantee substitutivity in intentional contexts. Nor does analytic identity of reference.[29] This suggests a third possibility. Two expressions may have the same sense, if and only if they are tokens of the same type.[30] Roughly, this means that the expressions, assuming that they are in English, consist of the same letters of the alphabet in the same order with the same spaces between them. Thus all tokens of 'the earth is round' would have the same sense, while the two expressions 'Peter is a bachelor' and 'Peter is an unmarried male' would express different senses. Frege explicitly rejects this proposal on the ground that it would cripple logic by making all definitions false.[31]

Frege's analysis of intentional contexts thus rests on two ideas. First, Frege holds that expressions have a sense—that is, intentional meaning. Second, he asserts that expressions in intentional contexts refer to their ordinary sense rather than to their ordinary reference.

Frege's discussion of intentional meaning appeared in 1892. In 1905, Russell criticized some of Frege's views in his famous essay

[29] Compare *Translations from the Philosophical Writings of Gottlob Frege*, 2nd ed. (Oxford, 1960), p. 29.

[30] Compare, for example, P. D. Wienpahl's "More about Denial of Sameness of Meaning," *Analysis*, 12(1951):19–23; R. Rudner, "On Sinn as a Combination of Physical Properties," *Mind*, 61(1952):82–84; and the review by Thomson in the *Journal of Symbolic Logic*, 18(1953):89.

[31] *Translations*, p. 46n.

"On Denoting." Both papers seem to be addressed, at least in part, to the problem of intentional contexts. But this impression is rather deceptive. A closer look reveals that Frege talks primarily about intentional meaning and intentional contexts, while Russell argues mainly against one special feature of Frege's ontology. Here is what happened.

Consider the two sentences (1) 'Scott is Scott' and (2) 'Scott is the author of *Waverley.*' Frege, in his paper, starts with an example of this kind. He observes that (2) is obtained from (1) by substituting 'the author of *Waverley*' for 'Scott.' This means, in Frege's terminology, that one name is replaced by another. He points out that the denotation of (1) is the same as that of (2); both are true. Yet these two different sentences have a different "meaning," for (1) is a logical truth, while (2) is contingent. He concludes that this change of meaning must be due to the fact that a name not only has a reference but also expresses a sense, and that the sense of 'Scott' must be different from the sense of 'the author of *Waverley.*' Notice that Frege treats both expressions as *names*. Russell, in his article, objects to this treatment. He thinks that any expression properly called a name must name an existent. If so, what, for example, is the existent denoted by 'the present king of France'? Clearly, there is no present king of France. Hence the expression cannot be a name. In order to avoid the ontological commitment to an entity denoted by 'the present king of France,' one must show that descriptions need not and cannot reasonably be treated as names. Russell tries to show this by using Frege's example for his own purpose; he argues that identity statements for names are either false or trivial.[32] If one treats 'Scott' as a name, then (1) is both trivial and analytic. Since (2), however, is neither false nor analytic, 'the author of *Waverley*' cannot be a name.

Russell's argument is quite impressive. His theory of descriptions and his use of 'name' enables him to avoid Frege's ontological commitment to referents of descriptions. But Frege has an equally impressive point. He used the example in order to prove that there are intentional meanings. In support of this contention,

[32] Compare also Wittgenstein's remarks on identity in the *Tractatus.*

Frege claims that the problem of intentional contexts can only be solved if one acknowledges that there are such intentional meanings. Russell, even with his theory of descriptions, cannot solve this problem.

Russell considers the following three sentences: (1) 'George IV wished to know whether Scott was the author of *Waverley*,' (2) 'Scott is the author of *Waverley*,' and (3) 'George IV wished to know whether Scott was Scott.' (1) and (2) are true, while (3) is taken to be false. Yet, (3) seems to follow validly from (1) and (2). This is the problem. Russell's solution of it rests on two ideas. He treats 'the author of *Waverley*' as a description; and he distinguishes between the primary and the secondary scope of this description. According to this distinction, there are two possible reformulations of (1)—namely, (1') 'Concerning the one man who wrote *Waverley*, George IV wished to know whether Scott was that man,' and (1'') 'George IV wished to know whether one man wrote *Waverley*, and Scott was that man.'

Now it can be shown that (3) cannot be deduced from (1'') and (2).[33] Hence, if we take the secondary scope of the description, the inference cannot be made.[34] Russell says that we would normally take (1) to mean (1''). The problem thus disappears for the "normal" reformulation of (1). However, if we take (1) to mean (1'), we can derive (3'): 'Concerning Scott, George IV wished to know whether he was Scott.' Russell claims, however, that (3') is no longer false, as (3) was supposed to be. Hence the problem disappears again.

It must be noted, though, that the problem of intentional con-

[33] *Principia Mathematica* contains the following theorem (14.15):
$$(\imath x)(fx) = b \,.\, \supset: g[(\imath x)(fx)] \,.\equiv.\, gh.$$
But this theorem can only be proven if one assumes that either g is a truth-functional context or g indicates the scope of $(\imath x)(fx)$. Since neither is the case for (1''), we cannot deduce (3) from (1'') and (2).

[34] Fitch and Smullyan apply similar considerations to a similar modal argument: (1) 'The morning star is identical with the evening star'; (2) 'The morning star is necessarily identical with the morning star'; (3) 'The morning star is necessarily identical with the evening star.' Compare F. B. Fitch: "The Problem of the Morning Star and the Evening Star," *Philosophy of Science*, 16(1949):137–41; and A. F. Smullyan's two articles "Modality and Description," *Journal of Symbolic Logic*, 13(1948):31–37, and "φ-Symbols," *Analysis*, 11(1951):69–72.

texts remains unsolved by Russell's analysis of this argument. To
see this, remember that (1') is of the form 'George IV wished to
know whether p.' Hence, if (1') were already the translation of
(1) into a truth-functional system like that of *Principia Mathematica,* it would violate the truth-functionality of this system. By
his reformulation of (1) as (1'), Russell has not as yet explained
how he would, or shown that he could reformulate intentional
contexts in a truth-functional language. This shows that the theory
of descriptions does not solve the problem of intentional contexts.[35]

It may be argued that (3') in the original argument is in fact
false. Russell's assertion to the contrary seems to indicate an implicit distinction between two different occurrences of 'Scott' in
(3'). If we mark these different occurrences by subscripts, then
(3') becomes: 'Concerning Scott$_1$, George IV wished to know
whether he was Scott$_2$.' Using 'Scott$_1$,' we refer to the person we
know to be Scott: that is, to the author of *Waverley.* Using 'Scott$_2$,'
however, we refer to the person whom George IV knew to be
Scott. Notice that Russell does not make this distinction explicitly.
Going beyond what is explicitly there, however, one may be
tempted to interpret what he does say as an anticipation of a
distinction between 'Scott' as it occurs in nonintentional sentences
and as it appears in intentional contexts. This amounts to making a
distinction between the sentence 'p' as it occurs in nonintentional
contexts and the expression 'that p' as it occurs in intentional
sentences. This, we remember, is also the line along which Frege
sets forth his solution of the problem of intentional contexts. However, in Frege this idea is quite explicit. Substitutivity *salva
veritate* is possible in intentional contexts, according to Frege, if
the expressions which are substituted for each other express the
same sense. Frege's solution, to repeat, rests on the acceptance of
intentional meanings as separate entities. But Frege did not try to
specify in greater detail under what condition two sentences ex-

[35] Russell clearly realized this. Compare his discussions of intentional contexts in
"The Philosophy of Logical Atomism" papers and in his introduction to the
Tractatus.

press the same sense. We have seen, however, that this condition must be stronger than equivalence and even stronger than analytic equivalence. What further possibility is there?

Church has tried to answer this question.[36] Following Lewis, he thinks that two sentences p and q can be substituted for each other *salva veritate* in intentional contexts, if and only if they are *intentionally isomorphic*.[37] Thus p and q have the same sense, if and only if they are intentionally isomorphic.

For the sake of simplicity, let us consider a specified language L which only contains certain kinds of expressions; and let us agree to consider only well-formed expressions of L which contain the same free variables. Church's definition of intentional isomorphism is then substantially the following.[38] Two well-formed expressions of L are intentionally isomorphic, if and only if one of them can be obtained from the other by a series of steps from the following list: (1) alphabetic change of bound variables; (2) replacement of one individual constant by another which is *synonymous* with it; (3) replacement of one predicate constant by another which is *synonymous* with it; (4) replacement of a definite description by a (individual or predicate) *synonymous* constant; and (5) replacement of a (individual or predicate) constant by a *synonymous* definite description.

Obviously, this definition requires one to specify what constituent expressions of the kinds mentioned in (1) to (5) are synonymous with each other. According to Church there are two ways of accomplishing this. Either one states (semantical) rules of synonymy and nonsynonymy, or one gives so-called rules of sense.

[36] Compare especially A. Church, *Introduction to Mathematical Logic* (Princeton, 1956), vol. 1, pp. 3–31; his "A Formulation of the Logic of Sense and Denotation," in *Structure, Method, and Meaning* (New York, 1951), pp. 3–24; and his "The Need for Abstract Entities in Semantic Analysis," *Proceedings of the American Academy of Arts and Sciences*, 80(1951): 100–12. Compare also R. Carnap, *Meaning and Necessity* (Chicago, 1956).

[37] See C. I. Lewis, *An Analysis of Knowledge and Valuation* (La Salle, 1946), and his "The Modes of Meaning," *Philosophy and Phenomenological Research*, 4(1943):236–50.

[38] See A. Church, "Intensional Isomorphism and Identity of Belief," *Philosophical Studies*, 5(1954):65–73. The following account is not quite the same as Church's. But it will do for our purposes.

Assume that a rule of synonymy has been given to the effect that the two expressions 'fortnight' and 'period of fourteen days' are synonymous. The following two sentences are then intentionally isomorphic according to the definition: (1) 'The seventh consulate of Marius lasted less than a fortnight,' and (2) 'The seventh consulate of Marius lasted less than a period of fourteen days.' Hence (1) and (2) must be interchangeable in intentional contexts *salva veritate*.

Mates has tried to show that Church's definition of intentional isomorphism does not assure substitutivity *salva veritate* in intentional contexts.[39] Let p and q be any two intentionally isomorphic sentences, and consider the two sentences 'Whoever believes p believes p' and 'Whoever believes p believes q.' Since p and q are intentionally isomorphic, these two sentences must also be intentionally isomorphic. Hence it should be impossible for Mates or any other person to believe the first and not the second of these two sentences. Yet Mates claims to believe that whoever believes p believes p, but not that whoever believes p believes q. In effect Mates argues that 'A believes p' may be true, and 'A believes q' false, even though p and q are intentionally isomorphic. Just as a certain person may believe one of two analytically equivalent sentences and not the other, because he does not know that they are analytically equivalent, so a certain person may believe one but not the other of two intentionally isomorphic sentences, because he does not know that they are intentionally isomorphic.

Church, however, thinks that his definition of intentional isomorphism is not open to Mates's criticism. He considers the following two sentences: (3) 'Whoever believes that the seventh consulate of Marius lasted less than a fortnight believes that the seventh consulate of Marius lasted less than a fortnight,' and (4) 'Whoever believes that the seventh consulate of Marius lasted less than a fortnight believes that the seventh consulate of Marius lasted less than a period of fourteen days.' Since (1) and (2) are intentionally isomorphic, so are (3) and (4). Next, Church con-

---

[39] Compare Mate's "Synonymity," in *Semantics and the Philosophy of Language* (Urbana, 1952).

siders the German translations of (3) and (4). Since German has
only one expression for what in English we call either a fortnight
or a period of fourteen days, these translations are identical: (5)
'Wer glaubt, dass das siebente Konsulat des Marius weniger als
einen Zeitraum von vierzehn Tagen gedauert hat, glaubt, dass das
siebente Konsulat des Marius weniger als einen Zeitraum von
vierzehn Tagen gedauert hat.'

Church now argues that whoever believes (3) must believe the
same sense as whoever believes (4), because the translation shows
that whatever is believed in either case is what is expressed by
(5). It is, so to speak, an accidental feature of English that (3)
and (4) look slightly different; but since what is believed is an
extralinguistic entity (namely, a sense), one believes in either case
the sense expressed by (5). According to Church, this shows that
Mates cannot really believe (3) and not believe (4), since to do so
would mean that Mates has to one and the same sense the two
attitudes of belief and disbelief.

Now it may be said that Church's argument does not lend any
additional force to his original contention that one cannot doubt
one and believe the other of two intentionally isomorphic sentences.[40] Assume that Mates professes to doubt (4) but not (3).
Church claims that this is impossible and that therefore Mates's
alleged doubt of (4) must be construed as a doubt of something
else. In support of this contention, Church cites the case of the
German translation. Now let us assume that (4) and (5) are
intentionally isomorphic. Then Mates's point can be restated for
these two sentences. Mates professes to doubt (4) but does not
doubt (5), even though (4) and (5) are intentionally isomorphic.
We see that the original situation has not changed. It seems that
Church has not given any additional reason for saying that Mates's
doubt must concern a different sentence. All he seems to be saying
is that we cannot doubt one and believe the other of a pair of
intentionally isomorphic sentences. And this assertion must be
based on the view that a comparison of the senses of (3) and (4)
shows clearly that they are the same. On the other hand, if Church

[40] The following point is made by I. Scheffler. See his "On Synonymy and
Indirect Discourse," *Philosophy of Science*, 22(1955):39–44.

does not wish to say that (4) and (5) are intentionally isomorphic, but that they have the same sense, he must know this by comparing their senses. If his argument from translation is based on such a comparison, he could have appealed directly to a comparison between (3) and (4), pointing out that the sense of (3) is in fact the same as the sense of (4).

However, whether or not Church's argument lends any additional force to his contention that one cannot doubt one and believe the other of two intentionally isomorphic sentences, it at least calls our attention to one very important point. Languages contain many expressions which are mere *abbreviations* of other expressions. They contain completely arbitrary stipulations to the effect that certain marks and noises can be used in place of other marks and noises. But if a certain expression is a mere abbreviation of a longer one, it cannot possibly have a different sense from the sense expressed by the longer one. For all the "meaning" which an abbreviation has, it derives from the expression of which it is an abbreviation. It is in the nature of an abbreviation that by means of it we never introduce a new or different idea or thought.

I speak of abbreviations, but what I say holds for all definitions, for definitions, properly understood, are nothing but abbreviations. Every definition simply introduces new strings of marks and noises for old ideas. Intentional meanings, though, are not linguistic entities. They do not consist, not even in part, of marks and noises. They can be expressed by marks and noises; they can even be accompanied by marks and noises or by images of marks and noises: but they are not to be identified with them. Hence we can change, arbitrarily as it were, the physical signs that comprise a language without changing in the least the intentional meanings expressed by these signs. The world remains what it is, whether we talk about it in English or in German. And our thoughts, beliefs, wishes, hopes, etc. remain what they are, whether we express them in English or in German.[41]

We understand now the point of Frege's remark that not every

[41] It must be kept in mind that the intentional meaning of an expression is not the sum of all the inner responses which that expression may evoke. These responses may vary, even if the intentional meaning does not.

two different expressions must have different senses, for otherwise all definitions would be false. Definitions serve one and only one purpose: they introduce different expressions for the same sense.

Now if it is true in general that every definiendum has the same sense as its definiens, then they must be interchangeable *salva veritate* in intentional contexts. If we assume, for example, that 'fortnight' is merely an abbreviation of 'period of fourteen days,' then the two sentences 'a fortnight is a fortnight' and 'a fortnight is a period of fourteen days' must have the same sense. Hence there could be no thought of the sense of the first sentence which would not *ipso facto* be a thought of the sense expressed by the second sentence. No one could believe that a fortnight was a fortnight without believing that a fortnight is a period of fourteen days. But could it not happen that someone thought that a fortnight was a fortnight without thinking that a fortnight was a period of fourteen days, simply because he did not know that 'fortnight' is a conventional abbreviation of 'period of fourteen days'? I do not think that it could. If he has the thought expressed by the first sentence, he has the thought which we also express by the second sentence, whether he knows about the abbreviation or not,[42] just as it makes no difference to a thought whether or not we know how this thought would be expressed, say, in Chinese. If someone claimed to know what the two sentences 'a fortnight is a fortnight' and 'a fortnight is a period of fourteen days' meant, and if he professed nevertheless to believe only the first sentence, then he must be mistaken about the meaning of 'fortnight.' He must think that this expression means, say, a period of forty days. In this case, it is not correct to say that he does not believe that a fortnight is a period of fourteen days. Instead, we must say that he does not believe that a period of forty days is a period of fourteen days; for the sense which he actually does not believe is the sense expressed by 'a period of forty days is a period of fourteen days.' Yet, there

---

[42] Of course, if he does not know about the abbreviation, he will not think that 'fortnight' is an abbreviation of 'a period of fourteen days.' For the following compare also R. Carnap, "On Some Concepts of Pragmatics," *Philosophical Studies,* 6(1955):89–91, where he makes a similar point.

might arise circumstances in which we would wish to convey that he did not believe that a period of forty days is a period of fourteen days and also that he expressed this disbelief in the words 'I do not believe that a fortnight is a period of fourteen days.' In such circumstances, we quote what he said word for word and then add some information about what he mistakenly thinks these words mean. We distinguish between what he said and what he actually thought. We distinguish between the words he uttered and what he meant by them. But what he thought was not that a fortnight is not a period of fourteen days, but rather that a period of forty days is not a period of fourteen days. What a person thinks is not always what he says he thinks, not because he is lying, but because he does not know the meaning of certain words.

I conclude, then, that there are different expressions which have the same intentional meaning. If p and q are two sentences and p is merely an abbreviation of q, then p and q have the same intentional meaning. Hence they can be substituted *salva veritate* in all intentional contexts. Is this the only condition under which different expressions have the same intentional meaning? I do not think so. Any two simple (undefined) expressions of a language which happen to name the same particular, or the same property, or the same relation, express the same intentional meaning.[43] If, for example, 'a' and 'b' are two names of the same particular, then the intentional meaning expressed by, say, 'a is green' is the same as that expressed by 'b is green.' And similarly for two simple predicates, 'F' and 'G,' which name the same property or the same relation.

It must be clear by now that the so-called intentional meanings are contents of mental acts. These contents are expressed by sentences. Intentional contexts of the form 'X believes that . . .', or 'X thinks that . . . ,' or 'X perceives that . . . ,' etc., report the contents of mental acts. Two different sentences express the same

---

[43] Such simple expressions are mere labels. In order to communicate by means of them, we must either *show* to someone else what things they label or we must *explain* to someone else what things they label by using description.

content if one is a mere abbreviation of the other or if one is exactly like the other, except that it contains a different simple expression for the same particular, property, or relation. Two such sentences can be interchanged *salva veritate* in intentional contexts.

Let us now assume that a certain language contains no definitional abbreviations and no two (undefined) expressions for the same property, particular, or relation. In other words, all its descriptive constants are undefined and there is one and only one such constant for each simple entity. It is clear that under these conditions no two simple descriptive signs could express the same intentional meaning. Consider next two sentences p and q: under what conditions may we say that they represent the same state of affairs? It is obvious that two sentences could not possibly express the same content unless they represented at least the same state of affairs. Hence, if we wish to inquire under what conditions two sentences in this language can express the same content, we have to consider only those cases in which sentences may reasonably be said to represent the same state of affairs.[44] There are three possibilities.

First, two sentences p and q may be said to represent the same state of affairs if they are equivalent. But equivalence is not a criterion for substitutivity *salva veritate* in intentional contexts. However, if we take a closer look at some of the conditions under which two sentences are equivalent, we shall understand quite well why equivalence could not possibly guarantee substitutivity in intentional contexts.[45] Consider, for instance, the following three conditions: (a) p contains a proper name for a certain entity which in q is represented by a (successful) definite description;[46] (b) p contains a (successful) description of a certain entity which

[44] For the time being, it makes no difference whether we talk about actual or merely possible states of affairs.

[45] We assume that the language does not contain defined signs and that it contains only one descriptive sign for every simple entity.

[46] We accept, of course, Russell's account of definite descriptions. Since we also assume that L contains no definitions, we think here of the sentence which according to Russell's analysis is the definiens.

in q is represented by a different (successful) description; (c) p contains a simple predicate which happens to be co-extensive with another simple predicate contained in q. In each one of these three cases, one of the pair of sentences mentions one or more simple properties not mentioned in the other sentence. Since the thought of a certain simple property f differs from the thought of a different simple property g, even if f and g are co-extensive, it is no wonder that p and q will express different mental contents, if they are merely equivalent.[47]

Second, two sentences r and s may be said to represent the same state of affairs if they are analytically equivalent. We have seen that analytical equivalence is not a criterion for substitutivity *salva veritate* in intentional contexts. In this case, r and s contain the same proper names and (undefined) predicates. They differ however in that they contain different logical signs or in that the logical signs connect or affect the descriptive constants in different ways. For example, r may be the sentence 'p or q,' while s is the sentence 'not- (not-p and not-q).' Since the thought of certain logical constants differs from the thought of different logical constants, even if their respective combinations are analytically equivalent, it is no wonder that r and s will express different mental contents.[48]

Third, two sentences u and v may be said to represent the same state of affairs if they contain the same descriptive constants and the same logical constants and if the latter connect or affect the same descriptive constants in the same manner in both sentences. A moment's reflection shows that if u and v represent the same state of affairs in this sense, they also express the same mental content.

These reflections allow us to formulate a criterion of substitutivity *salva veritate* in intentional contexts. Two sentences p and q can be substituted *salva veritate* in intentional contexts, if and

---

[47] Compare Gustav Bergmann, "Meaning" in *Logic and Reality*.

[48] We take for granted that all the connectives and operators are undefined. Bergmann has argued that, say, a conjunction is not a complex consisting of disjunction and three negations. See his "Generality and Existence," *Theoria*, 28(1962):1–26; reprinted in *Logic and Reality*.

only if either p is an abbreviation of q, or p and q differ only in that they contain different expressions for the same descriptive entities and logical entities. In all other cases p and q express different mental contents and hence are not interchangeable *salva veritate* in intentional contexts. A language L, which contains no definitional abbreviations and no different signs for the same undefined entities, contains no two sentences which express the same mental content.

They also allow us to make a precise distinction between intentions on the one hand and what I earlier called ultimate objects of acts. Two sentences which express the same mental content represent the same intention. If they do not express the same mental content, they represent different intentions. But in this latter case, they may represent states of affairs which are either equivalent or analytically equivalent. If we say that two sentences represent the *same* state of affairs if they are either equivalent or analytically equivalent, then we can say that two mental acts which have different intentions nevertheless intend the same state of affairs. This state of affairs is the ultimate object of both mental acts.

In summary, we hold that there are mental contents. These contents are properties of mental acts. Sentences express contents and represent states of affairs. Two sentences which express the same mental content can be interchanged *salva veritate* in intentional contexts. Two sentences express the same content, if and only if they are either abbreviations of each other or contain different expressions for the same simple entities.

THE BEHAVIORISTIC APPROACH

Some contemporary philosophers reject this approach to intentional contexts. They try to replace all such contexts by truthfunctional ones. This program requires that one provide purely behavioristic descriptions of mental phenomena. Quine, for example, wishes to separate meaning from reference. The point of this distinction is to emphasize that meanings, unlike denotations, are not to be construed as entities. He claims that one can explain why expressions are meaningful or, as he prefers to say, significant, without resource to intentional meanings.[49] But if meanings are not things or entities, what are they? Tentatively, Quine answers that they are ideas in the mind.[50] However, such ideas, as our analysis shows, are entities. Quine therefore hastens to amend his answer. Meaning must be and can be explained in behavioristic terms.[51]

In *Meaning and Necessity* Carnap treated beliefs (and similar mental acts) as relations between persons and sentences.[52] Later, however, he changed his view. He subsequently introduced belief as a theoretical construct into the language of science.[53] Consider the sentence 'John believes that the world is round.' This sentence is now interpreted in such a way that it must and can be inferred only with probability from some description of John's behavior. For example, it would be confirmed by the fact that John made an affirmative response to the English sentence 'the earth is round.' Carnap's reconstruction of intentional contexts involves the following steps. Assume that '$U(X, t, R)$' means that the person X produces at time t a series of audible sounds R. Suppose that R is a token of the sentence S. Then we write instead of our original sentence: '$U(x, t, S)$.' Assume further that we have in our scientific language a theoretical construct called asserting such that '$A(X, t, S, L)$' means: X at time t wills to utter a token of S as a sentence of L in the sense of an assertion. It may then be possible to infer this last sentence from '$U(X, t, S)$.' Suppose further that one has defined behavioristically the notion of intension so that '$\text{Int}(p, S, L, t, X)$' means: the proposition p is the intension of S in L for X at t. Finally, let '$T(X, t, S, L)$' mean: X at t takes S of L to be true. Given certain additional premises formulating some observable features of the situation, one may then be able to infer

[49] Compare his "Semantics and abstract objects," *Proceedings of the American Academy of Arts and Sciences*, 80(1951):90–96.

[50] *From a Logical Point of View* (Cambridge, 1953), pp. 47–48.

[51] This program is carried out in his *Words and Objects*. For an analysis of W. V. O. Quine's behaviorism see H. Hochberg, "Of Mind and Myth," *Methodos*, 11(1959):123–45; reprinted in *Essays in Ontology*.

[52] See Carnap, *Meaning and Necessity*, pp. 53–64.

[53] See R. Carnap, "On Some Concepts of Pragmatics," *Philosophical Studies*, 6(1955):89–91.

this last sentence from '$A(X, t, S, L)$.' Similarly, one may be able to infer '$B(X, t, p)$,' where 'B' refers to the theoretical construct of belief.

Notice, though, that this analysis is not truly behavioristic. It still contains the two intentional contexts '$B(X, t, p)$' and 'Int(p, S, L, X, t).' However, Carnap is quite aware of the possibility of avoiding intentional contexts altogether; for he states that these two expressions could be translated into a nonintentional language. Let us therefore try to give a purely behavioristic definition of beliefs.[54]

First, we define the sentence 'the mark or noise A means p to the person P at t' to mean the same as 'If the person P stands in certain relations to A and is in the state S_1, then P will be in the state S_2.' The states S_1 and S_2, for example, could be described in purely physiological terms. In this case, their descriptions will undoubtedly be very complicated. At the present time, we may not even know how to describe them. Assume, therefore, that S_1 and S_2 are defined in terms of verbal stimuli and responses. For example, assume that A consists of an instance of the verbal stimulus 'dog,' that the relations between P and this stimulus assure, as we ordinarily say, that P perceives A, that S_1 is defined in terms of the verbal stimulus 'Say what this word means,' and that S_2 is defined in terms of the utterance of 'dog.' Schematic as this definition is, it provides us with a general idea of how a behavioristic definition could be constructed.

Notice that the left-hand side as well as the right-hand side of the definition state individual facts rather than generalities or laws. The following expression, on the other hand, states a law: 'for all t, whenever P stands in certain relations to A and is in the state S_1, P will be in the state S_2.' The difference between the right-hand side of the definition and this law is rather important. One may express this difference by saying that the former attributes to P a dispositional property, while the latter attributes to

[54] For the following compare my "Propositional Attitudes," *Philosophical Quarterly*, 10(1960):301–12.
[55] Compare Gustav Bergmann, "Dispositional Properties and Dispositions," *Philosophical Studies*, 5(1955):77–80.

P a *disposition*.[55] The difference is important, because the former may be true, while the latter is false. For example, it may well be the case that a certain stimulus means *dog* to P at a certain time t_1, while it is false that this stimulus always meant *dog* and always will mean *dog* to P. It may therefore happen that the behaviorist attributes to P at t_1 a certain dispositional property, but that he does not attribute to P the corresponding disposition. The behaviorist must discover through empirical investigations the circumstances in which the law will hold for given values of t.

Second, we define, again most schematically, the sentence 'P at t has the property of believing p' as 'if P at t stands in certain relations to A and if P is in state S_3, then P will be in state S_4.' For example, assume that S_3 is described by reference to the stimulus 'Do you believe A?,' that A is the stimulus 'Scott was the author of *Waverley*,' and that S_4 is defined in terms of the verbal response 'Yes.' The definition then states that the sentence 'P believes at t that Scott was the author of *Waverley*' means the same as the sentence 'if P is presented at t with the question "Do you believe this?" followed by the utterance "Scott was the author of *Waverley*," P will utter the noise "Yes." ' Again, the general principle of this definition should be clear.

If 'P believes-p at t' means that P at t believes that Scott was the author of *Waverley*, it cannot also mean that P at t believes that Sir Walter was the author of *Waverley*. For this sentence is defined in terms of the stimulus A, and A is the expression 'Scott was the author of *Waverley*.' If one replaces A by another stimulus, for instance, by the sentence 'Sir Walter was the author of *Waverley*,' one defines a property which is different from *believes-p*. Call this property *believes-q*. It follows that P may have the property *believes-p* but not the property *believes-q*, or conversely. However, if we assume that 'Scott' and 'Sir Walter' are proper names, P could not possibly have the one belief and not have the other. This shows that the behavioristic definition must be supplemented by many further definitions, or, rather, it shows that it must be expanded in greater detail. For example, we must incorporate somehow that P means by 'Scott' and 'Sir Walter' the same person. We could say, for instance, that P has the property believes-p, that he does not have the property believes-q, and that he has the (relational) property of meaning Sir Walter Raleigh by 'Sir Walter.' This last property must, of course, also be defined in behavioristic terms. In this fashion we could explain in behavioristic terms that P believes that Sir Walter as well as Scott was the author of *Waverley*, but that he misunderstood the expression 'Sir Walter.' It is quite obvious, at any rate, that the behavioristic reconstruction of intentional contexts will have to be rather complicated. In effect, it will have to consist of a complete theory of human behavior. At the present time, we do not possess such a theory. One could therefore argue that the behavioristic reconstruction of intentional contexts is at the present time at best a program. One could object that no one has as yet shown in detail how to translate intentional contexts into a truth-functional language.[56]

But let us waive this objection. Let us assume that the behavioristic program had been carried out. Nothing, I claim, would have been gained thereby in respect to the problem of intentionality and intentional meaning. This problem concerns the nature of mental acts and their contents. A complete behavioristic theory, however, would tell us nothing about mental phenomena. All its descriptive terms refer to stimuli, behavior patterns, and the like. Even such expressions as 'believes-p,' 'A means p to P,' etc. are merely definitional abbreviations of descriptions of behavior patterns in observable situations.[57] When one replaces intentional contexts by such truth-functional descriptions, one merely stops talking about mental phenomena. If one identifies mental phenomena with behavior or physiological processes, then one's philosophy of mind reduces to a behavioristic theory. If one is only interested in a science of psychology, then one may well be satisfied with a theory of behavior. But the philosophy of mind does not coincide,

---

[56] Compare R. M. Chisholm's detailed discussion of several proposals to reduce intentional contexts to truth-functional ones in *Perceiving*, pp. 173–85. Chisholm seems to think, however, that Brentano's thesis (that mental phenomena are distinguished from nonmental ones through their intentionality) stands or falls with the success of a behavioristic description. I do not think so.

[57] This assumes of course that such terms are not introduced as so-called theoretical constructs.

not even in part, with either materialism or behavioristic psychology.[58]

We must keep apart two completely different problems. One problem consists in the formulation of an adequate theory of human behavior. The other concerns a philosophically satisfactory analysis of mental phenomena. The topic of intentional contexts has therefore two sides. There is, on the one hand, the challenge of translating intentional contexts into behavioristic terms. On the other hand, there is the question of how certain mental phenomena give rise to the occurrence of intentional contexts. Our concern has been to show that intentional meanings are contents of mental acts. We must next investigate how mental contents are related to their intentions.

[58] I think that certain sentences about mental phenomena are *equivalent* to certain other sentences about physiological processes. In a sense, the latter may be said to represent the same states of affairs which are represented by the former. In another sense, though, there are two quite different kinds of states of affairs. Compare also the discussion of spatial and temporal analyses below.

INTENTIONALITY 5

IN THE LAST CHAPTER I discussed the nature of mental contents. Such contents are expressed by sentences. But language, as I remarked earlier, does not merely express the contents of our mental acts. We use it in order to describe the world. What makes this descriptive function possible?

Two things, I think, are essential for the occurrence of language. There must be minds which can perceive and contemplate the world, and there must be marks and noises which can picture the world. Unless we could think about and perceive states of affairs, we would have nothing to talk about; and unless we had marks and noises which pictured these states of affairs, we would have nothing to talk with. In addition to the connection between linguistic expressions and the mental contents which they express, language presupposes two further connections. One of these connects linguistic expressions with what they represent; the other connects mental contents with what they intend.

What is the connection between linguistic expressions on the one hand and what these expressions represent on the other? What is the significance of the picture metaphor? How can certain perceptual objects represent others? Wittgenstein, I think, hinted at the correct answers. Language has its representative function because there is an *isomorphism* between language and reality. This isomorphism, simple as it may be in the case of an artificial language, is extremely complicated in the case of natural language. Its precise structure, far from being obvious, is only revealed in the detailed investigations of linguists.

Of course, to say that language and the world are isomorphic is not to say that the former is a naturalistic picture of the latter. Nor is it to claim that there is a simple one-to-one correspondence between the elements of the two structures. However, a philosopher need not concern himself with the detailed features of the isomorphism; that, as I said, is the proper concern of linguists. The philosopher only has to answer the question of what there is in the world that accounts for there being isomorphic structures in general. This question has been answered. That two structures are isomorphic is a *logical* fact of the world. When two structures are isomorphic, then there holds between them a certain (definable) logical relation. This logical relation obtains whether or not there are minds.[1]

This last fact shows quite clearly that there is a difference between the connection between language and world and the connection between thought and reality. Certain marks are isomorphic with the world even if no one uses them in order to talk about the world. The isomorphism would still obtain, even if there were no mental acts. The intentional nexus, on the other hand, since it always connects mental acts with their intentions, could not exist in a world without minds. If we take for granted that we can use marks and noises in order to talk about the world, because these marks and noises are isomorphic with the world, then we must ask how minds can intend what we wish to talk about. This question concerns the nature of the intentional nexus. It is this question which I wish to discuss in the present chapter.

POSSIBLE PARTICULARS

Mental contents are expressed by whole sentences rather than by isolated words. They must therefore intend states of affairs

[1] For a more precise definition of 'isomorphism' compare, for example, R. Carnap, *The Logical Syntax of Language* (London, 1937). A philosophical discussion of different kinds of isomorphisms can be found in E. Stenius, *Wittgenstein's Tractatus: A Critical Exposition of Its Main Lines of Thought* (Oxford, 1960).

rather than "things." [2] The problem of nonexistent objects thus arises only in regard to whole sentences. If we assume, as we shall, that every mental content has an intention, then the question arises: what do those mental contents intend which are expressed by false sentences? Formulated differently, if we assume that every sentence represents something, there arises the question what it is that false sentences represent. Obviously, both formulations will have to receive the same answer.

Now I cannot accept the answer that certain contents, those expressed by false sentences, intend propositions instead of states of affairs. For I do not think that there are such entities as propositions—that is, entities which are different from mental contents and states of affairs and which somehow intervene between contents and states of affairs. Nor can I hold that the contents expressed by false sentences simply have no intentions. For I think that it is an essential characteristic of all mental acts that they "point beyond themselves." Let us therefore take a look at the view which was first outlined by Twardowski and then elaborated by Meinong into a coherent theory. According to this view, there is an entity for every mental content which the content intends. But this entity, depending on the case, may have different modes of being. In some cases, it does not exist, but merely subsists. In other cases, it does not even subsist, but merely has "Aussersein." Does this view solve the problem of nonexistent objects?

Before we try to answer this question, we must call attention to one peculiarity of Twardowski's and Meinong's view. The problem of nonexistent objects arises for them primarily in connection with so-called presentations. Presentations intend "things" rather than states of affairs. Hence they approach the problem by asking whether or not there are nonexistent "things." If we adopt their point of view, we shall be able to dismiss certain parts of their position as incorrect.

According to Twardowski, every presentation has an object.[3]

[2] This is somewhat rough. One must keep in mind, of course, that according to our analysis such things as chairs, disks, etc., are really states of affairs.

[3] Twardowski, *Zur Lehre vom Inhalt und Gegenstand der Vorstellungen* (Vienna, 1894), p. 29.

Consider, for example, the expression 'the round square.' Twardowski holds that it not only expresses a mental content (of a presentation), but also represents something. What the expression represents is the *object* of the corresponding presentation. This object is something which has contradictory properties and something the existence of which one immediately denies, if one makes a judgment about it.[4] He argues for this view by claiming that in order to judge that the round square does not exist, one must have a presentation of the round square. In order to have a presentation of the round square, one must conceive of the property of being round and square as inhering in an object. Hence one must have a presentation of this object. Furthermore, it is this object which is presented as being both round and square and not the mental content. For the mental content exists, while it could not possibly exist, if it were both round and square.[5]

I mentioned that one can formulate the problem of nonexistent objects in two different ways. One can ask what certain mental acts intend, or one can ask what certain expressions represent. Let us raise this latter question: what does the expression 'the round square' represent? Consider the sentence 'Round squares do not exist.' Must we assume that this sentence mentions particular round squares? Obviously not. It mentions, among other things, the two properties round and square, but it does not mention particulars which are round and square.[6] This fact becomes quite obvious when we reformulate the sentence as follows: 'It is not the case that anything has the property of being both round and square.' Hence, if the judgment that round squares do not exist involves a presentation, it must be the presentation of the property of being round and square rather than a presentation of round square individuals. When we consider the sentence 'Round squares are round and square,' we come to the same conclusion.

---

[4] *Ibid.*, p. 23. Twardowski, in agreement with some Brentano students, holds that the essence of judgment consists in affirmation or denial of existence. (See also F. Hillebrand, *Die neueren Theorien der kategorischen Schluesse* [Vienna, 1891].)

[5] Twardowski, *Zur Lehre vom Inhalt und Gegenstand der Vorstellungen*, pp. 25, 26, 30–31.

[6] Compare also Gottlob Frege, *Foundations of Arithmetic* (New York, 1960).

Transform this sentence into 'If anything is round and is square, then it is round and it is square' and you will see that it does not mention individual round squares. Finally, consider the sentence 'The round square does not exist.' According to Twardowski and Meinong, it mentions an individual round square. But if we analyze the sentence according to Russell's theory of descriptions, we see once again that it mentions the property of being round and square, but not an individual round square.[7]

These considerations seem to show that we are not forced to accept nonexistent particulars. Russell's theory of descriptions shows us how to get rid of nonexistent round squares and similar entities. However, if we apply this theory to the sentence 'The round square is round and square,' the resulting sentence turns out to be false. Meinong, though, holds that it is true.[8] If it is true, we must concede that the theory of descriptions is not applicable to this and similar sentences. Hence we might have to consider nonexistent particulars after all. Is this sentence false, as Russell claims, or is it true, as Meinong alleges? Obviously, our answer will depend on what we take the sentence to *mean*. If we interpret it in the Russellian fashion, it is undoubtedly false. On the other hand, if, with Meinong, we reject this interpretation, we may be inclined to say that it is true. We cannot decide whether it is true or false without first interpreting it in some way. But just these different interpretations are at stake in the controversy between Meinong and Russell.

I think that Russell was aware of this situation. He therefore tried to argue indirectly against Meinong's view by showing that it violates the law of contradiction.[9] Meinong replied that this violation of a logical principle must be expected in connection with

---

[7] See Bertrand Russell, "On Denoting," and his review of Meinong's *Ueber die Stellung der Wissenschaftstheorie im System der Wissenschaften* in *Mind*, 16(1907):439.

[8] Compare A. Meinong, "Ueber Gegenstandtheorie," *Gesammelte Abhandlungen*, vol. 2, pp. 493–94.

[9] See Bertrand Russell's review of the *Grazer Untersuchungen zur Gegenstandstheorie* in *Mind*, 14(1905):533.

"impossible" objects.[10] What else could one reasonably expect but that such entities as round squares should combine contradictory properties? However, Russell's position does not need to be fortified by his argument that certain nonexistent objects would violate the principle of contradiction. He had clearly shown that one can avoid Meinong's commitment to nonexistent particulars if one accepts the kind of analysis contained in his theory of descriptions.

But Findlay not only thinks that Meinong's view can be defended against Russell's argument, but that Russell's position must be false.[11] Assume that someone wishes that there were such a thing as the philosopher's stone. In Russell's view, Findlay argues, this person really wishes some object in the universe to possess the property of being a stone that turns baser metals into gold. "But it is perfectly clear that the man might wish nothing of the kind. He might be perfectly satisfied with all the objects in the universe, ... But he might wish, not that any of the objects in existence should be other than it is, but that *some other object*, some object not comprised among the objects of the universe, but whose nature is nevertheless determined in various ways, *should* be comprised in that universe, that is, should exist."

Findlay's argument needs some clarification. First, we must note that he speaks of *objects* whose *natures* are determined. The philosopher's stone, for example, would be such an object. However, Russell's theory of descriptions rests on the assumption that such objects are really states of affairs consisting of particulars which exemplify various universals. Russell's theory only shows how one can avoid a commitment to nonexistent *particulars*. It does not show that one can also avoid a commitment to nonexistent (complex) properties and states of affairs. But let us assume that Findlay meant to argue that there must be nonexistent par-

---

[10] *Ueber die Stellung der Wissenschaftstheorie im System der Wissenschaften* (Leipzig, 1906–7), p. 62; and *Ueber Moeglichkeit und Wahrscheinlichkeit* (Leipzig, 1915), p. 278.

[11] J. N. Findlay, *Meinong's Theory of Objects* (London, 1933), p. 53.

ticulars rather than that there must be nonexistent states of affairs.

Second, the point of Findlay's argument then seems to be that the person wishes that there were an *additional* particular (in the world), a particular not comprised among the existent ones. It is of no real importance that the additional particular should have certain specified properties. Quite similarly, we could imagine a person who wishes that there were an additional (simple) property in the world. Of course, this second person could not tell us what this property would be. Nor, of course, could the person of Findlay's example tell us which particular he wishes to have added to the inventory of the world. In either case, there is a wish for an additional entity of a certain kind: in the first case, for a particular; in the second, for a property.

When we adopt this point of view, we see clearly that Findlay's argument does not refute Russell's position. Nevertheless, his argument calls our attention to the fact that there are, in addition to particulars and universals, also the *categories* of *particularity* and *universality*. To wish for the existence of an additional particular or simple universal is to wish for an entity of a certain kind—that is, for an entity of a certain category. When we talk about existent particulars (or universals), we talk about *what there is;* when we talk about nonexistent particulars (or nonexistent simple universals), we talk about *what there could be.* And what there could be in this sense is determined by the categories of particularity and universality which exist. In addition to existent particulars, there are thus no further nonexistent particulars which enjoy some peculiar ontological status. But there are the categories, and these categories exist in the very same sense in which everything else exists and some things do not exist. Findlay's argument against Russell does not show that there must be nonexistent particulars. However, it may induce us to recognize that the categories of particularity and universality exist.

We can avoid a commitment to nonexistent particulars, if (1) we heed the important distinction between particulars and so-called objects, (2) we accept Russell's theory of descriptions, and

(3) we recognize the existence of the category of particularity. But Russell's theory, as I said, does not show that we can also do without nonexistent complex properties and nonexistent states of affairs. Even if we exclude "additional" particulars and properties from our considerations and eliminate all definite descriptions in the manner prescribed by Russell's theory, there will still be false sentences and complex predicates which represent no actual properties. The problem of nonexistent objects arises anew for these types of expressions.

Consider, then, the predicate 'round and square.' What does it represent? We know that nothing exemplifies this property. The property of being round and square does not exist. Twardowski and Meinong, as I have said, hold that there is nevertheless such a property, even though it does not exist. Let us say that this predicate represents a *possible property*. The case of false sentences will be similar. Twardowski and Meinong hold that they, too, represent certain entities. Let us call these entities *possible states of affairs*. In this view, the sentence 'The round square is round and square' represents a possible state of affairs and mentions a possible (complex) property.[12]

But if we are willing to consider the possibility that possible properties and possible states of affairs exist, why should we not also consider this possibility for possible particulars? Findlay, in fact, raises an objection of this type.[13] He says that if we consider the fact that there are no ghosts, we admit the possible circumstance that something is a ghost. If we must therefore talk about such nonexistent entities as the possible circumstance that something should be a ghost, "there seems to be no reason why we should not admit ghosts themselves as genuine objects." Before I answer this objection, let us note once again that Findlay confuses particulars with "objects." If we admit possible properties and

---

[12] Clearly, we could call the "additional" particulars and (simple) universals *possible* entities. A "possible world," for example, would differ from ours in that it contains different simple properties. However, I shall only speak of possible entities in connection with complex properties and states of affairs. Compare our discussion below.

[13] Findlay, *Meinong's Theory of Objects*, pp. 54–55.

possible circumstances, it is misleading to say, as Findlay does, that we do not admit ghosts themselves as possible "objects." For we admit "ghosts themselves" in the form of the possible property of being a ghost. What we deny is not that there is such a possible property, but rather that there are possible particulars. Possible particulars, if there were any, would not be ghosts. But let us disregard this permanent confusion. Let us assume that Findlay meant to argue that we might just as well talk about possible particulars. How can we meet this objection?

There are simple and complex properties. A brief reflection shows that all possible properties must be complex. More precisely, it shows that they would be complex entities were it not for the fact that they are mere possibilities. For example, the simple property round and the simple property square yield such complex properties as round-and-square and round-or-square. The former is a possible property, while the latter is an actual property. Nothing has the property of being round-and-square, but some particulars exemplify the complex property round-or-square. What this example shows may be expressed by saying that all the ingredients of a possible property are ultimately actual entities. All possible properties consist ultimately of actual simple properties and actual logical relations. A property is not a possible one because it contains ultimate possible entities. Rather, it is a possible property because the simple properties of which it consists are not exemplified in a certain combination prescribed by the logical relations which enter into it. Similarly for possible states of affairs. Every possible state of affairs must be complex. More precisely, a possible state of affairs would be a complex entity if it were actual rather than merely possible. All of its ultimate ingredients are actual entities. But it may happen that these actual entities are not combined in a certain way. For example, there may be a particular a and a property f, but it may not be the case that a exemplifies f: a may exemplify some other property and f may be exemplified by some other particular (s).

These considerations show that there can be no possible particulars *in the same sense* in which there are possible properties and possible states of affairs. In this sense, every possible entity would necessarily be complex if it were actual. But there are no complex particulars, not even actual ones. Two or more particulars forming a possible combination yield a possible state of affairs, not a possible particular. Findlay and Meinong do not see this, because they constantly confuse so-called objects with particulars. Meinong, for example, distinguishes between objects and objectives. This distinction seems to correspond to our distinction between particulars and states of affairs. But this appearance is deceptive. For Meinong holds that such things as tables or stones are objects, while we hold that they are states of affairs—that is, particulars which exemplify certain properties and relations. If one clearly distinguishes between particulars, properties, and states of affairs, it is obvious that there can be no possible particulars, even though there may be possible properties and possible states of affairs.

Now in what sense are there possible properties and possible states of affairs? In order to answer this question, we must inquire into the inner structure of states of affairs.[14]

POSSIBLE STATES OF AFFAIRS

Consider the "complex whole" C consisting of two green disks, one to the left of the other. What are the constituents of C? There are two particulars, a and b, which exemplify certain properties and stand in a spatial relation, R, to each other. Let us neglect the properties exemplified by a and b and assume, for the sake of simplicity, that C consists of a and b in the relation R. Upon this assumption, C seems to consist of the three elements a, b, and R. But these three constituents do not just stand side by side. They form the whole C. Hence there must be a connection between them. There must be a further entity, say R', which binds a, b, and R together. But C cannot consist of a, b, R, and R' standing side by side. These four entities in turn must be connected in some fashion. Otherwise, they could not yield the whole C. Hence there

[14] I shall in the following concentrate on states of affairs only, for possible properties can of course be reduced to possible states of affairs.

must be a fifth entity, say R'', which connects a, b, R, and R'. And so on. The assumption that the complex whole C consists of the three entities a, b, and R thus seems to lead to an infinite regress. I shall call it the Bradley regress.[15] I think that there is only one satisfactory way of avoiding this regress. Meinong, however, proposes a different solution of the problem posed by the Bradley regress.

Meinong claims that only a and b are constituents of C.[16] The relation R must not be counted as a constituent of C. But he also thinks that we can discover in C further complexes which contain relations as constituents. For example, in the complex C we can discover another complex, C', which contains not only a and b, but also R. In C' we can discover a third complex, C'', which contains a, b, R and R'—that is, the relation R' which connected a, b, and R into C'—and so on. Every complex thus contains infinitely many further complexes. In this respect there is some similarity between the Bradley regress and what we may call the Meinong regress. Yet, according to Meinong, there is an important difference. The Bradley regress is a vicious one in the following sense. We try to explain how a and b form a whole. For this purpose, we invoke the relation R. But now we are faced with the question of how a, b, and R form a whole. If we introduce a second relation R', then the same question arises once again for the four constituents a, b, R, and R'—and so on. No matter how many relations we introduce, the original question finds no answer. Even if there were infinitely many relations involved in the complex C, none of these relations could explain how a and b form a whole. Now according to Meinong, there are in fact infinitely many relations contained in C. But Meinong claims that the existence of this infinite series does not lead to a vicious regress. He claims that each one of the infinitely many relations R, R', R'', etc. does in fact connect its respective terms. What is the basis of this claim?

[15] See F. H. Bradley, *Appearance and Reality* (Oxford, 1930), p. 18.
[16] Compare A. Meinong, *Ueber Annahmen*, p. 261; "Ueber Gegenstaende hoeherer Ordnung," *Gesammelte Abhandlungen*, vol. 2; and Findlay, *Meinong's Theory of Objects*, pp. 145–46.

One may be tempted to propose the following interpretation of Meinong's position. The complex whole C consists of only two *constituents*, namely, a and b. Yet, a and b do not just stand side by side, as it were. They are connected by the relation R. But R is not a constituent of C. If we ask how a and b can form a whole, the answer is that they stand in the relation R. But if we now ask how a, b, and R can form a whole, we have treated R as if it were a constituent of C. But it is not a constituent of C. Hence the second question cannot arise. Therefore, the Bradley regress cannot arise. Upon this interpretation of Meinong's view, there is a distinction between two kinds of entities: constituents and nonconstituents. While it makes sense to ask what there is that connects constituents, it makes no sense to ask what there is that connects nonconstituents. Hence, while it makes sense to ask how a and b are connected, it makes no sense to ask how the nonconstituent R is connected with a and b. It is not an entity that is connected, but rather a connection between entities. Instead of talking about constituents and nonconstituents, we could say that R as well as a and b are constituents of C. But R is a peculiar kind of entity, different from a and b. It is different from a and b in that it needs no connection in order to be connected with a and b, while, for example, a could not be connected with b unless there were a third entity that connected them. We could in this manner distinguish between *saturated* and *unsaturated* elements of C. If we make some such distinction, we can avoid the Bradley regress; for this regress rests on the assumption that all constituents of a whole are alike in that they need to be connected with each other.

But this cannot be Meinong's view. For if it were, then Meinong's regress could not arise. We could not discover in C infinitely many further complexes and infinitely many further relations. The complex whole C would simply consist of a, b, and R. When Meinong says that R is not a constituent of C, he does not just characterize R as a peculiar kind of entity. As a matter of fact, he does not treat a and b as being in any sense different from R. For even though R is not a constituent of C, it is a constituent of C'. Each complex of the infinite series C, C', C'', etc., arises out of its predecessor when the relation which makes it a complex is *turned into* a constituent of another complex.[17] Even though *C* does not contain *R*, we can *discover* in *C* another complex *C'* which does contain *R*. This view, I think, leads straightforwardly to Bradley's regress, if we interpret the two italicized phrases in an objective rather than a subjective sense. Presumably, we *discover C'* in *C*. Unless we *create C'* by discovering it in *C*, *C'* must be contained in *C*. If it is contained in *C*, then all its constituents must also be contained in *C*. Hence *C* must contain *R* in addition to *a* and *b*. Since *C'* in turn contains *C''*, *C* must also contain *R'*, and so on. Hence *C* must consist of *a*, *b*, and the infinite series *R*, *R'*, *R''*, etc. Does *C* contain anything else? Does it contain, for example, a relation which connects *a* and *b* but which is not identical with one of the relations in the infinite series? Obviously not; for each complex arises from its predecessor when the relation which makes it a complex is *turned into* a constituent of another complex. Unless we can just turn entities into entirely different entities, *R*, for example, must be the relation which connects *a* and *b*. But if it is, then the question arises how *R* is connected with *a* and *b*. If we assume that the relation *R'* does this connecting, then the same question arises for *a*, *b*, *R*, and *R'*, and so on. Upon this interpretation of Meinong's view, there is no escape from the Bradley regress.

However, there is still a third interpretation of Meinong's position. I think that this one comes closest to what Meinong actually had in mind. Assume that the relation *R* which is a constituent of *C'* is not the relation which connects *a* with *b* in the complex *C*. Similarly, assume that *R'* which occurs in *C''* does not tie *a*, *b*, and *R'* together. According to this view, there are infinitely many complexes *C*, *C'*, *C''*, and so on. *C* contains as elements *a* and *b*; *C'* contains *a*, *b*, and *R*; *C''* contains *a*, *b*, *R*, and *R'*; etc. Now *R* is not a connection at all; it is a constituent of *C'*. *R'* is not a connection, but a constituent of *C''*, and so on. But *a* and *b* are in fact connected, and so are *a*, *b*, and *R*, and all the other constituents of

---

[17] Compare Findlay, *Meinong's Theory of Objects*, p. 146.

the different complexes. What connects these constituents is a series of further entities which must not be identified with the constituents R, R', etc. In order to keep these two series of entities apart, let us follow Meinong and distinguish between *relate* and *relations*. The constituents R, R', R'', etc. are called relate; the connections between, say, a and b or a, b, and R are called relations. For example, the relation r ties a and b together into the complex C; the relation r' ties a, b, and R together into C'; the relation r'' ties a, b, R, and R' together into C'', and so on. The relate R, R', R'', etc. are constituents of the complexes C', C'', C''', etc., while the relations r, r', r'', etc. are not constituents of any complex.

According to this view, what we ordinarily call relations are relate. For example, if we think of the relation to the left of as a constituent of the complex formed by two particulars which exemplify this relation, then this relation would correspond to Meinong's relat R.[18] But if relate are what we call relations, what kind of entities are the so-called relations r, r', r'', etc.? Meinong's answer is that these are objectives. For instance, the so-called relation responsible for the complex C is the objective which we ordinarily represent by the sentence 'R (a, b).' Similarly, the relation r' responsible for the complex C' is the objective represented by the sentence 'R' (a, b, R).' In general, what ties objects and relate together into complexes are objectives. But this means that complexes are different entities from objectives. In Meinong's view, the complex formed from two particulars which stand in a spatial relation must be distinguished from the corresponding objective. There are both complex entities and states of affairs. Once again, we come across the confusion between particulars and so-called objects. Meinong's distinction between a complex object and the corresponding state of affairs (objective) only makes sense if we overlook the fact that a so-called complex object is really a state of affairs.

Be that as it may, can Meinong in fact avoid Bradley's regress?

[18] Compare *Ueber Annahmen*, p. 283.

If objectives were simple irreducible entities, he could avoid the regress. His view could then be summarized as follows. There are complex objects. These objects contain relate. In addition to complex objects, there are also relational objectives. Objectives produce complex objects by connecting the constituents of these objects. However, objectives are different from objects (and relate) in that they need no connection in order to connect objects. In order that two or more objects be connected, there must be an objective which connects them. But an objective is a connection and hence needs no further connection in order to be connected with objects. Complex objects and their constituents are saturated entities, while objectives are unsaturated.

But objectives cannot possibly be simple entities. Meinong holds that a and b are constituents of the complex C by virtue of a relational objective in which they stand to each other. Conversely, if a and b stand in a relational objective to each other, then there is *ipso facto* a complex of which they are constituents. Hence the same terms which are constituents of the complex C also occur in the objective which "produces" C. Meinong calls this the principle of the coincidence of parts.[19] According to this principle, objectives must be complex rather than simple entities, though they do not have to be complexes in Meinong's technical sense. But, as the objective which "produces" C will be itself complex, if it contains at least a and b, we can then ask how a and b can form the complex objective in which they occur. It was this very same question in regard to the complex C which first threatened to lead to Bradley's regress. Meinong could only avoid the regress then because he distinguished between complexes and objectives. This time, there is no similar way out. Obviously, one cannot say that an objective is "produced" by another objective; for this answer leads to a vicious regress. Nor can one answer that in addition to complexes and objectives there is still a third kind of entity which produces objectives just as objectives produce complexes. For this type of answer also leads to a vicious regress.

[19] See "Ueber Gegenstaende hoeherer Ordnung," *Gesammelte Abhandlungen*, vol. 2, p. 389; and Findlay, *Meinong's Theory of Objects*, pp. 138–39.

How, then, do the two objects a and b form the objective which produces C? If in order to form an objective there would have to be a connection between them, we would be faced with the regress which Meinong avoids the first time around for complexes. Hence the objective cannot contain an additional ingredient. It must consist of a and b and of nothing else. In the objective, a and b must not be connected by a third entity. Rather, a and b must hang together like two links of a chain.[20] An objective does not consist of a, b, and *a connection*. Rather, it consists of a and b *in connection*. The Bradley regress cannot arise for objectives, because such objects as a and b need no connecting link in order to be linked together in an objective.

But this account of Meinong's view raises the following questions. If Meinong held that a and b could form an objective by hanging together like two links of a chain, why did he not avoid the Bradley regress in the same way for complexes? Why, in other words, did he distinguish between complexes and relational objectives in the first place? Furthermore, why did he not hold that in the objective which "produces" C three entities a, b, and R hang together like links of a chain? Why, in other words, did he not need R as a link in the objective? The answer to the first question is by now obvious. The distinction between complex objects and objectives was not introduced in order to help avoid the Bradley regress. It rested on the conviction that a complex object, say, a table, was not the same as a state of affairs. But whenever a and b or a, b, and R hang together like links of a chain, they form an objective rather than a complex. Hence, complexes which are different entities from objectives cannot consist of entities *in connection*. The answer to the second question is somewhat more complicated.

Assume that someone holds that there are no complexes in Meinong's sense, but only states of affairs. Consider the state of affairs represented by '$R(a, b)$.' How are a and b connected in this state of affairs? The answer that they hang together like links of a

---

[20] Compare Wittgenstein's *Tractatus*, 2.03: "Im Sachverhalt haengen die Gegenstaende ineinander, wie die Glieder einer Kette."

chain will not do, for how are we then to distinguish between $R(a, b)$ and, say, $R'(a, b)$? There is only one way in which two links can hang together, while there are many different relations in which two particulars can stand. If we stretch the metaphor of the chain and say that two links can be arranged, say, either one to the left of the other or one above the other, and that these different arrangements account for the difference between $R'(a, b)$ and $R(a, b)$, then we have acknowledged that a state of affairs cannot be completely analyzed into particulars alone. Hence we must hold that it is not just a and b which hang together, but rather a, b, and R. According to this view, there is a distinction between $R(a, b)$ and $R'(a, b)$. Both states of affairs consist of three constituents. But the first contains the link R, while the second contains the link R'. The Bradley regress cannot arise, however, because there is no further relation which connects the three entities in each case.

By this last account, "ordinary" relations like R and R' are treated as constituents of states of affairs. They need to be linked just like the particulars a and b. But they can be linked with a and b without there having to be a further link, while particulars cannot be linked with each other without a relation. This view presupposes a distinction between relations and related particulars. But this distinction occurs in Meinong's view in the form of the distinction between relate and relational objectives. Structurally speaking, Meinong can hold that a and b are linked in an objective like two links of a chain, because he also acknowledges the existence of relate as constituents of complexes. The two objectives which we ordinarily represent by '$R(a, b)$' and '$R'(a, b)$' are different, because the first produces a complex with the constituent R, while the second produces a complex with the constituent R'.

To sum up. According to Meinong, a state of affairs such as $R(a, b)$ consists of particulars (objects) which are linked like two links of a chain.[21] The Bradley regress can therefore not arise for

[21] There is a certain roughness here. Objects, we noted, are not particulars. However, in *Ueber Annahmen*, Meinong seems to come close to holding that relations obtain between particulars. See *Ueber Annahmen*, p. 283.

objectives. Meinong, however, avoids the standard objection against this account by holding that there are also relate which distinguish between different objectives.[22] These relate do not occur in objectives, but are constituents of complexes. A complex must therefore always be distinguished from the objective which *produces* it. Hence objectives and complexes are two different kinds of entities. However, the connection between these two kinds remains obscure. There is an ontological gap between objectives and their corresponding complexes which is verbally bridged by saying that objectives "produce" complexes. The Bradley regress cannot arise for complexes, because they are "produced" by entities which are not constituents of them.

In our view, complex "objects" are states of affairs. The state of affairs $R(a, b)$ consists *at least* of the two particulars a and b and of the relation R. Similarly, the state of affairs $f(a)$ consists at least of the particular a and the property f. If these states of affairs are actual (facts), their constituents do not just stand side by side, but form a complex entity. How can we avoid the Bradley regress?

I think that Frege gave the correct answer.[23] According to him a and b *fall under* the relation R, if the sentence '$R(a, b)$' is true. The complex entity $R(a, b)$ contains not only two particulars and the relation R, but also the nexus of falling under.[24] Particulars and relations (as well as properties), Frege holds, are *saturated* entities, while the nexus of falling under is an *unsaturated* entity. Now this distinction can of course be made in different words. One could say, for example, that only certain entities are *constituents* of $R(a, b)$, while the nexus of falling under, though contained in $R(a, b)$, is not a constituent of it. Or one could say that particulars

---

[22] I say that *there are* relate. But Meinong distinguishes between different kinds, according to whether they exist, subsist, or have *Aussersein*. Besides, his view that almost all relations are ideal relations casts some doubt on whether these entities can have any ontological status at all.

[23] Compare especially Gottlob Frege, "Ueber Begriff und Gegenstand" (*Translations from the Philosophical Writings of Gottlob Frege*, 2nd ed. [Oxford, 1960], pp. 42–55).

[24] However, Frege later dispensed with the nexus of falling under. Yet, the distinction between saturated and unsaturated entities remains: universals are unsaturated.

and relations are *things connected,* while the nexus of falling under is a *connection.* But the point of this distinction is in every case the same. One distinguishes in each case between entities which need to be connected in order to form a state of affairs and another entity which is the connection and hence needs no further connection in order to connect entities of the first kind. Particulars and universals have to be connected in order to yield an actual state of affairs. The nexus of exemplification, on the other hand, is not tied to particulars and universals, for it is the tie between them. Particulars and universals may be compared to wooden boards which can be glued together. Two or more boards cannot stick together without glue, but the glue—that is, the nexus of exemplification—sticks to a board without having to be glued to it. We can ask what there is that holds two or more boards together, but we cannot ask what there is that holds the glue and a board together.

This metaphor of the boards may tempt us to dispense with the nexus of exemplification. We might follow Frege and hold that besides particulars and universals there is no unsaturated nexus. Rather, the distinction between saturated and unsaturated entities coincides with the distinction between particulars and universals. Some boards (namely, particulars) come without glue, while others (namely, universals) have the glue already on them. But even this metaphor shows that there must be some glue. We have not really dispensed with the nexus of exemplification, but merely added it on to the universals. If, on the other hand, we substitute the chain analogy for the board metaphor, the following difficulty arises. If the two particulars a and b and the relation R really resemble three links of a chain, there is no reason why the two particulars alone should not be linked together under certain circumstances. Yet, two particulars by themselves never form— nor could they—a complex.[25] They could only form a complex if they exemplified a relation. A relation is thus necessarily involved in every complex formed from particulars. But it would not have

---

[25] I assume, of course, that the state of affairs R (a, b) cannot just consist of a and b in connection. See the argument given above against this possibility.

to be necessarily involved if particulars really resembled links of a chain. To put it differently, if we take the chain metaphor seriously, there is no essential difference between particulars on the one hand and relations on the other as far as their ability to connect is concerned. Whatever other difference there may be between different kinds of entities, they all are like links and each link can be linked to any other link. If we reject this view, as we surely must, there are only two possibilities. Either we must agree with Frege that particulars differ from universals in that the former are saturated, while the latter are unsaturated; or we must hold that both particulars and universals are saturated, while the nexus of exemplification is unsaturated. But even in Frege's view the nexus of exemplification does not just disappear; it is merely incorporated into every universal.[26]

The Bradley regress thus forces us to realize that there is an important ontological distinction between particulars and universals on the one hand and the nexus of exemplification on the other. No matter how we express this difference, once it is recognized, the Bradley regress cannot arise, for this regress depends on the assumption that all entities which enter into a state of affairs require a connection between them. The two particulars a and b are connected with the relation R by the nexus of exemplification. But the nexus is not an entity on a par with particulars and universals. Particulars exemplify universals, universals are exemplified by particulars, but the nexus of exemplification is not exemplified, nor does it exemplify anything. The distinction between particulars and universals does not exhaust the ontological inventory of the world. The nexus of exemplification is neither a particular nor a universal. It constitutes a unique ontological kind. This is the most important lesson which the Bradley regress teaches us.

After this lengthy preparation, let us return to the problem of nonexistent states of affairs. I said tentatively that false sentences represent possible states of affairs. This seems to imply that there

---

[26] Frege's distinction between saturated and unsaturated entities has also other sources than the Bradley regress.

are in addition to actual states of affairs also possible ones. And this may sound as if there were two kinds of states of affairs, actual and possible ones, just as there are, say, green disks and red disks. It may give rise to the mistaken impression that states of affairs somehow resemble Frege's propositions in that for every sentence, be it true or false, there is one of these entities. According to Frege, there is no difference in ontological status between a proposition expressed by a false sentence and a proposition expressed by a true sentence. Both propositions subsist. They only differ in that the former is somehow connected with the False, while the latter is connected with the True. One may think that actual states of affairs differ from possible ones only in a similar fashion. But this is not the case.

In our analysis, there is an actual state of affairs if at least one particular exemplifies a universal. If the sentence '$f(a)$' is true, there is a complex entity formed from a and f by the nexus of exemplification. However, if the sentence is false, there is no such complex entity which the sentence could represent. If '$f(a)$' is false, then no complex entity exists which consists of a and f connected by exemplification. Of course, there are other complexes [say, $g(a)$ and $f(c)$] but the complex $f(a)$ does not exist. It does not even subsist. It has no ontological status at all. Therefore, to say that certain sentences represent possible states of affairs does not mean that *there are* certain complexes which are represented by these sentences. If a sentence is true, *there is* a certain complex entity which it represents. If it is false, *there is no* complex entity which it represents.

But a well-formed false sentence is not just a jumble of letters and spaces. Since it is well-formed, it could represent a state of affairs. Even though there is no complex which it represents, *there could be* such a complex. To talk about actual and possible states of affairs is to talk about what *there is* and what *there could be*. To say that there are possible states of affairs is not to say that there are complex entities of a certain peculiar kind, but rather that there could be complexes of the ordinary kind. In what sense of 'could' could there be a state of affairs?

There are particulars and universals. Particulars are the kind of entities which can and do exemplify universals. Universals, on the other hand, are not the kind of entities which can and do exemplify particulars. That is, '$f(a)$' whether true or false is a well-formed expression; '$(a)f$,' on the other hand, is merely a jumble of letters. Similarly, *and* is a connection in the world which can and does conjoin states of affairs. But it does not and cannot conjoin, say, a state of affairs with a particular. The expression '$f(a)$ and not-$f(a)$,' though it expresses a contradiction, is well formed; but the expression '$f(a)$ and b' is nonsense. The existents of the world have a "logical form"; they form different categories.[27] In other words, the world has *categorial features*.[28] And these categories obey certain *categorial laws*. Now when we say that there is no such complex as $f(a)$, but that there could be one, we call attention to certain categorial laws of the world. We say in effect that these categorial laws allow for this particular combination of entities. On the other hand, if we say that there could be no such state of affairs as $(a)f$, we claim that the categorial laws of the world exclude such a combination of entities. It is quite obvious that the rules which determine which expressions are well formed and which expressions are not rest on the categorial laws of the world. To say that '$f(a)$' represents a possible state of affairs is to say merely that a could exemplify f according to the categorial laws of the world. To say that there are possible states of affairs is to mean merely that *there are* categorial laws of the world and that these laws allow for certain combinations of entities which as a matter of fact do not exist. To distinguish between actual and possible states of affairs is to distinguish between what there is and what there could be according to the categorial laws of the world.

We now see clearly that possible states of affairs have no onto-

[27] Compare Ludwig Wittgenstein's *Tractatus*. However, Wittgenstein does not give ontological status to the logical form of the world. For a discussion of this feature of Wittgenstein's philosophy, compare Gustav Bergmann, "Stenius on the *Tractatus*," *Theoria*, 29(1963):176–204; reprinted in *Logic and Reality*.

[28] We must distinguish between the categories on the one hand and the laws which govern these categories on the other, just as we must not confuse the type-distinction with the type-rules.

logical status whatsoever. They do not exist, they do not subsist, nor do they have any other kind of being, not even so-called *Aussersein.*[29] When we talk about what there could be, we are not talking about what there is in some peculiar sense of what there is. I remarked earlier that there are no different modes of being, there are only entities which differ from each other in certain ways. There are particulars, there are universals, there is the nexus of exemplification, there are certain connections like *and* and *or,* there are even categorial features like particularity and universality.[30] All these entities *are there,* even though they are quite different from each other. For example, particulars exemplify spatial and temporal relations, while universals do not; the nexus of exemplification differs from both particulars and universals in that it is an entity which needs no connection in order to be connected. The sense in which there are actual states of affairs does not differ from the sense in which there are particulars and universals, even though actual states of affairs are of course quite different from universals and particulars. Just as most philosophers mistake a difference between entities as a difference between modes of being, so they mistakenly view the difference between what there is and what there could be as a difference in being. But there is only one such mode of being. When we assert that certain complex entities could exist, we call attention to the fact that the world has categorial features.

We see now also that the sense in which there could be certain states of affairs which as a matter of fact do not exist must be distinguished from two quite different senses in which certain states of affairs are possible. I called the contradiction represented by a sentence of the form '*p* and not-*p*' a possible state of affairs. Thus I claim that there could be such a state of affairs. But this is likely to arouse some misgivings, for if any state of affairs is impossible, it is a contradictory one. We must therefore distin-

[29] In this respect Russell's rejection of propositions and subsistent possible states of affairs is justified.

[30] About the ontological status and nature of categorial features see Gustav Bergmann, "Ineffability, Ontology, and Method," *The Philosophical Review,* 69(1960):18–40; reprinted in *Logic and Reality.*

guish among three different cases. (1) By a possible state of affairs, one can mean a state of affairs that does not exist, but which could exist without contradicting known laws of nature. (2) One can mean a state of affairs which does not exist, but which could exist without contradicting the principles of logic. (3) One can mean a state of affairs that does not exist, but which could exist without violating the categorial laws of the world. When I talked about possible states of affairs, I had quite obviously this third kind of possibility in mind. A contradiction of the form p and not-p, even though it is impossible because it violates the logical structure of our world, could exist in the sense that it does not violate the categorial laws of the world.

When Meinong first talked about such contradictory entities as round squares, he assigned to them a certain mode of being, *Quasisein*. Later, however, he changed his view and formulated the so-called doctrine of the independence of so-being from being.[31] Certain entities, according to this doctrine, neither subsist nor exist, but have *Aussersein*. He gave up his earlier view, because he thought that *Quasisein* as a mode of being had no opposite. Presently I shall argue that even *Aussersein* is a mode of being in Meinong's system. But let us first ask whether or not possible states of affairs, in our sense of the expression, have an opposite.

Possible states of affairs which do not contradict known laws of nature can be contrasted with states of affairs which do contradict known laws of nature. Hence there are possible as well as impossible states of affairs in this sense of the term. The same holds for possible states of affairs which do not contradict the principles of logic. They, too, can be contrasted with impossible states of affairs—namely, states of affairs which would violate the principles of logic. In our sense of the term, however, even contradictions are possible states of affairs. What are their opposites? The answer follows immediately from what I said just a moment ago. Possible states of affairs are to be contrasted with states of affairs which violate the categorial structure of the world. These are the

[31] Compare Meinong, "Ueber Gegenstandstheorie."

impossible states of affairs which correspond to the possible ones.

As a corollary we may note that one can distinguish among three kinds of *possible worlds*. By a possible world, one could mean a world that shared with ours the same laws of nature, the same logical principles, and the same categorial structure. It would only differ from ours in that it consisted of different states of affairs. Or one could mean a world which shared with ours the same logical principles and the same categorial features, but which differed from ours in that it obeyed different laws of nature. Finally, by a possible world one could mean a world which shared with ours the same categorial structure but differed from ours in that it contained different logical principles. Of course, we cannot imagine such a world. But as Frege correctly remarks, the imaginable does not coincide with the intelligible.

Meinong's objectives are either factual or unfactual. Factual objectives *subsist,* while unfactual ones have *Aussersein*. From our point of view, this position involves at least two mistakes. First, Meinong distinguishes between existence and subsistence as two modes of being. Certain objects and certain complexes, in his view, exist, while objectives at most subsist. I have argued that actual states of affairs exist in exactly the same way anything else does. Second, even though he seems to claim that unfactual objectives have no mode of being, that they neither exist nor subsist, he really holds, as a close examination shows, that *there are* such things. His view is therefore not very different from Frege's. Meinong has two kinds of objectives, factual and unfactual ones, while Frege has two kinds of propositions, those connected with the True and those connected with the False. How do factual objectives differ from unfactual ones?

Let O be a certain objective and let P be the objective represented by 'O is factual.' Meinong argues that P cannot get its factuality simply by being the material of a higher objective.[32] If it could, O would have to be factual, because it serves as the material for P. What holds for O, holds for any objective whatsoever:

---

[32] Compare *Ueber Annahmen,* pp. 70–71; Findlay, *Meinong's Theory of Objects,* pp. 75–76.

there is always a higher objective which would confer factuality on it. Hence all objectives would have to be factual. On the other hand, if one holds that O is factual if and only if P is factual, one is faced with an infinite regress. P confers factuality on O, but P itself must receive its factuality from a still higher objective Q, and Q in turn must receive its factuality from R, and so on. Meinong concludes, therefore, that factuality cannot be bestowed on any objective by a higher objective; factuality must reside in O itself. If it does, P will be factual, and therefore the objective represented by 'P is factual' will be factual, etc. He holds that factuality is an indefinable property which certain objectives have and others lack. The presence or absence of this property distinguishes factual from unfactual objectives.[33]

According to Meinong, then, *there are* both factual and unfactual objectives. The former have a certain indefinable property which the latter do not have. If an objective has this property, it subsists; otherwise it has *Aussersein*. Nothing could show more clearly that a difference between entities is turned into a difference between modes of being. We also see that objectives are quite different from states of affairs. There is only one kind of state of affairs, actual, while there are two kinds of objectives, factual and unfactual.

Meinong accused philosophers of having a prejudice in favor of the real. Metaphysicians, he claimed, confine themselves all too often to an investigation of what exists. Yet there are also entities which do not exist. Some of these merely subsist; others have *Aussersein*. Insofar as the theory of objects pays attention to these kinds of entities, its scope is much wider than that of traditional metaphysics. I think we now understand Meinong's mistake as well as his achievement. He is mistaken in thinking that metaphysics could ever inquire into anything else but what there is. The prejudice in favor of the real is no prejudice at all. The metaphysician's task is completed if he has listed all the entities there are. However, Meinong's achievement consists in having called attention to the fact that there are possibilities. He insisted,

[33] Compare *Ueber Annahmen*, pp. 70–71.

to be more precise, that the possibilities in the world must have some ontological foundation. But he did not grasp that this foundation consists of the categorial features of the world which are as real as anything. Instead, he populated the universe with possible entities. It remained for Wittgenstein to put the ontology of possible entities into the right perspective.

THE INTENTIONAL NEXUS

Descriptive sentences express mental contents and represent states of affairs. Sentences can be used to represent states of affairs because their elements are isomorphic with elements of reality. But the existence of such an isomorphism between marks and noises on the one hand and elements of reality on the other is only a necessary, not a sufficient, condition for the occurrence of language. A structure of this kind becomes a language only if people use it in order to describe what they have in mind, what they mean, what they perceive or think of, and so on. It is also necessary that there be minds which intend states of affairs. In addition to the isomorphism between expressions and reality, there must be an intentional nexus which connects minds with reality. This relation is not a linguistic one, for it obtains between mental contents and states of affairs. But even though it is not linguistic, without it language would be impossible. What is this intentional nexus?

I agree with those philosophers who hold that the intentional nexus is not one of similarity or resemblance.[34] Nor does it merely consist of an isomorphism between contents and states of affairs.[35] Neither one of these two possible answers does justice to the intimate connection which we all feel obtains between our mental acts and what they intend. The intentional nexus must be a unique kind of connection. It seems to be irreducible to anything which

[34] This includes almost all of Brentano's students. Compare, for example, Twardowski, *Zur Lehre vom Inhalt und Gegenstand der Vorstellungen.*

[35] This is not to deny, though, that there is a one-one correspondence between contents and intentions. Remember how we explicated different intentions above.

we find in the nonmental world.[36] Its occurrence truly distinguishes between a world with minds and a world without minds.[37] But to say merely that the intentional nexus is indefinable and the hallmark of mind is not all one can do. We must try to describe its most important characteristics.

Recall the problem of nonexistent objects. It arises from the assumption that a relation can only obtain between two or more existents. If there is a relation between a mental content and its intention, both the content and the intention must exist. Yet, some contents intend nonexistent entities. This is the problem. Brentano, it will be recalled, proposed successively three different solutions. At first, he held that so-called nonexistent objects do exist after all, but they exist in minds, they exist immanently. Then he gave up this view and solved the problem in a different way. He agreed with the assertion that relations can only obtain if their terms exist. But he also asserted that the intentional nexus is an entity of a different kind. It differs from relations in that it can hold even if one of its two terms does not exist. Brentano's view at this point amounts to making a distinction between relations on the one hand and entities which are somewhat similar to relations on the other. The latter kind of entity differs from relations in that it can hold between an existent and something that does not exist. Still later, however, he gave up this view in favor of the position that there are no relations whatsoever, but only so-called relational attributes. We discussed his latest view in detail and saw that it led to idealism. The nexus of intentionality simply disappears.[38]

In Frege's general view, the problem of nonexistent objects cannot arise. Assuming, of course, that all acts are propositional,

[36] This would be our explication of Brentano's distinction between the mental and the nonmental in terms of intentionality.

[37] Compare, for example, S. Witasek, *Grundlinien der Psychologie* (Leipzig, 1923).

[38] Compare also Twardowski, *Zur Lehre vom Inhalt und Gegenstand der Vorstellungen*, p. 27, where he claims that a relation can subsist, even if one of its terms does not exist.

every mental content can be related to an intention, for there are false as well as true propositions.[39] Every sentence, be it true or false, expresses a proposition. There are both false and true propositions, but they are called subsistents because they are not localized in space and time. Meinong's view is not entirely different from Frege's. He held that factual objectives like Frege's true propositions subsist, but that unfactual objectives merely have *Aussersein.* Yet, they are not just nothing; they have some ontological status. Hence the intentional nexus always connects two entities. In some cases it holds between a mental content and a subsistent factual objective; in other cases it holds between contents and unfactual objectives which have *Aussersein.* Whereas Brentano avoids the problem of nonexistent objects by rejecting the intentional nexus, Frege and Meinong attempt to solve it by attributing some kind of ontological status to nonexistent entities.[40]

It is clear that we cannot follow in their footsteps. We cannot accept Brentano's way out, because we hold that every mental content is related to an intention. On the other hand, we cannot accept the Frege-Meinong solution, because possible states of affairs have no ontological status whatsoever. There simply are no such things. When we say that certain contents intend possible states of affairs, we mean only that they intend states of affairs which could exist, but do not in fact exist. The intentional nexus, in this view, can obtain not only between a content and a state of affairs which is there, but also between a content and a state of affairs which is not there, but could be there. In brief, instead of conferring some ontological status on nonexistent states of affairs, we hold that states of affairs either exist or do not exist and that the intentional nexus can connect a mental content even with a mere possibility.

[39] Compare also Bertrand Russell, *The Principles of Mathematics* (London, 1956), p. 450: "Now the truth of a proposition consists in a certain relation to truth, and presupposes the being of the proposition. And as regards being, false propositions are on exactly the same level, since to be false, a proposition must already be."

[40] Frege, of course, does not consider this problem explicitly. We are interpolating what kind of answer his system contains.

This solution of the problem of nonexistent objects was antici-
pated by Brentano's second view. Like Brentano, we have to
distinguish between different kinds of "relations." Ordinary descriptive relations—for example, spatial and temporal ones—can
only obtain if their terms exist. I shall continue to use the term
'relations' in order to refer to these kinds of connections. Even the
nexus of exemplification can only hold between existents. The
intentional nexus differs, therefore, not only from (ordinary) relations, but also from the nexus of exemplification. On the other
hand, there is also a similarity between the nexus of exemplification and the nexus of intentionality: both connections can connect
entities without having to be connected to the entities which they
connect. Furthermore, there are connections (in the world)
which resemble the intentional nexus in that they can obtain
between existents and states of affairs that could exist. For example, *if-then* and *or* are two such connections. The sentence
'$f(a)$ or $g(b)$' is true, for instance, if '$f(a)$' represents an actual
state of affairs while there is no state of affairs $g(b)$.[41] The intentional nexus resembles therefore certain logical connectives.
These various similarities and differences among connections can
be summed up in the following dichotomies. First, descriptive
relations are "saturated," while the nexus of exemplification, the
intentional nexus, and the logical connections are all "unsaturated." By this we mean that of all the connections, only descriptive relations need to be tied to their terms. The tie is of course the
nexus of exemplification. Second, descriptive relations and the
nexus of exemplification can only obtain between existents, while
the intentional nexus and certain logical connectives can hold
between an existent and a mere possibility. Third, logical connections differ from the intentional nexus in that they may yield
tautologies if they hold. For example, '$f(a)$ or not-$f(a)$' is a tautology, while a sentence to the effect that the content f intends the
state of affairs p is never a tautology, even though it may be true,
of course.

[41] We assume here that these logical connectives cannot be reduced, say, to *and*
and *not*.

This last point deserves some special attention. Let f be a certain mental content and let p be an actual or possible state of affairs. If f intends p, the sentence 'f intends p' is true. Otherwise it is false. But if it is true, it is never a logical truth. Yet some philosophers have held that sentences about contents and their intentions if true are in some sense *necessarily* true.[42] They have argued that it is not just a matter of brute fact that a certain content f intends a certain state of affairs p. But if it is necessarily true that f intends p, then there must be some explication of the kind of necessity involved in intentional states of affairs. One particular explication, however, offered by Meinong and implicit in Husserl's view, threatens to destroy the ontological status of the intentional nexus.

According to Meinong, the intentional nexus is an *ideal* relation. All ideal relations hold with *necessity* between their terms.[43] They hold necessarily, because they are founded on the *natures* of their terms. Two terms, being what they are—that is, having the natures which they have—must necessarily stand in the ideal relations in which they stand to each other. Husserl held a similar view in regard to mental contents. According to him, the intentional nexus must be understood as the *intrinsic nature* of the mental content.[44] But to say that the intentional nexus holds necessarily between a given content and its intention because it is grounded in the natures of the terms which it connects, is to claim that the intentional nexus is an *internal relation*.[45] Meinong's explication of the necessity attached to the intentional nexus rests on the assertion that the intentional nexus is an internal relation.

What does it mean to say that a certain relation R is *founded* on or *grounded* in the nature of its terms? Put differently, what does

[42] Compare, for example, Meinong, *Ueber Annahmen*, p. 265; "Ueber Gegenstaende hoeherer Ordnung"; and also Gustav Bergmann, "Analyticity," *Theoria*, 24(1958):71–93; reprinted in *Meaning and Existence*.

[43] Compare "Ueber Gegenstaende hoeherer Ordnung," *Gesammelte Abhandlungen*, vol. 2, p. 399.

[44] Compare E. Husserl, *Logische Untersuchungen* (Halle, 1913), vol. 2, pp. 368, 435.

[45] Compare G. E. Moore, "External and Internal Relations," *Philosophical Studies* (London, 1922), p. 308.

it mean to say that from the natures of the two terms A and B it *necessarily* follows that A and B stand in the relation R? What is the ontological difference between external and internal relations? I think that the following explication will answer these questions and do justice to what some philosophers, at least, have meant by internal relations.

Let '$R(A,B)$' represent the fact that A and B stand in the relation R. What are the ontological constituents of this fact? Obviously, this fact will contain all the constituents of A and B. But are there in addition to these constituents any further ones? There are two possible answers. According to the first, the fact $R(A,B)$ contains at least one further constituent. This constituent is the ontological ground for the relation R. According to the second possible answer, the fact does not contain any further constituent. The relation R is grounded ontologically in the constituents of A and B. If R is grounded in the constituents of A and B, R is an internal relation. Otherwise, it is an external relation. This is our explication.[46] By this explication, to say that R is grounded in the nature of its terms is to say that a complete ontological assay of the fact $R(A,B)$ would yield the various constituents of A and B *and nothing else*.[47] To say that R holds necessarily between A and B because of the natures of A and B is to say that the assertion of '$R(A,B)$' does not tell us *anything more* than that A and B consist of certain entities.

By this explication, internal relations have no ontological status. A complete description of the world, if I may put it so, would have to mention things and their natures but not, in addition, certain relations. If the intentional nexus is an internal relation in this sense, it is not an ontological constituent of the world. There are, then, mental contents (with their natures) and intentions (with their natures), but not a third entity irreducible to these two kinds of things. This is what I meant when I said that Meinong's explica-

[46] Compare Gustav Bergmann, "Synthetic *a priori*," in *Logic and Reality*.

[47] Notice how well this fits in with our previous analysis of Meinong's position. In the objective $R(A,B)$, A and B hang together like two links of a chain. There is no further constituent. Insofar as Wittgenstein thinks of relations in this way, he holds the view that all relations are internal.

tion of the necessary connection between content and intention threatens to destroy the ontological status of the intentional nexus.

If the intentional nexus is an internal relation, it does not exist. If it is an external nexus, it does exist. Are there internal relations? More precisely, can certain entities which have been called internal relations really be internal relations? Consider one of Meinong's examples. According to Meinong, two local determinations (*Ortsbestimmungen*) could not possibly stand in any other spatial relation to each other than the one in which they stand.[48] Whatever spatial relation obtains between them obtains necessarily between them. In brief, the spatial relation in which they stand is an internal relation founded on the natures of the two local determinations. Let A, B, C, and D be four local determinations (on a plane). Assume that A is to the left of B, C to the left of D, and C directly below B. If 'R' stands for the relation of being to the left of, the following two sentences are true: (1) '$R(A, B)$' and (2) '$R(C, D)$,' while (3) '$R(B, C)$' is false. Now the relation R is presumably grounded in the natures of the terms between which it obtains. This allows for three possibilities.[49] First, its ground is contained in only one of the two terms of each pair (A, B) and (C, D). Let us assume its ground is the constituent of A in the one case and C in the other. Second, it is grounded in a constituent which is shared by both terms of each pair. For example, there is a constituent which occurs in A and B and also, of course, in C and D. Third, the relation is grounded in two entities—say, X and Y—so that A contains X, while B contains Y; similarly, C contains X, while D contains Y.

According to the first possibility, A and B stand in the relation R, because A contains X. Similarly, C stands in the relation R to D, because C contains X. If so, then the pair C and B should also stand in the relation R, for C contains X. Yet, C is directly below B

[48] Compare A. Meinong, *Hume Studien, Gesammelte Abhandlungen*, vol. 2, pp. 47–49.

[49] Compare Bergmann's "Synthetic *a priori*," in *Logic and Reality*, p. 276.

and not to the left of B. According to the second possibility, R is grounded in the entity X which is shared by A and B as well as by C and D. Since both B and C contain this entity, they should also stand in the relation R. But they do not. Finally, the third alternative provides two further possibilities. First, if the four entities A, B, C, and D were simple, X and Y would be identical with A and B. But they also would have to be identical with C and D. Yet, A is different from C, and B is different from D. Second, if A, B, C, and D are complex entities which contain X and Y, C should stand in the relation R to B, for C contains X and B contains Y. Yet C is directly below B and not to the left of it.

We can give a similar argument to show that the intentional nexus cannot be an internal relation. Let the content A intend the intention B and the content C intend the intention D. If the intentional nexus is founded on these four terms, there are again the three possibilities mentioned above. According to the first, the content C should also intend B—but it does not. And similarly for the other two cases. We conclude, therefore, that the intentional nexus cannot be an internal relation. It must be an external nexus. Furthermore, if one wishes to hold that a given content necessarily intends a certain intention, this view cannot be based on the doctrine that internal relations hold necessarily between their terms. We remarked earlier that it was not a logical truth that a certain content intends a certain intention. Nor, of course, is it simply a definitional truth. Yet it differs in important respects from those truths which rest on exemplification. If we wish to indicate this difference, we may speak of intentional truths.[50]

Meinong had still a further reason for holding that the intentional nexus was an ideal relation. Relations, it will be remembered, generate complexes. Ideal relations generate ideal complexes, while real relations produce real complexes. Now one difference between these two kinds of complexes is that ideal complexes, as distinct from real ones, are not intimate wholes.

[50] Compare also Bergmann's "Intentionality," reprinted in *Meaning and Existence* (Madison, 1960).

Ideal relations, as distinct from real relations, do not bind their terms into any intimate unity. They leave their terms completely unaffected.[51] The intentional nexus does not bind an intention and a mental content into an intimate whole. Whether or not it obtains between a certain content and a certain intention, neither the content nor the intention is affected in the slightest. The intention is in this sense *independent* of the mental content. In short, it makes no difference to an intention whether it is intended or not. The world is not affected by being known.

Insofar as this view rests on the assumption that the intentional nexus is an ideal (that is, an internal) relation, we cannot accept it. The fact, correctly stated by Meinong, that intentions are independent of minds, can be explained in a different way. First of all, it is clear that the intentional nexus is not a causal connection. A state of affairs or possible state of affairs does not causally depend on "its" mental content. If there is any causal connection between content and intention at all, it obtains in the opposite direction: the occurrence of a certain content may causally depend on there being a certain state of affairs. Hence intentions are causally independent of contents. Secondly, the intentional nexus is not a connection of logical implication. If the sentence 'If A, then B' is a logical truth, we say that A (logically) implies B. In this case A and B are connected by logical implication. But it is clear that a sentence of the form 'f intends p' is never a logical truth. Hence f does not logically imply p. Nor, of course, does the true sentence 'f intends p' imply p. Intentions are thus logically independent of mental contents.

To sum up. The intentional nexus has at least three important characteristics. First, it can obtain between a content and a possible state of affairs. It can connect a content with what is not there but could be there. This fact distinguishes it from "ordinary" relations and the nexus of exemplification. Second, if the intentional nexus obtains between a content and a state of affairs, it never obtains with logical necessity. This fact distinguishes it from logical connectives. Yet intentional truths must be counted as unique

[51] Compare Meinong's *Ueber Annahmen*, p. 266.

among purely descriptive truths, for they do not rest on the nexus of exemplification.[52] Third, the intentional nexus expresses neither a causal nor a logical dependence of intentions on mental contents. Mental contents neither cause nor logically imply the existence of intentions.

[52] '$f(a)$ or $g(b)$' is true, if, say, a exemplifies f. 'f intends p' may be true, however, even if p is merely a possible state of affairs.

REALISM

THERE ARE perceptual objects. Some I know because I have perceived them. I know of others because even though I myself have never seen them, other people have. There are even perceptual objects which no one has ever perceived; and a long time ago, long before there were human beings, there existed still others which no one will ever be able to perceive. Our knowledge of these things is necessarily indirect: we infer their past or present existence from other perceptual objects with which we are acquainted.

There are also sense-impressions, images, feelings, and mental acts. Some of these I have had myself. Of others I know only indirectly. But whether or not these things occurred in me, in my contemporaries, or even in persons of the distant past, they are quite different from perceptual objects. The most obvious difference is that there would be no sense-impressions, images, feelings, mental acts, and the like, if there were no organisms, while the same does not hold for perceptual objects in general.

Idealism, in any of its many forms and guises, has to deny one or more of these facts. Or it has to reject some facts which follow from the ones I mentioned. Phenomenalism, for example, holds that perceptual objects consist of phenomenal ones. Hence it denies the obvious fact that sense-impressions are not in any sense of the word constituents of perceptual objects. Of course, there is more to idealism than the mere rejection of some common-sense fact. If not, it would have little to recommend it. There is, in addition, the traditional philosophical dialectic: there are issues and arguments. But the burden of proof rests, as it were, on the idealist. He has to raise issues which cast doubt on our most firmly established beliefs; he must produce arguments which prove his position. This feature of the dialectic defines the task of the realist. The philosophical realist does not have to defend his position unless it comes under attack. He need not convince us that his view is correct; he need only show that the arguments of the idealist are not sound. In short, the realist need not argue for his position, but must defend it against the arguments of the idealist.

What are the relevant issues and arguments? I shall raise these issues and produce those arguments presently. But my presentation will be much clearer and more convincing if I first indicate what issues are definitely *not* at stake in the realism-idealism controversy.

First of all, this controversy has nothing to do with what is known as the problem of our knowledge of other minds. That there is such a problem I do not wish to deny. But it is not one of the problems with which we have to be concerned in our defense of realism. It will suffice if we merely consider such inanimate things as tables and chairs. Are there such things? Are they independent of our perceptions? Do we perceive them directly or do we merely infer their existence? These are the kinds of questions which we have to deal with.

Secondly, the issue is not whether or not there are in fact sense-impressions, images, feelings, mental acts, and the like. Of course there are. But given that there are these entities, given also that there are perceptual objects, how can we show that the arguments of the idealist do not lead to his conclusions? Lately, some philosophers have tried to discredit phenomenalism by denying that there are phenomenal objects. Others have argued against it more subtly by admitting that there are phenomenal objects, while insisting that these entities are not important or that one cannot talk about them. This kind of cure, however, is as bad as the disease. If realism could not be defended in any other way it would not be worth a defense at all.

Lastly, the relevant issues do not concern the existence and nature of physical objects—that is, the existence and nature of those entities which, according to the latest theory of physics, constitute the ultimate elements of the universe. That there are such entities cannot be denied. Nor can it be denied that perceptual objects consist of them. But in what sense a chair, say, consists of these physical entities and what these entities are precisely, are not questions that matter to the realism-idealism controversy.[1]

However, this last assertion does not agree with a definite trend in modern philosophy. Just consider what many modern philosophers have said about colors. The objective, real, or physical world, they claim, does not contain colors. "Out there" are perhaps atoms in motion or light-rays, but certainly no colors. And since they also contrast the objective, real, or physical world with the subjective, phenomenal, or mental world, colors could necessarily only exist in the latter. As a consequence, the realism-idealism issue took on a very special form. It was based on the dichotomy between the mental and the physical world. But this point of view, I submit, confuses the real issues. There are not only color-sensations and light rays, there are also colors. And colors are as objective and nonmental as light-rays or atoms in motion. From this point of view, the realism-idealism controversy centers around the dichotomy between color-sensations and colors, and not around the distinction between color-sensations and light-rays.

These brief remarks, I hope, may help to separate the relevant issues and arguments from the irrelevant ones. Perhaps, they merely explain why I shall discuss certain problems and not others. But even if the reader should disagree with my assessment of the philosophical situation, he will be in a better position to understand why I choose to approach it in the way I do.

DIRECT AND INDIRECT KNOWLEDGE

The Cartesian revolution led within a hundred years to the idealistic systems of Berkeley and Hume. A closer look at the

---

[1] For a discussion of some of these questions see Gustav Bergmann, "Physics and Ontology," *Philosophy of Science*, 28(1961):1–14; reprinted in Bergmann's *Logic and Reality* (Madison, 1964).

Cartesian philosophy reveals that it contained the seeds for this development.[2] A closer look also throws considerable light on the problems which confront the contemporary representative realist just as they confronted his Cartesian precursor.

Cartesianism is truly a philosophical turning point because it introduced a new ontology.[3] According to the Cartesians, there are two (created) substances which differ essentially: thinking is the essence of mind; extension is the essence of matter. Moreover, thought and extension are not merely modifications of mind and matter, respectively. They are these substances themselves: thinking is the substance of mind; extension is the substance of matter.[4] The two substances also have different modifications. Matter is modified by size, shape, and motion or rest. Mind is modified by volition, passions, sensations, and ideas. The two categories of substance and modification are taken to be exhaustive: everything there is, is either a substance or the modification of a substance.

Our knowledge or perception of material objects is explained in the following way. Sensations and ideas are caused by the interaction between mind and matter.[5] However, only ideas represent objects external to the mind; sensations do not.[6] Hence material objects and their modifications are known through *ideas* which *represent* these objects and modifications.

This representative account of perception was challenged by two arguments; the first ontological, the second epistemological. These arguments were thought to be decisive. Philosophies which developed out of Cartesianism were a direct result of the challenge and were designed to escape the objections.

---

[2] An excellent account of the Cartesian philosophy can be found in R. A. Watson, "The Breakdown of Cartesian Metaphysics," *Journal of the History of Philosophy,* 1(1964):177–97; and in his forthcoming book *The Downfall of Cartesianism, 1673–1712* (The Hague).

[3] When I speak of Cartesians, I do not have just Descartes in mind. I include such philosophers as Robert Desgabets, Louis de la Forge, Jacques Rohault, Pierre Sylvain Régis, Antoine Le Grand, and Antoine Arnauld.

[4] However, Descartes does not always identify a substance with its essence.

[5] This assertion invited the objection that two substances which are essentially different could not causally interact with each other.

[6] Our view is therefore rather similar to the Cartesian view. Our mental contents resemble Cartesian ideas.

The ontological argument was first advanced by Simon Foucher.[7] He pointed out that the Cartesian philosophy denies that there is any similarity between mind and matter and their respective modifications. Mental and material substances, according to the Cartesian, are essentially different. But if there is no *resemblance* whatsoever between ideas on the one hand and material substances and their modifications on the other, then ideas could not possibly *represent* material substances and their modifications. Hence there could be no knowledge of material objects if the Cartesian ontology were correct.

Faced with this internal inconsistency of their system, the Cartesians looked for a way out. The only one they saw was to reject Foucher's argument on the ground that ideas must be able to represent material things without having to resemble them. They argued that since ideas cannot resemble material objects and since we nevertheless know material objects through ideas, ideas must represent without resemblance. This kind of representation, they conceded, may very well be inexplicable. But to deny its possibility is to deny that God could make such knowledge possible. Foucher responded by pointing out that to speak of nonresembling representation is merely to use a phrase for something that is allegedly possible, without explaining in any way how it is possible. The Cartesians themselves conceded that such representation is unintelligible.

The key to this controversy is contained in this admission. Foucher charges, and the Cartesian admits, that nonresembling representation is unintelligible if one accepts the Cartesian ontology. Why it should be unintelligible can best be seen if we ask what possible explanations of the "knowing relation" the Cartesian ontology contains. Restricted by his ontology, the Cartesian can only give one explanation. The "knowing relation" must be the relation which obtains between a mental substance and its modifi-

---

[7] See Foucher's *Critique de la Recherche de la vérité où l'on examine en meme-tems une partie des Principes de Mr Descartes: Lettre, un Academicien* (Paris, 1675).

cations. No other relation or connection occurs in his ontology.[8] To say that a mind knows something can only mean that it has certain modifications.[9] What is known, is always *in* the mind in the sense of being a modification of the mind. The mind can thus know its own sensations and ideas (as well as passions and volitions). But it cannot know anything else, for nothing else is a modification of the mind. If we use the term 'direct knowledge' in order to refer to the relation which a mind has to its own modifications, we see that all knowledge of material objects must necessarily be indirect. The Cartesian problem is how to explicate indirect knowledge, given that ideas cannot resemble material things.

But why would this problem be solved, as both Foucher and the Cartesians seemed to assume, if ideas could resemble material objects? I think that the most plausible explanation is the following. If ideas resembled material things, indirect knowledge could be reduced to direct knowledge. For if there is a resemblance, an idea will share something with whatever it represents. Whatever is shared by the idea and the material object will be known directly by the mind, for it will not only be exemplified by the material object, but also by the mind which exemplifies the idea.

In the light of this consideration, we can reconstruct the ontological argument against the Cartesian position as follows. Since the Cartesian holds that minds and material things have nothing in common, indirect knowledge of material objects cannot be reduced to direct knowledge of ideas. But given the Cartesian ontology, only direct knowledge is possible. Hence, given the Cartesian ontology, we can know material objects neither directly nor indirectly.

We understand now why Foucher is justified in rejecting the way out proposed by some Cartesians. If the only "knowing relation" is the relation between a mental substance and its modi-

[8] Of course, not even this nexus was clearly recognized as an ontological constituent of the world.

[9] Compare Brentano's later view. Brentano's idealism has the same root as the problem which confronted the Cartesians: their ontologies contain no other relation than that between substance and modification.

fications, it is all well and good to claim that ideas can represent without resemblance, but there is no explanation of how such representation is possible. The Cartesian claims that something is the case, but he has not modified his ontology so that it can be the case. Nonresembling representation may well be a fact; but according to the Cartesian ontology, it is "unintelligible." The point, then, is not that there could be no representation without resemblance, but rather that such representation is not provided for in the Cartesian ontology. This is the important lesson of Foucher's objection.

Quite obviously, our view is not subject to Foucher's criticism. There is an ontological constituent, in our view, which connects mental contents with their intentions. The intentional nexus holds between contents and intentions, even though contents do not resemble intentions. But this solution of the problem did not occur to the Cartesians and their critics. Nor is this surprising. The ontological status of all connections has been suspect for the last few hundred years.[10] Even such recent defenders of intentionality as Brentano, Meinong, and Husserl were under the influence of the traditional prejudice against the existential status of relations. The critics of orthodox Cartesianism, at any rate, searched for a different way out. Some of them—we may call them Aristotelians—accepted the ontology of substances and modifications, but denied Descartes' assertion that mental and material substances have nothing in common. Others followed Descartes' innovation, but tried to modify the pattern of traditional metaphysics.

The Aristotelians claimed that knowledge of material things could not come through ideas, but only through *notions*.[11] Notions are not, as are ideas, similitudes of material objects. Rather, they are the very natures of material objects as these natures exist in the mind. Material things, as some put it, exist materially outside the

[10] Compare Frege, Russell, and Moore, on the one hand, with Brentano, Meinong, and Husserl on the other.

[11] Compare, for example, Sir Kenelm Digby, *Two Treatises, in one of which the nature of bodies; in the other, the nature of mans soul is looked into: in way of discovery of the immortality of reasonable souls* (London, 1665); and John Sergeant, *Solid Philosophy, asserted against the fancies of the ideists . . .* (London, 1697).

mind and immaterially in the mind. To know a material thing is not to have a likeness of it in the mind but to have its very nature in the mind. In brief, material and mental substances are sufficiently alike, contrary to the Cartesian view, to allow them to have common modifications. In this view, all knowledge is direct, for knowledge of material things consists in the direct knowledge of notional modifications of the mind.

Malebranche proposed a different view. He held that ideas were not modifications of the mind, as the Cartesians assumed, but were *in* God.[12] These ideas are neither mental nor material. Our knowledge of material things is mediated by ideas, but our knowledge of these ideas is not mediated by anything else. Knowledge of ideas is direct. This account breaks with the Cartesian ontology, for ideas, being neither mental nor material, neither substances nor modifications of substances, constitute a new ontological kind. But even this drastic break with the tradition does not solve the Cartesian problem. The direct knowledge of ideas in God remains "unintelligible." For Malebranche thinks of direct knowledge, in accordance with the Cartesian system, as exemplification by a mental substance, even though the ideas in God are not exemplified by mental substances.

Berkeley's break with the Cartesian ontology is even more radical. He denies that there are material substances and hence that ideas are representative. However, he does not deny that all existents are either substances or modifications of substances. Ideas, in particular, are modifications of mental substances.[13] For an idea to exist, it must be exemplified by a mental substance. Its *esse* is

[12] See N. Malebranche, *De la recherche de la verité où l'on traite de la nature de l'esprit de l'homme, et de l'usage qu'il en doit faire pour éviter l'erreur des sciences,* ed. G. Lewis (Paris, 1945).

[13] However, there are two interpretations of Berkeley's view on ideas. According to one interpretation, Berkeley modeled his ideas on Malebranchian ideas; according to the other, Berkeley's ideas are modifications of minds (as here suggested). For the first interpretation compare, for example, A. A. Luce, *Berkeley and Malebranche: A Study in the Origins of Berkeley's Thought* (London, 1934); R. Popkin, "The New Realism of Bishop Berkeley," in *George Berkeley* (Berkeley and Los Angeles, 1957); and H. Bracken, "Berkeley and Malebranche on Ideas," *The Modern Schoolman,* 41(1963). The second interpretation is defended in Watson's article and in Edwin B. Allaire, "Berkeley's Idealism," *Theoria,* 29(1963); reprinted in *Essays in Ontology.*

percipi. His view explains how knowledge of material things is possible, even if the only "knowing relation" is that which obtains between a mental substance and its modifications. Indirect knowledge is reduced to direct knowledge.[14] But the price Berkeley pays is high: material things, he must also hold, are nothing but collections of ideas.

What is the crucial step that leads to Berkeley's idealism?[15] Surely it does not consist in the assertion that an idea can only exist when it is perceived. This doctrine, as we have seen, was also part of the representative realism of the Cartesians. Since ideas are modifications of minds, they could not possibly exist apart from minds. Obviously, the crucial step consists in Berkeley's reduction of material things to collections of ideas. This step was taken, because the Cartesian ontology could only account for knowledge in the form of direct knowledge. Moore's refutation of idealism must be evaluated with this pattern in mind.

In his famous essay, Moore distinguishes between the sensation blue (object) and the awareness of this sensation (act).[16] He claims that the relation between an act and its object is not the same as the relation between a thing and its properties. The sensation blue, for example, is said not to be a "content" (property) of the act of awareness of blue. A "content," Moore agrees, could not exist apart from the act of which it is a "content." This is just a special case of the general principle that a property could not exist apart from all things of which it is a property. However, since the relation between act and object is not the relation of exemplification, Moore concludes that it is logically possible for an object to exist apart from mental acts. The sensation blue, for instance, could exist apart from the awareness of this sensation. Hence it is false to assert that for a sensation to exist, it must be

---

[14] But there arise certain well-known problems in regard to notional knowledge.

[15] We can distinguish between idealism and phenomenalism in the following way. Keeping in mind that there is a distinction between sensations and ideas, a phenomenalist reduces material objects to sensations, while an idealist reduces them to ideas.

[16] G. E. Moore, "The Refutation of Idealism," in *Philosophical Studies* (London, 1922).

perceived. This is Moore's refutation of the principle that *esse* is *percipi*.

Even if we agree that this refutation is sound, we may nevertheless feel that something else is needed in order to refute idealism. Sensations, Moore has shown, can exist unperceived. But how do we know perceptual objects? To deny that there are such objects to be known is not to refute but to accept idealism. Thus the question must be answered.

At the very end of his paper, Moore claims that he has shown that there is no question of how we are to get outside the circle of our own ideas and sensations. "Merely to have a sensation is already to be outside that circle. It is to know something which is as truly and really *not* a part of *my* experience, as anything I can ever know." This claim seems rather confused: merely to have a sensation (or idea) is obviously not to be outside the circle of our own sensations (and ideas). What Moore must have had in mind was something quite different. Moore seems to have argued that only mental acts are experienced. Hence only mental acts deserve to be called experiences. If so, then there can be no question as to how we get outside the circle of our own experiences, for to be aware of a sensation means already to be aware of something which is not an experience. To get outside the *mind* means to Moore to get outside our *experiences*. And we get outside the mind, in this sense, by having sensations. But even if we refuse to call sensations experiences, even if we refuse to say that they are *in* the mind, as long as we distinguish between sensations on the one hand and perceptual objects on the other, the question arises as to how we know perceptual objects.

In the very last paragraph of his paper, Moore hints at an answer to this question. He says that the peculiar relation of awareness is equally involved in sensing, perception, and reflexion. He claims, further, that this relation is such that its objects are precisely what they would be if we were not aware of them. According to this account, direct awareness is involved not only in the awareness of sensations, but also in our knowledge of perceptual objects. We are not only directly aware of sensations, but also of perceptual objects. In this paper, Moore accepts direct realism.

Whether or not this position is defensible is a question we shall lay aside. Let us ask instead what the structure of Moore's refutation of idealism is. On the surface it looks as if he had done nothing more than refute the dictum *esse est percipi*. And even this refutation is only carried out for sensations. If one looks no closer, one may conclude that his claim to have refuted idealism is rather exaggerated. For idealism, as we have seen, does not stand or fall with this dogma; even the Cartesians accepted it for sensations and ideas. However, this conclusion does not do justice to Moore's achievement. His achievement does not consist in the refutation of *esse est percipi*, but in the particular manner in which he attacks the dogma. He argues against it by introducing a certain irreducible relation of awareness, thereby rejecting the Cartesian ontology of substances and modifications. If we acknowledge the existence of such a relation, we have solved the ontological problem of knowledge contained in Cartesianism. But it was this problem which gave rise to the later idealistic systems. Moore's refutation really goes to the root of the traditional realism-idealism controversy. Direct knowledge, Moore argues, against the whole tradition, does not consist in exemplification by a mental substance (or a mental act).

Yet Moore also claims that our knowledge of perceptual objects is direct rather than indirect. Having added the irreducible relation of direct awareness to the Cartesian ontology, Moore discards another of its basic entities, ideas. Between a mental substance or mental act on the one hand and its object on the other, there intervenes no further entity, neither an idea, nor a mental content (of an act). Moore argues, quite explicitly, that there are no such contents of acts. Try as he may, he simply cannot find mental contents in his experience in addition to mental acts themselves and their objects. For this empirical reason, he rejects representative realism. But one may well wonder whether there was not a further reason in his mind. To understand this reason, we must turn to the second, epistemological, argument against Cartesianism.

In one sense, this argument is more fundamental than the one we have so far considered. It applies not only to the kind of representative realism defended by the Cartesian metaphysician, but to every view that can properly be called representative realism. It applies even if we assume that the relation between ideas and what they represent is not one of resemblance, but the intentional nexus. The argument runs as follows.[17] (1) In order to know that a certain idea (or mental content of an act) represents, we must know both the idea and what it represents. We must be able to compare the idea with its intention. (2) But in order to compare an idea with its intention, we must not only know the intention as well as the idea, we must also know it by means other than the idea. (3) However, the only way in which we can know an intention is by way of "its" idea. (4) Hence we cannot compare an idea with an intention. (5) Therefore, we cannot know that a certain idea represents a certain intention.

It is obvious that premise (3) is false, if knowledge of material things is direct rather than indirect. Direct realism is not affected by this argument. Perhaps this is one of the reasons why Moore, in his early papers, accepted direct rather than representative realism. Be that as it may, can a Cartesian answer this alleged refutation? If not, how does our version of representative realism differ from the Cartesian one, so that we can reject the argument?

According to the Cartesian metaphysics there is only one "knowing relation." This is the relation between a mind and its modifications. To compare two things with each other, we must obviously know them both. This means that any two objects of comparison must be modifications of the mind. Ideas can be compared with each other, for they are modifications of the mind. But in order to know a material thing (or its modifications), it would have to be a modification of the mind. Since material objects are not modifications of the mind, we cannot know them in order to compare them with ideas. In this way the epistemological argument refutes the representative realism of the Cartesian.

Does it also refute our version of representative realism? Per-

---

[17] This is Sergeant's formulation. Sergeant concludes from this argument that knowledge of material things cannot be by way of ideas, but must be by way of notions.

ception, in our view, involves the occurrence of a mental act with its content as part of a conscious state. Since the content is part of and not the object of a conscious state, it may be said to be *experienced*. Now assume, for the sake of the argument, that a comparison between two *perceptual objects* presupposes the occurrence of two acts of perception. If so, then it involves the experience of two mental contents. These contents, being experienced, are not the objects of their respective conscious states. They can therefore not be compared when we experience them. In order to compare them, they must not be merely experienced— that is, there must not occur two perceptions of perceptual objects—but different contents must be experienced, contents which intend the contents we wish to compare. This means that we can only compare a content with something else if the content is no longer a part of a conscious state, but rather the object of a conscious state.

Now in order to compare a perceptual object with a content, the perceptual object must first be perceived. This involves a certain content, say, f. Then the conscious state must shift. We must next focus our attention on the content f which was previously experienced. Hence there will now occur a second content, g, as part of the new conscious state which intends the content f. Since we can both perceive a perceptual object and inspect "its" content, although not simultaneously, a comparison of the perceptual object and its content is possible.

This description of the actual comparison shows where the argument against representative realism goes wrong. Premise (2) asserts that a comparison is only possible if the perceptual object is known by means other than a content. This premise, we now see, is false. What is true is that a comparison is only possible if the content to be compared is not merely experienced, but is the object of a further content—that is, the object of a conscious state. To *experience* a mental content is not to *know* it, but to know a perceptual object. The problem of the representative realist is not, if I may so put it, that of how to get a perceptual object into the mind (into the conscious state), so that it can be compared with some other part of the mind (conscious state). Rather, if there is a problem at all, it is how to get a content outside the mind, so that it becomes an object which can be compared with other objects. What is merely experienced is as such never known; what is known is never merely experienced. Any part of a conscious state can only be known through a different conscious state. The model of knowledge is not experience but representation.

The idealistic conclusion that we cannot get outside the circle of our own sensations and ideas is false, because it follows from a false premise. One asserts, first, that we can never *experience* anything but our own sensations and ideas. This premise we accepted in the very first chapter. But it is also asserted that to *know* something is to *experience* it. And from this false premise one then concludes that we can never know anything but our own sensations and ideas.

Quite a different argument from the one we just considered, but also directed against the representative realist, is the following one. In our explanation of how a comparison between perceptual object and content is possible, we claimed that it involved both the perception of an object and the inspection of a content. But how do we know, so the argument begins, that the experienced contents really represent the objects which we believe they represent? How can we be *sure* that we are really comparing this perceptual object with that content and not two other things? Of course, we can be *certain* that the contents we experience in perception and inspection are what they appear to be. But we cannot be *certain* in the same way about their objects. We cannot be *certain* that the objects are as we perceive them to be; nor can we be *sure*, as the example of hallucination shows, that there are these objects at all.[18]

Now it is clear that this argument is not directed against our

[18] This argument is not about a subjective feeling of certainty. We may have that feeling, even if we are wrong; and we may have it about logical as well as factual matters. Rather, by certain or infallible knowledge is meant a *kind* of knowledge—namely, knowledge which is not subject to mistakes. For example, perceptual knowledge and logical reasoning are not certain in this sense, for we all know that there are perceptual mistakes as well as mistakes of reasoning. The only knowledge which is held to be certain in this sense, is knowledge of our own sensations and ideas. In our terminology, certain knowledge is supposed to concern momentary conscious states.

view that a comparison between perceptual objects and contents is possible, but rather the view that perception and inspection are infallible. We might therefore be inclined to dismiss it rather cavalierly with the remark that the search for certain knowledge, the search for some elusive kind of absolute certainty, is simply a matter of the past. Those battles have all been fought; the proper distinctions have been drawn; and the rather obvious philosophical lessons have been learned. But in doing so, we would forgo the opportunity to draw attention to two interesting and important points.

First, behind the argument lurks one of the most powerful traditional reasons for denying the status of knowledge to anything that is not direct knowledge. The experience of contents, it is assumed, is certain. In regard to the mere experience of sensations and ideas no mistakes are possible. However, perception and inspection are not infallible. That alone sets direct knowledge apart from all sorts of indirect knowledge. Furthermore, if anything at all deserves to be called knowledge, it is infallible experience. Hence experience is the paradigm of knowledge, and not, as we have claimed, representation through mental contents. We only know what we experience; we do not know anything else. The quest for certainty leads in this fashion to a rather arbitrary redefinition of the term 'knowledge.' Only philosophers who do not realize the twin follies of skepticism and dogmatism can be easily persuaded to march through the gate which this redefinition opens.

In addition, however, the argument also fulfills the useful task of calling our attention to a certain laxity of expression which up to now we could tolerate because it was of no particular consequence. Previously, I talked about the comparison between a perceptual object and its content. But, obviously, what we compare is an *intention* and a mental content. And this fact has far-reaching consequences in regard to the objection just considered. This objection was based on, among other things, the fact that perceptual error is possible. But does the indubitable existence of such error show that we cannot be *certain* when we compare an intention with the content whose intention it is?

Assume, for example, that I mistake a table in front of me for a chair. There occurs then an act of perception whose content is expressed by the sentence, 'This is a chair.' Its intention is the possible state of affairs represented by the same sentence. Am I then mistaken about the intention of my act of perception? Obviously not. Similarly, in a case of hallucination. If I see a dagger in front of me when there is nothing at all in that place, I am not mistaken about the intention of my act of perception. Rather, I am mistaken in both situations because of the intentions which these acts of perception have. I am mistaken because my acts of perceptions have the intentions they have and not different ones. The fact that we can be mistaken about perceptual objects has no bearing on the question as to whether or not we can be mistaken about the intentions of our acts. A comparison between an intention and its content is possible, even if the original perceptual act was not veridical. Even in the case in which I see a chair when there is a table in front of me, I can compare the intention represented by the sentence 'This is a chair' with the content whose intention it is. Nor would such a comparison yield different results for veridical and nonveridical situations: in both cases there is the same intention as well as the same content. It "feels the same" to see a real dagger as to see a hallucinatory dagger. That is why we cannot distinguish between a veridical and a nonveridical perception on the basis of that very perception itself. That is why we can make perceptual mistakes.[19]

This analysis also shows that the following regress cannot occur. Someone may argue that in order to be certain that a particular content C_1 intends the intention I_1, one must compare C_1 with I_1. Such a comparison presupposes that a new conscious state with the content C_2 occurs, where C_2 now intends the previous content

---

[19] This is not intended to be an answer to the so-called arguments from illusion and hallucination. These arguments are discussed in the last section of this chapter.

C_1. But this means that in order to be *certain* that C_1 intends I_1, we must be certain that C_2 intends C_1. In order to be certain that it does, we must now compare C_2 with C_1. Such a comparison presupposes that a further conscious state with the content C_3 occurs. And so on.

The regress does not arise, because in order to be certain that C_1 intends I_1, we need not compare them. We saw that we cannot be mistaken about the intention of C_1. One must shift from a conscious state which contains C_1 to one which contains C_2, not in order to make *certain* that C_1 intends I_1, but in order to *compare* C_1 with I_1.

But a different objection may still be raised. It may be argued that even though we cannot be mistaken about the intentions of our mental contents, we can be mistaken in comparing an intention with a content. We cannot compare a content C_1 with anything while we experience the content. First, we must switch to a different conscious state. But such a switch involves *memory*. The content C_2 which intends C_1 must be the content of an act of memory. But memory is not infallible. Hence any *comparison* which is based on memory is not infallible. Thus we may be mistaken in our comparison.

The best way to answer this objection is to grant its point. Memory is indeed not infallible; nor is, therefore, any comparison which is based on memory.[20] But I have never claimed that the comparison between an intention and its mental content is infallible; I merely claimed that such a comparison is possible. The objection, if it is to apply to the latter claim, must therefore contain a further, hidden, premise to the effect that nothing short of an infallible comparison deserves to be called a comparison. However, this premise, like the one mentioned earlier that only certain knowledge deserves to be called knowledge, seems to me unacceptable.

So far, we have considered some of the traditional objections against the kind of representative realism we wish to defend. But we have as yet not discussed the most formidable idealistic argu-

[20] Compare our discussion in the last chapter.

ments against realism—namely, the so-called arguments from illusion and hallucination. However, discussion of these arguments and the problems connected with them presupposes a somewhat lengthy preparation. We must first clarify in considerable detail the difference between phenomenal and perceptual things. This in turn will force us to touch upon some purely ontological issues.

PERCEPTUAL AND PHENOMENAL OBJECTS

Consider the following argument for phenomenalism.[21] All perceptual objects are *continuants*. They have a *duration* and may *change* their properties while they last. On the other hand, all sense-impressions are *momentary* entities. They undergo no change while they last. Now a certain perceptual object A, being a continuant, may change its color from green to red and hence be green at one time and not green at another. Obviously we cannot describe this situation by the sentence 'A is green and A is not green.' The only *prima facie* satisfactory description introduces time in the form of absolute moments: 'A is green at t_1 and not green at t_2.' [22] Therefore, if one holds that perceptual objects are unanalyzable continuants, one must introduce absolute moments in order to describe without contradiction a changing perceptual object. Hence one is committed to hold that time is *absolute*. But time is *relational*. It follows that perceptual objects cannot be unanalyzable continuants. They must consist of momentary entities which undergo no change while they last. A perceptual object must consist of a series of momentary sense-impressions. The perceptual object A, for example, must consist of at least two sense-impressions, a and b, the first of which is green, the second of which is red; and a occurs earlier than b.

Let us assume, for the sake of discussion, that a philosopher who starts his analysis with unanalyzable continuants will in fact be committed to absolute time. Let us further assume that time is

[21] See Bergmann, *Meaning and Existence* (Madison, 1960), pp. 182–88, and 230–39. However, compare also his different approach in *Logic and Reality*, especially the last chapter.

[22] One can, of course, introduce tenses. But this creates ontological problems of a different kind.

indeed relational rather than absolute. Even if we make these two assumptions, the argument outlined above does not prove that perceptual objects must consist of sense-impressions. If it shows anything at all, it shows that perceptual objects must somehow consist of series of momentary entities. But whether or not these momentary entities are sense-impressions remains an open question. *A* may indeed consist of two momentary entities *a* and *b*, but nothing forces us to identify *a* and *b* with sense-impressions, even if we assume that sense-impressions are momentary entities.

We must therefore distinguish between two quite different philosophical problems. The first of these problems concerns the nature of continuants. How can we reconcile the apparent fact that there are continuants with certain philosophical accounts of *space* and *time?* What is the nature of *change?* These two important questions arise in connection with the first problem. The second problem, structurally speaking, presupposes a solution of the first. It concerns the relationship between perceptual objects and phenomenal ones. Do perceptual objects consist of sense-impressions? If not, how are these two kinds of entities related to each other? These two are among those questions which arise in connection with the second problem. By keeping the first and the second problem apart, we shall be able to avoid some of the mistakes which invariably occur in traditional arguments for or against phenomenalism.

At the beginning of Chapter 3, I said that a green disk consists of a bare particular which exemplifies certain properties and relations. This analysis was offered against the background of the nominalism-realism controversy. In this context, my account was quite adequate. The problems of the existence and nature of universals do not depend on the problems of the existence and nature of continuants. Neither time nor space, I think, need be discussed in connection with the first set of problems. However, now that I am attempting an analysis of continuants, my previous account has to be supplemented.

A green disk is both a continuant and a spatial object. It lasts through time and is extended in space. One's ontological assay of such an object will therefore in part depend on one's ontological assay of space and time. What is the nature of time? What is the nature of space? A full answer to these two questions would require a separate book. I must therefore limit myself to a few important points. I must take certain preliminary answers for granted. For example, I shall take for granted that time and space are *objective* rather than *subjective*. This leaves us with the second traditional dichotomy between *absolute* and *relative* space and time. According to the relational view, the temporal and spatial entities of the world are relations which hold between nontemporal and nonspatial entities. According to the absolute position, time and space consist of nonrelational entities. I shall at first only consider one of the many possible relational views and one of the many possible absolute views. Let us refer to the two views which I single out as *the* relational view and *the* absolute view.

According to the relational view, bare particulars exemplify temporal and spatial relations. For example, the particular *a* may be *to the left of* the particular *b,* and it may occur *earlier than* the particular *b*. In the first case, *a* and *b* exemplify a spatial relation; in the second, a temporal relation. Temporal and spatial relations are, of course, external relations. Bare particulars have no natures; hence temporal and spatial relations cannot be "founded" on the natures of their terms.

According to the absolute view, time and space consist of absolute moments in time and absolute places in space. In addition to these entities, there are also temporal and spatial relations. There must be such relations, because moments and places are ordered and this order can only be achieved through relations. Hence the absolute place *A* may be to the left of the absolute place *B*; and the absolute moment *C* may be earlier than the absolute moment *D*. Are these relations between moments and places external or internal? Many philosophers held, I believe, that they are internal.[23] However, I argued in the last chapter that there are no internal

[23] Compare, for example, Meinong's view that spatial relations are ideal relations between local determinations.

relations. If my argument is sound, the temporal relations between moments and the spatial relations between places must be external relations. But this means that absolute moments and absolute places must be bare entities; they cannot have natures.

Having narrowed down the field of possible views in this fashion, we shall now turn to the question of how to analyze continuants. But let us, for the moment, disregard certain questions about space. With this restriction in mind, consider the following four views.

(1) If one began with the assumption that time is relational, one could hold that a perceptual object A consisted of a temporal series of changeless (momentary) particulars.[24] These particulars must be changeless, because otherwise one could give a contradictory description of them of the form 'a is f and a is not f.' Further, such particulars are held to *last* as long as no change occurs. If there is change—for example, if A changes from green to red—there also occurs a different particular in the temporal series which is A.

But what precisely is a changeless or momentary particular? It is clear that particulars *as such* cannot undergo any change. This is what we mean when we speak of *bare* particulars. We must mean, therefore, that one and the same particular cannot *exemplify* a certain universal at one moment and not exemplify this universal at another moment. With this fact in mind, we can distinguish among three different kinds of change. First, an entity may be said to have changed$_1$, if it exemplifies at one moment a nonrelational property f and at another moment does not exemplify f. Second, it may be said to have changed$_2$, if it exemplifies at one moment a certain spatial relation and at another moment does not exemplify this relation. Third, it may be said to have changed$_3$, if it exemplifies at one moment a certain temporal relation and at another moment does not exemplify this relation. Now a changeless (momentary) particular must obviously fulfill all three conditions: it must neither change$_1$, nor change$_2$, nor

[24] Compare, for instance, Gustav Bergmann, "Duration and the Specious Present," *Philosophy of Science*, 27(1960):39–47.

change$_3$. To see this clearly with respect to change$_3$, assume that there are two things which do not change their properties and which are not in space. Assume that the first thing lasts, while the second appears and then disappears. Even though the first thing changes neither its properties nor its spatial relations, we cannot hold that it contained one and the same particular a, while a second particular, b, appeared and then disappeared. For, if we hold this, then we get presumably a contradictory description: 'a is earlier than b and a is not earlier than b.' To avoid such a contradiction, a particular must be changeless in all three senses of 'change.'

But from this it follows that a particular can only *last* until another particular occurs. And this means that a particular cannot last at all, if time is relational. For, if time is relational, as we assume, there can be no *duration* unless at least one particular occurs later (or earlier) than another particular.[25] A particular cannot last, if I may so put it, because duration is generated by the occurrence of different particulars which exemplify the temporal relation of being earlier than (or of being later than). One particular by itself cannot last for even the smallest length of time; and if there occurs a second particular, there is no longer the first particular. In short, particulars must be *instantaneous* and not merely *momentary*—that is, not merely changeless in respect to change$_1$ and change$_2$. Particulars cannot have any duration. Hence it seems that if we wish to avoid the contradiction mentioned above and hold a relational view of time, we are committed to instantaneous particulars.

(2) The second view takes its cue from the first.[26] The latter holds, as we have just seen, that a particular lasts as long as there is no change$_1$ and no change$_2$. Now the second view introduces, first of all, the notion of an *event*. For example, A's being f or A's being to the left of B are called events. Then it claims that we can distinguish directly between different events. Finally, it asserts

[25] This is one explication of the assertion that change is the measure of time.

[26] Compare, for example, F. E. Dretske, "Particulars and the Relational Theory of Time," *The Philosophical Review*, 70(1961):447–69.

that temporal relations do not hold between particulars, but rather between events. It is argued that one must distinguish between different particulars on the basis of distinguishable events. A particular lasts as long as "its" event lasts. For instance, to distinguish between A's being (first) green and (then) red, one must assign different particulars to these two events. A's being green would involve the particular a, while its being red would involve the particular b. Since A's being green occurs earlier than its being red, one assigns the same temporal relation to the two particulars a and b.

There are at least two objections to this view. First, it assumes that there can be lasting events without change. But if time is relational, there can be no duration unless there are at least two events, one earlier (or later) than the other. This is of course the same objection which I raised against the first view. Secondly, the view holds that all particulars must be distinguished in terms of different events, while it can be shown that some events must be distinguished in terms of particulars. Consider, for example, the following situation. Assume that a thing A with the property f lasts while another thing B appears and then disappears. According to the second view, there are then at least three events: namely, A's being f, B's appearance (say to the right of A), and A's still being f. Furthermore, these three events are temporally related. Now, the first and second events are presumably distinguishable in terms of the spatial relation mentioned. But there is nothing that distinguishes the first from the third event. Yet, the proponent of the second view would insist that there are three events, and hence three different particulars.

It may be argued that the first event is distinguished from the third event because it occupies a different *temporal position*. But this explanation introduces absolute moments, and one of the purposes of the second view is to avoid a commitment to absolute time. Moreover, if there were such moments, temporal relations would have to obtain between these moments rather than between events.

It may be thought that events can be distinguished in terms of their *temporal relations*.[27] The first event, for example, would be different from the third event, because one occurs before the other. But how could the occurrence of a temporal relation differentiate numerically between two events, if its occurrence presupposes that there are at least *two* distinguishable events? If the first event is *otherwise* indistinguishable from the third event, we could not know that there were *two* events, and hence we would have no reason to think they might exemplify a temporal relation. Furthermore, if it were possible to distinguish numerically between entities on the basis of temporal relations alone, there would be no point to the second view; one would not have to introduce events as the basis for this distinction.

Events must therefore be distinguishable by themselves if the second view is to make sense. But we saw that the first event in our example could not be distinguished from the third event. There is only one way out: these two events must be numerically different because they contain different particulars. But this means that events must be distinguished in terms of particulars, and not conversely.

(3) The third view accepts absolute time (and absolute space). According to this view, the perceptual object A contains one particular which lasts through time. Time consists of a series of instantaneous moments which are ordered by the temporal relation of being later than (or of being earlier than). Notice that our objection against the lasting particulars of the first view and the lasting events of the second view does not apply to the particulars of this analysis. For, to say that the particular *a* lasts, means according to this analysis that *a* exists at any given moment of a *continuous* series of moments.[28] The objection mentioned above could only arise if it were claimed that moments themselves lasted for some time. Notice also that no moment can be numerically the same as any other moment—or, rather, two moments, presented to us at different times, are never numerically the same. This shows

---

[27] Dretske seems to have this possibility in mind. Compare the remark on p. 461 of his article.

[28] It does not matter for our purposes what kind of continuity may be involved.

that the question of numerical sameness cannot arise for *instanta-neous* entities. It can only arise if the entity under consideration has a duration.

According to the third view, particulars have a duration. They are continuants. One can therefore ask whether or not a particular presented at one moment is numerically the same as a particular presented at a different moment. One can also ask how one recognizes that one and the same particular was presented at two different moments. A brief reflection shows, though, that the recognition of particulars cannot be immediate or direct. Assume, for example, that you see a green disk at a certain moment. A little later, you see again such a disk. If the two disks look sufficiently alike you cannot tell whether or not the two disks are numerically the same unless you have some additional information. Hence you cannot recognize the particulars "in" the disks as being numerically the same or different. We may express this fact by saying that particulars are not recognizable as such.[29]

Now, the third view holds that the numerical sameness of *things* (perceptual objects) is to be explained in terms of the numerical sameness of *particulars*. Since we cannot establish directly that one and the same particular occurred on two different occasions, we must go one step further back: we need a criterion of numerical sameness for particulars. Traditionally, for "things," spatio-temporal continuity is accepted as a criterion of numerical sameness. Can we apply this criterion to the particulars of the third view? And what precisely must we mean by spatio-temporal continuity in regard to particulars?

Two things are obvious. First, if spatio-temporal continuity is to serve as the criterion of numerical sameness for particulars, it must be presented to us directly. It must not, in turn, depend on some other criterion. Second, the spatio-temporal continuity of a particular cannot be explained in terms of the repeated occurrence of the *same* particular. We cannot say that it obtains whenever one and the same particular occupies successive moments (and

---

[29] Compare Allaire's article on bare particulars.

places). For this would presuppose that we could recognize particulars as such.

Particulars differentiate numerically betweeen simultaneous things. How many things there are at a given moment depends on how many particulars there are at that moment.[30] How many particulars there are, though, does not depend on anything else. Thus we know *directly*, not on the basis of some criterion, whether or not there is at least one particular at a given moment. But since this is all we can know, on the basis of particulars alone, temporal continuity of particulars must be based on this kind of knowledge and on nothing else. One may therefore propose the following explication: *the* particular *a* is temporally continuous, if and only if there is a particular at any given moment of a continuous series of moments. The explication of spatial continuity is similar. We know immediately whether or not there is a particular at a given place for a continuous series of moments. We also know immediately whether there are successively particulars at any given place of a continuous series of places. In the first case we say that one and the same particular remained at a certain place for some time; in the second case, that one and the same particular moved from one place to another.

Let us interrupt this analysis of the third view for a moment, in order to round out the account. Up to now I have ignored certain complications which arise in regard to space. Let us briefly consider these complications. A perceptual object—say, a green disk—is, of course, a spatial object. It has spatial parts. One may, therefore, be tempted to say that it consists of a whole "volume" of particulars. I think that the general idea of this account is clear: a continuous volume of absolute places is filled with particulars. If the disk does not move, there will be a particular at every place of the volume for a continuous series of moments. On the other hand, if the disk moves, there will be successively particulars at every place of a continuous series of such volumes. How many things

---

[30] This is not quite correct. According to the third view, a spatial thing is really a volume of particulars. See below.

there are will therefore not depend, contrary to what I said a moment ago, on how many particulars there are at a given moment, but rather on how many such volumes of particulars there are at a given moment. Moreover, what kinds of volumes we will count as separate things will depend on the purpose we have in mind. For example, we may for certain purposes think of the green disk as consisting of two half-disks. But in order to avoid contradictions of the form 'a is to the left of b and a is not to the left of b,' one assumes that (absolute) places have no (spatial) extension. Just as moments must be instantaneous, so places must be extensionless.

The numerical sameness of particulars can thus be explained in terms of spatio-temporal continuity. The latter must be explicated in terms of unrecognizable particulars, continuous series of moments, and continuous series of volumes of absolute places. We arrive therefore at the following version of the third view. (1) There are instantaneous moments and extensionless places. Time and space are absolute rather than relative. (2) Moments form a continuous series; places form a continuous volume. Hence there are also temporal and spatial relations. (3) There are unrecognizable particulars. (4) Numerical sameness of such particulars is defined in terms of spatio-temporal continuity. (5) There are (perceptual) things which consist of particulars. (6) Numerical sameness of these things is defined in terms of numerical sameness of particulars.

(4) The fourth view rejects absolute time and absolute space. Time consists of temporal relations among particulars; space consists of spatial relations among particulars. Particulars are thus *instantaneous;* they have no duration. Nor do they have any extension. Since, as we have seen, it makes no sense to raise the question of numerical sameness for instantaneous entities, this question cannot arise for particulars. One and the same particular cannot be presented at different times or at different places. Numerical sameness of things is explained, as before, in terms of spatio-temporal continuity. The latter is explicated in terms of temporally continuous series of volumes of particulars. This explication

is in all essential respects the same as that given by the third view. For example, a moving green disk consists of a temporally continuous series of spatially continuous volumes of particulars.[31]

If we compare this view with the third, we notice that it can account for all the facts which the third view explains. But it avoids the commitment to absolute time and space. Moreover, it does away with the lasting particulars of the third view. Numerical sameness of things is not explained in terms of numerical sameness of particulars. Rather it is explained directly in terms of instantaneous particulars and spatio-temporal continuity. Structurally, the instantaneous moments and unextended places of the third view correspond to the instantaneous and unextended particulars of the fourth. This suggests the following modification of the third view. Eliminate from it the lasting particulars. Instead, call the absolute places particulars. Let these places be instantaneous and let them exemplify not only temporal relations, but also "ordinary" universals like colors. The result of this modification is a view which is similar to the fourth view.

The fourth view can avoid the contradictions mentioned earlier. It agrees well with the notion that there can be no duration without some kind of change. Yet, as an account of phenomenal (perceptual) space and time it seems to have one fatal shortcoming. It claims that, in perceiving a lasting and extended perceptual object, one perceives a class of instantaneous and extensionless entities. Many philosophers reject this claim. They usually base their objection on a so-called *principle of acquaintance*. According to this principle, a philosopher must start from what he is acquainted with. The undefined entities of his ontology must not comprise entities with which he is not acquainted. But instantaneous and extensionless particulars are presumably not among the objects of our acquaintance. Hence they cannot be among the undefined constituents of the world.

Now, often there are added to the priniciple of acquaintance

[31] It follows from this view (as well as the third view) that in cases of interrupted observation, there is no inductive or deductive argument for numerical sameness.

two further principles which we have already criticized. The first holds that a philosopher must start from what he is *directly* acquainted with—namely, such things as sense-impressions, feelings, images, etc. All the undefined entities of his ontology must be mental and phenomenal objects. But it is clear that this principle merely expresses a phenomenalistic prejudice. If adopted, it can but lead to phenomenalism. Perceptual objects can only be constructions out of sense-impressions and similar entities. For this reason as well as others, we find the principle of *direct* acquaintance unacceptable. We hold that one is acquainted not only with phenomenal and mental objects, but also with perceptual ones. Generally speaking, every intention is an object of acquaintance. Every mental act is an act of acquaintance. The principle of acquaintance, in distinction to the principle of direct acquaintance, asserts that a philosopher must not introduce undefined entities which are not contained in any intentions.

The second additional principle holds that only simple (undefined) entities deserve to be called existents. All complex entities are merely logical fictions or constructions. For example, if it were possible to define instantaneous and extensionless particulars in terms of objects of acquaintance, these particulars could not be said to exist, since they would be mere constructions. Insofar as this principle implies that only simple entities exist, that there are only simple entities, we must reject it. An actual state of affairs, for example, though it is not a simple entity but a complex, has the same ontological status as its constituents. However, if the principle merely contains the recommendation that we call only simple entities existents, we have no objection to it, because it expresses only an apparent disagreement with our view.

The principle of acquaintance, in the form which we *can* accept, merely states that one must be acquainted with all the simple entities which occur in one's ontological inventory of the world. On the basis of this principle, certain philosophers reject instantaneous and extensionless particulars. They assert that we are not acquainted with such entities and hence that we can only introduce them as defined entities. If it is impossible to define them in terms of objects of acquaintance, there can be no such things. Before we evaluate this line of reasoning, it will be helpful to survey the traditional dialectic which seems to force us to talk about instantaneous and extensionless entities.

I said earlier that if we hold that temporal duration can be analyzed into temporal relations between particulars, we cannot possibly hold that particulars themselves have a duration. They must be instantaneous entities. Not only must they undergo no change$_1$ and change$_2$, they cannot even change$_3$.[32] The same point can be made in a slightly different form.[33] As long as our analysis of a certain duration D merely yields a series of "particulars" of smaller duration, our analysis is not complete. Time has not as yet been reduced to temporal relations between nontemporal entities. If it is to be complete, our analysis must end with terms that are not durations but are related to each other by temporal relations. Hence particulars cannot have any duration: they must be instantaneous. And this same conclusion also seems to follow as long as we try to avoid contradictions of the form 'a is earlier than b and a is not earlier than b.' But if these arguments are sound, they show that the relational view of time must always be open to the objection based upon the principle of acquaintance. The relational view requires that particulars are instantaneous. Yet we are presumably not acquainted with instantaneous entities.

On the other hand, we could assume that there are particulars which have durations. This assumption yields a fifth view. Durations are (undefined) properties of (at least some) particulars. Stressing the fact that according to the fifth view some undefined temporal entities are not relations, one may wish to call this view absolute rather than relative. On the other hand, stressing the fact that none of the temporal entities could exist without particulars, one may wish to emphasize that it is not absolute in one historically important sense of the term. At any rate, this view seems to

[32] Similar considerations hold for space: according to the relational view, particulars cannot have any extension.

[33] Compare Bertrand Russell, *Our Knowledge of the External World* (London, reprinted 1952), p. 158.

take care of the phenomenal facts: (many) particulars are not instantaneous (and extensionless) entities, but have durations (and extensions). However, we saw that the fifth view seems to clash with the attempt to get rid of the bothersome contradictions and the principle that there can be no duration without change.

At this point, one could attempt to reconcile the view that particulars are instantaneous with the view that we are not acquainted with instantaneous entities in the following way. One could try to *define* instantaneous entities in terms of entities with a finite duration.[34] If such a definition were possible, one could say that things consist of instantaneous particulars, even though one is not acquainted with such particulars. The principle of acquaintance would not be violated, because instantaneous particulars are defined in terms of things with observable durations. However, a definition of instants in terms of durations seems to be possible only if certain conditions are fulfilled; and it may reasonably be argued that whether or not these conditions are in fact fulfilled cannot be decided on the basis of "acquaintance." [35]

It seems to me that those philosophers are mistaken who claim that we are never acquainted with instantaneous entities. Most likely, they fail to distinguish between phenomenal duration on the one hand and physically measurable duration on the other. A flash of light, for instance, though it may actually last for a fraction of a second, has no phenomenal duration. It has no temporal parts; we cannot phenomenally distinguish between an earlier and a later "phase" of it. An act of perception, to cite another example, has no phenomenal duration. It is not a "process" that goes on for some time. These examples, I think, could easily be multiplied. But it is also true that many perceptual objects are not phenomenally instantaneous, but have durations. The green disk of our favorite paradigm certainly has a duration. I shall therefore main-

[34] Compare, for example, Whitehead's method of extensive abstraction. According to this method, space-time points can be defined as converging series of space-time regions.

[35] See Bertrand Russell's article, "On Order in Time," in *Logic and Knowledge,'* ed. R. C. Marsh (London, 1956).

tain that there are some things which are phenomenally instantaneous and others which have durations.

Furthermore, many perceptual objects have no phenomenal
extension or shape. A tiny white dot on the blackboard has no
extension. It has no spatial parts; we cannot distinguish between a
left and a right "half" of it. On the other hand, there can be no
doubt that many perceptual objects are extended. The green disk
just mentioned has a shape. Hence I shall also maintain that there
are some entities which have no spatial extension (although they
are spatial in nature) and others which are extended.

Earlier, we saw that as long as we talk only about instantaneous,
extensionless entities, no contradictions of the form 'a is to the left
of b and a is not to the left of b' arise. But now I have asserted that
there are particulars which have durations and shapes. How can
we reconcile this assertion with the earlier considerations? Moreover, does my view not clash with the notion that there can be no
duration without change and no extension without spatial diversity?

Let us begin with the last question. Every extended object, it
seems, has *spatial parts*. One cannot even imagine a perceptual
object of a certain shape which does not also have certain spatial
parts. Hence there can be no doubt that spatial extension depends
on spatial diversity. But if this is so, does it not follow that every
extended object *consists* of certain spatial parts? Does it not follow
that every extended object can be *analyzed* into a class of spatial
parts (and the spatial relations between these parts)? Do we not
once more arrive at extensionless particulars and spatial relations
as the ultimate constituents of so-called extended objects? Extension or shape as a kind of property of particulars simply disappears under analysis. The truth that there can be no extension
without related spatial parts seems to force us to reject the view
that shapes can be (undefined) properties of particulars.

In what sense do *categorial* entities *consist* of other categorial
entities? A certain fact, for example, consists of a particular, a
universal, and the nexus of exemplification. But none of these

three entities is a spatial or temporal part of the fact. Similarly for complex universals: green, for instance, is part of the complex property green-and-square. But it is obviously not a spatial or temporal part of that property. Furthermore, there are no complex particulars comparable to complex universals. All particulars are simple. Categorial entities thus form complexes either by entering into the nexus of exemplification, as in the case of states of affairs, or by being jointly exemplified, as in the case of universals. These are the only two possibilities.

Contrast this kind of categorial analysis with the analysis of a perceptual object into its spatial parts. Assume that there is a certain object A which has a certain shape. Then there is a particular which exemplifies a certain shape and other universals. A is said to consist of the spatial parts B, C, etc., if and only if the particular in A stands in certain spatial relations to the particulars in B, C, etc. (and the latter stand in certain spatial relations with each other). Thus even though A is said to consist of B, C, etc., the particular in A does not consist of the particulars in B, C, etc. If B is a spatial part of A, B has a certain spatial relation to A; and this means that the particular in B stands in a certain relation to the particular in A.[36]

It is true that every extended object has spatial parts. For whenever there is a particular of a certain shape, there are also particulars which stand in certain spatial relations to each other and to the first particular. But from this we must not conclude that an extended object can be analyzed into its spatial parts. Or rather, we must not conclude that 'analysis' here means the same thing as in the case of categorial analysis. It does not mean that an extended object consists of a class of (unextended) particulars which stand in spatial relations. Rather it means that whenever there is a certain set of categorial entities (namely, a particular which exemplifies a shape) there is also a further set of categorial entities (namely, particulars in relations), and conversely.

Similar considerations apply of course to temporal analyses. Whenever an object of a certain duration is said to consist of two

[36] Compare Bergmann, *Logic and Reality*, p. 289.

objects of shorter durations, there are three particulars which stand in certain temporal relations. Every object which has a duration does indeed contain temporal parts. But from this fact we must not conclude that a particular of a certain duration is really a class of particulars which are temporally related.

A sentence which states that a certain particular has a certain extension or duration is thus *equivalent* to a sentence which states that certain other particulars exemplify certain spatial or temporal relations. The spatial or temporal analysis of a perceptual object consists in the discovery of such an equivalence between two sentences. But a spatial or temporal analysis of an object always involves *two* states of affairs. Even though we say that one state of affairs (the object to be analyzed) *consists* of another state of affairs (the partial objects in relation), strictly speaking there is no reduction of the former to the latter. Shapes and durations are phenomenally simple properties of particulars. However, since as a matter of fact certain *equivalences* hold, it is possible for certain purposes to replace sentences which mention spatio-temporal properties of particulars by sentences which mention spatio-temporal relations among different particulars.

Next, we must ask whether or not we can avoid contradictions of the form 'a is to the left of b and a is not to the left of b,' even though we hold that some particulars exemplify (undefined) shapes (and durations). I think that the foregoing considerations show how we can avoid such contradictions. First of all, we shall use relational terms in a certain restricted way. For example, 'a earlier than b' must be understood to mean 'a wholly earlier than b.' No temporal part of a overlaps with a temporal part of b. Similar restrictions must be placed on other temporal and spatial relational terms. Now, as long as we talk only about particulars which exemplify these relations, no contradiction arises. But what happens when we wish to talk, say, about a green disk that lasts for some time, while a red disk appears and disappears? How can we describe this situation without getting involved in a contradiction?

The particular a in the green disk is neither earlier nor later nor (strictly) simultaneous with the particular b in the red disk. However, a temporal part of the green disk which contains the particular c is earlier than b; another temporal part of the green disk, with the particular d, is simultaneous with b; and a third temporal part of the green disk, containing the particular e, is later than b. Furthermore, c is earlier than d, d is earlier than e, and c, d, and e stand in certain temporal relations to a. In this manner we can describe the situation without contradiction. To say that one and the same green disk exists both before and after the red disk is to say that certain particulars occur before, simultaneous with, and after the red disk and that these particulars are temporal parts of the green disk. To say that they are temporal parts of the green disk is to say, as we remarked, that they stand in certain temporal relations to each other and to the particular in the green disk.[37]

To sum up: I maintained that perceptual objects contain bare particulars. Some particulars are extensionless and/or durationless, while others have durations and/or spatial extension. We are acquainted not only with the latter kinds, but also with the former. Whenever there is a particular which has a shape and a duration, there are also further particulars which stand in certain spatial and temporal relations. This fact constitutes the sound core of our pre-analytic conviction that there can be no duration without change and no extension without spatial diversity. I tried to show further that this fact does not lead to the conclusion that all statements concerning spatial and temporal properties of particulars can be analyzed into statements which only mention spatial and temporal relations among particulars. Finally, I proposed a certain type of analysis which does not lead to the paradoxes discussed earlier.

One last point must be cleared up. All particulars, I emphasized repeatedly, are *bare*. Most philosophers, though, claim that we are never acquainted with such bare entities. Recall, for example, Berkeley's discussion of the meaning of the term 'substratum' or Russell's claim that a bare particular is "an unknowable something

[37] Our view that certain particulars have durations (and extensions) does not, however, contradict the earlier observation that particulars are unrecognizable.

in which predicates inhere." [38] Put differently, most philosophers have claimed that the assumption that there are bare particulars violates the principle of acquaintance. Notice, however, that this criticism of bare particulars does not at all depend on whether or not particulars are instantaneous or have a duration, or whether or not they are extensionless or have a shape. Even if we assume that all particulars have a duration and a shape, the problem of whether or not we are ever acquainted with bare particulars still arises. It is the "bareness" of the particular that raises the problem, not whether or not such bare particulars have certain properties. Consider once more the example of the green disk. According to our ontological analysis, the disk contains a bare particular which exemplifies a certain shape and a certain duration. I can point out to you the shape and the duration, so the criticism goes, but I cannot point out to you the particular which exemplifies these two properties. We are acquainted with a certain shape and duration when we are acquainted with the disk, but we are not acquainted with something that is neither a property (of the disk) nor a relation (between the disk and certain other things).

I think that most philosophers who deny the existence of particulars are looking for the wrong kind of thing when they try to find the particular. They expect to find, I suppose, something very much like another universal or like another thing. Since they do not find either, they claim to have searched in vain for that elusive kind of entity called a particular. But, of course, particulars are neither universals nor states of affairs. One must look for them with a different mental set. Thus, as I remarked some time ago, one is never acquainted with redness alone or in isolation, but always with red things. This does not mean that redness always occurs together with certain other properties. Rather, it means that we are always acquainted with *something* that is red and not with redness. Nor are we ever acquainted with redness together with roundness and heaviness. Rather, we are always acquainted with *something* that is red, round, and heavy. In brief, we are

[38] See George Berkeley, *Treatise*, part 1, sections 16 and 17, and Bertrand Russell, *An Inquiry into Meaning and Truth* (London, 1948), p. 97.

never acquainted, I wish to claim, with just a "bundle of properties," but rather with *something* that has these properties.[39] And insofar as this is the case, we are presented with particulars. The shoe is on the other foot, as it were: the assertion that there are bare particulars does not violate the principle of acquaintance; what violates the principle is the claim that we are ever acquainted with a mere bundle of universals.

If we assume, then, that perceptual objects consist of particulars which exemplify certain properties and relations, the question arises as to how phenomenal objects differ from perceptual ones. The realist must insist that there is a difference. Perceptual objects simply do not consist of phenomenal ones. This is a common-sense truth which every realist must take for granted. It is as obvious as the fact that if there were no conscious states whatsoever, there would still be perceptual objects. It is as obvious as the fact that sense-impressions are "subjective," while perceptual objects are not. But even though we may take for granted that a perceptual object always differs from a phenomenal one, the precise nature of this difference is not easy to discern in every case.

Two things may differ only numerically, or they may differ in their properties and relations as well. In the first case, they consist of different particulars; in the second case, they differ in having different properties and/or relations too. On the other hand, two particulars can only differ numerically; two different simple properties can only differ qualitatively. Keeping these facts in mind, we see immediately that a certain perceptual object P and a certain phenomenal object O cannot differ because they contain different *kinds* of particulars. They differ numerically, they are two rather than one, because they contain different particulars. The sense-impression which we experience when we perceive the perceptual object P is numerically different from P. It differs from P as one green disk differs from another one. The oval-shaped sense-impression which we experience when we look at the sun on a winter evening contains a different particular from the one

---

[39] Neither the analysis of a thing into its spatio-temporal parts nor a listing of a thing's many properties can yield a bare particular.

contained in the sun. The sun is not the sense-impression. There are two entities and not just one.

Earlier I distinguished between mental and nonmental entities. This distinction was based on an obvious qualitative difference. Mental—and only mental—entities have the two properties of quality and content. Mental and only mental entities are perceptions, rememberings, experiences, etc.; and mental—and only mental—entities exemplify those properties which I called mental contents. According to this distinction, mental acts are not only numerically different from phenomenal and perceptual objects, they also differ qualitatively from the latter. Is there a similar obvious qualitative difference between sense-impressions and perceptual objects?

In fact, many phenomenal objects have qualities which are never exemplified by perceptual objects. A pain, for example, may be stabbing or dull, but no perceptual object has these same qualities. Of course, we often borrow the terms with which we describe certain phenomenal objects from those situations in which we describe properties of perceptual objects. But we do not for a moment confuse the properties of a pain with the properties of a knife. We do not ever mistake a pain for a knife. However, there is also qualitative sameness between certain phenomenal and perceptual objects. For example, visual sense-impressions have many properties which are also exemplified by perceptual objects. They have color, shape, and size just as perceptual objects have. The property green can be exemplified by a sense-impression or by a perceptual object. There are not two properties, one exemplified by sense-impressions, the other by perceptual objects. There is only one such property which can be shared by sense-impressions and perceptual objects. This does not mean, of course, that the color of a sense-impression which we receive from a certain perceptual object must be the same as the color of this perceptual object. The sense-impression may be green, while the perceptual object which we see is red. But colors are exemplified by sense-impressions and perceptual objects.

These considerations account for some obvious facts. First, they account for the fact that the distinction between mental and nonmental entities has almost never been denied by philosophers. That a chair does not consist of thoughts, acts of perceiving, acts of memory, etc., has seldom if ever been denied. Second, they account for the fact that certain phenomenal objects like pains have hardly if ever been confused with perceptual objects. Third, these considerations explain why many philosophers confused sense-impressions and perceptual objects. Since their obvious properties are of the same kind (for example, color, size, and shape), and since, moreover, numerical difference is easily over-looked in the case of perception, there has always been a tendency to reduce perceptual objects to sense-impressions or to reduce sense-impressions to perceptual objects.

If we turn from ontological considerations to epistemological ones, we notice the following difference. Phenomenal (and mental) entities are experienced, while perceptual objects are never experienced, but always perceived. As a matter of fact, acts with a certain quality intend phenomenal objects, but never perceptual objects. This is of course an epistemological difference between phenomenal and perceptual objects. But for that very reason, it may appear to many the most obvious difference between the two kinds of objects. For we all feel that there is a difference between the way in which a sense-impression is presented to us and the manner in which we are acquainted with a perceptual object. If we inspect a sense-impression the difference is somewhat blurred. The "immediacy" with which sense-impressions are usually presented to us when we perceive a perceptual object is not present in inspection. In this regard, inspection resembles perception. Yet, even in inspection there is a felt difference. When we inspect a sense-impression, we experience mental acts of experience; when we perceive a perceptual object, we experience acts of perception.

How well does our distinction between sense-impressions and perceptual objects agree with the facts of perceptual situations? How well does it stand up under dialectical probing? Let us test it by defending it against one traditional argument. Before I outline this argument, however, we must clear up one minor but strategic point.

According to our analysis, a penny may be said to have temporal parts. When you look at the penny at a certain time from a certain point of view, you cannot see all these parts. You can only see a certain temporal slice of it. Nor can you see all the spatial parts of the penny. You can only see one side of it. Nor, finally, can you perceive all the properties which the particular in the penny has at a given moment. You can only see, for example, that the side turned toward you is brown, that it has a certain size, and that it is round. In brief, from where you stand at a given moment, you can only see the top of the penny at the present time. No one, I think, will deny these obvious facts.

However, we are also inclined to say that when you see the penny, the "whole" penny is presented to you at once. In one sense of the term, it is not at all misleading to say that you *see* the penny even though only one side of it is turned toward you. We may follow common sense and distinguish between what you see and what you actually see (at a given moment, from a certain point of view). Now the sense in which you actually only see one side of the penny needs no further explication; we all know what that means. But we must try to explicate the sense in which you see the "whole" penny. I think we can explain this feature of perceptual situations in terms of certain perceptual intentions. When you see that there is a penny in front of you, the intention of your act of perception is properly represented by the sentence 'This is a penny.' It would not be properly represented by sentences like 'This is brown,' 'This is the side of a penny,' etc. Of course, there may occur further perceptual acts which have these latter intentions—or such acts may precede your perception that there is a penny in front of you. But when these latter acts occur, it would be more precise to say that you perceive, say, that this is brown or that this is the top of a penny. Your perception of the penny, at any rate, does not consist of these further mental acts. It consists of one single act, and this act has the intention represented by 'This is a penny.' To say that you see the penny is to say that there occurred this particular mental act. To say that you actually only see a brown round surface with certain markings on it is to say that at a certain time and from a certain point of view you could only make out these properties of the perceptual object before you. Notice, however, that what you actually see are not sense-impressions. The distinction between what you see and what you actually see is not a distinction between seeing perceptual objects and sensing sense-impressions. The top of the penny may look oval to you, but you see that it is round. When we ask you to describe what you actually see, we are not asking for a description of your sense-impressions. Rather, we are asking for a description of the perceptual properties of the perceptual object before you, as you can make out these properties from where you stand at a given moment.

Consider now one of the traditional arguments as formulated by Broad.[40] Broad claims that if we wish to adhere to the common-sense notion of perceptual objects, we *must* either accept the view that the objective constituents of some perceptual situations have certain properties which differ from and are inconsistent with those which they seem on careful inspection to have; or we must accept the view that one and the same surface can vary and remain constant in shape, size, and color within the same stretch of time. But this means, according to Broad, that we are tied down to three alternatives, each as distasteful to common sense as the others. We may try to keep the common-sense view that objective constituents of some visual situations are literally spatio-temporal parts of certain perceptual objects, which we are said to be "seeing." But, if we do this, then we must hold either (a) that this perceptual object can be both variable and constant in its properties during the same stretch of time, or (b) that the objective constituents of the visual situations can have properties which are different from and inconsistent with those which they seem on careful inspection to have. Or (c) we may drop the common-sense view that the objective constituents of a visual situation may

[40] Compare C. D. Broad, *The Mind and Its Place in Nature* (New York, 1925), pp. 158–83. The following sentences are almost literally from Broad's book.

be, and in some cases actually are, literally a spatio-temporal part of a certain perceptual object which we are said to be "seeing."

According to view (a), one and the same perceptual object can be, say, both round and oval, brown and red, within the same stretch of time. According to (b), the objective constituents of a perceptual situation can be, say, brown and oval, even though on careful inspection they seem to be red and round. According to the third view (c), the objective constituents of perceptual situations are not parts of perceptual objects, but rather sense-impressions.

Broad seems to think that perceptual situations are such that only these three views can reasonably be expected to agree with the facts. No other view will be even *prima facie* satisfactory. I think, though, that we cannot possibly accept any of these three views. We must reject the third view, because the objective constituents of *perceptual situations* are perceptual objects rather than sense-impressions. When we perceive the top of a penny, we perceive a spatio-temporal part of a certain perceptual object. But if we reject the third view, if we insist with common sense that we perceive perceptual objects rather than sense-impressions, we are allegedly tied down to the two alternatives (a) and (b). However, we cannot possibly accept (a), because one and the same perceptual object could not possibly have incompatible properties within the same stretch of time. No particular can be both red and brown. Nor can we accept the alternative (b). If the top of a penny turns out to be brown *under careful inspection,* then it is brown and could not possibly have any other color.[41] Since we cannot accept any one of these three views which, according to Broad, are the only alternatives open to us, we may well wonder whether Broad has described the perceptual facts correctly.

A penny, Broad says, is believed by common sense to be a round flat object whose size, shape, and color are independent of the observer, his position, and his movements. With this assertion we can certainly agree. Next, Broad claims that a certain observer

[41] It must be kept in mind that we assume for the time being that all perceptions are veridical.

who moves about while looking at a penny will certainly find that
the objective constituents of his successive perceptual situations
seem to vary in size, shape, and color, if he carefully inspects these
constituents. Furthermore, if we suppose that there are two observers, one standing still, while the other moves about, then the
objective constituents of the stationary observer's perceptual
situation will seem constant in size, shape, and color, while the
objective constituents of the moving observer's successive perceptual situations will seem to differ in size, shape, and color. From
these and similar cases, Broad deduces the conclusion which we
already mentioned: if we accept the common-sense notion of
perceptual objects and if we identify the objective constituents of
the various perceptual situations with the neutral and public top
of the penny, then we must hold either that the top of the penny
can be both constant and variable in its properties during the same
stretch of time, or that the objective constituents can have
properties which are inconsistent with those which they seem on
careful inspection to have. Or else we must give up the assumption
that the objective constituents of the perceptual situations are
identical with the top of the penny. We must give up, in other
words, the notion that we see the top of the penny.

It is not very difficult to spot the flaw in Broad's argument.
When Broad claims that the single observer who moves around
will certainly find that the objective constituents of his successive
perceptual situations vary in size, shape, and color, he must
identify objective constituents with sense-impressions. The same
thing happens when he claims that the objective constituents of
the perceptual situation of the stationary observer will remain
constant in size, shape, and color, while those of the moving
observer will vary in size, shape, and color. It is quite true that the
single observer will have different sense-impressions when he
moves around the penny. His sense-impressions will vary in size,
shape, and color. It is equally true that the sense-impressions of
the stationary observer will remain constant, while those of the
moving observer will vary in size, shape, and color. Hence, if we
identify these sense-impressions with the objective constituents of

the various perceptual situations, as Broad does, it is true that these objective constituents will remain constant or differ, depending on whether or not the observer is stationary. But then we must not identify the objective constituents with the top of the penny. The top of the penny does not change its size, shape, or color when we move around it.

However, if we do not identify the objective constituents of the perceptual situations with the top of the penny, we are allegedly forced to accept the third view—namely, that what we really see when we walk around the penny are sense-impressions; we do not literally see a spatio-temporal part of the penny. It is at this point that Broad's argument goes wrong. Broad seems to assume that sense-impressions are the only objective constituents of perceptual situations; they are the only entities which we really see. Hence, if these entities are not identical with the top of the penny, we do not really see the top of the penny at all. But his assumption is false. There are other objective constituents—namely, the various intentions of the various acts of perceiving. These intentions are identical with a spatio-temporal part of the penny.[42] What we see when we walk around the penny is the top of the penny—that is, we see that it has a certain shape, a certain size, and a certain color. What happens, in outline, is this. The single observer who moves around the penny experiences successively different sense-impressions. From one point of view, he has, say, a round and brown sense-impression; from another point of view, he has, say, a red and oval-shaped sense-impression. However, he perceives from both points of view a round and brown top of a penny. Even when his sense-impression is oval-shaped and red, his act of perceiving has the intention represented by 'This is round and brown.' Hence, what he perceives remains the same, even though his sense-impressions vary. Similarly, the stationary observer perceives a round and brown top of a penny and so does the moving observer. They observe the very same thing, even though the sense-impressions of the stationary observer remain constant,

[42] Strictly speaking, we would have to distinguish between seeing the top of the penny while walking around it, and seeing the penny.

while those of the moving observer vary. If we used Broad's term, we should say that the *objective* constituents of the successive perceptual situations remain constant, while their *subjective* constituents vary. The objective constituents are the shape, size, and color of the top of the penny; the subjective constituents are the shape, size, and color of various sense-impressions.

Broad's mistaken argument rests on the assumption that a perceptual situation consists only of acts of sensing and sense-impressions. Before he starts his proof that we must accept one of three views which are equally distasteful to common sense, he has already succumbed to phenomenalism. It is no wonder that all the alternatives he comes up with clash with our notion that we see perceptual objects which have properties independent of any observer. I think that no phenomenalistic account can possibly agree with our notion.

But even though our view seems to be satisfactory when we consider the straightforward facts of veridical perception, how can we reconcile it with the further fact that there are delusive perceptual situations? Phenomenalism, as we know, has always been defended by the claim that no alternative view can satisfactorily account for delusive perceptions.

DELUSIVE PERCEPTUAL SITUATIONS

Turning to the topic of delusive perceptual situations, we are confronted by two problems. Or perhaps I should say that we must approach the topic from two different directions. Approaching it from one direction, we take for granted that there are both veridical and delusive perceptual situations and that we can usually determine whether or not a given situation is delusive. The problem which we then encounter consists in giving satisfactory ontological analyses of both kinds of perceptual situations. When we approach the topic from the other direction, we assume that the ontological problem has been solved. The question that arises now is how we in fact determine whether or not a certain situation is delusive. I think that realists and phenomenalists alike give substantially the same answer to this question. Their disagreement centers around the ontological and not the epistemological problem posed by the occurrence of delusive perceptual situations.

What is the correct ontological analysis of a veridical perceptual situation? Phenomenalists inevitably arrive at their answer by first considering delusive perceptual situations. Indeed, were it not for the so-called arguments from illusion and hallucination, very few philosophers could be persuaded to embrace phenomenalism. What, then, is the correct ontological analysis of an *hallucinatory* perceptual situation? Assume that someone sees a pink rat while hallucinating. How are we to analyze this (momentary) state of affairs? A pink rat is most certainly not a constituent of the situation. That, quite clearly, is why we call it an hallucinatory situation. But the situation can and does contain (visual) sense-impressions. Sense-impressions, we know, can be experienced in the absense of the relevant perceptual stimuli. The phenomenalist therefore concludes that the only "objective" constituents of hallucinatory situations are sense-impressions.[43] Depending on what kind of phenomenalist he is, he may or may not hold, in addition, that hallucinatory perceptual situations contain certain mental acts as "subjective" constituents. But all versions of phenomenalism agree that hallucinatory perceptual situations contain no other "objective" constituents than sense-impressions, and that they contain therefore no perceptual acts as distinguished from acts of sensing.

Next, consider a veridical perceptual situation. Assume that someone sees a penny. How are we to assay this state of affairs? There seems to be no doubt that this situation does not merely contain sense-impressions. We all believe that it contains a penny or, at least, a temporal slice of a penny. We are fully convinced that this situation differs from the hallucinatory one in that it contains a perceptual object, while no such object is present in the hallucinatory situation. But the phenomenalist calls our attention to the fact that there is no phenomenal difference between veridical and hallucinatory perceptual situations.[44] A veridical situation,

---

[43] I borrow this use of the term "objective" from Broad.

[44] This does not mean that every hallucination is indistinguishable from a veridical process. We are talking here about perceptual *situations* as distinguished from *processes*. Coherence, for example, is one criterion that distinguishes delusive processes and veridical ones.

he argues, must therefore contain the same kinds of entities as an hallucinatory situation.[45] This means that it must consist of sense-impressions, certain mental acts, and nothing else. It means that a veridical perceptual situation cannot contain a perceptual object. No perceptual situation, be it hallucinatory or not, contains a perceptual object in addition to sense-impressions. This view, however, is so preposterous that the phenomenalist feels obliged to add one final twist to his argument. He assures us that there is after all some truth in our conviction that we sometimes see perceptual objects, for, as he explains, we do sense sense-impressions, and perceptual objects, contrary to our naïve convictions, are formed by series, or bundles, or families of sense-impressions. But this assurance should merely reinforce our suspicions in regard to the phenomenalistic argument. Perceptual objects, no matter how they may have to be analyzed, certainly do not consist of sense-impressions; and sense-impressions, no matter what kinds of families they may form, certainly do not yield perceptual objects.

The phenomenalistic argument from hallucination which I just outlined is quite familiar. I shall therefore not elaborate on it. Instead, let us try to get to the heart of the matter. No doubt, there are sense-impressions and acts of sensing. But plain experience also shows that there are perceptual mental acts. The mental act of, say, seeing a penny is quite different from sensing a brown round patch. Plain experience shows, moreover, that perceptual acts occur not only in veridical perceptual situations; they even form the essential ingredient of every hallucinatory perceptual situation. The man who sees a pink rat in his hallucination does not just experience sense-impressions. Nor does he inspect sense-impressions. He truly *sees* something. Every perceptual situation, be it veridical or not, contains a perceptual act. One of the crucial (factual) mistakes of the phenomenalist consists in his asserting that hallucinatory perceptual situations cannot contain perceptual acts, but (at most) mental acts of sensing.[46]

[45] Compare, for example, C. D. Broad, *The Mind and Its Place in Nature*, p. 156, and A. J. Ayer, *The Problem of Knowledge* (London, 1956), pp. 98–99.

[46] Of course, phenomenalists who acknowledge the existence of acts usually also hold that every perceptual situation contains an act of believing or judging. But notice that these acts intend in every case states of affairs which contain nothing

However, there is one standard objection to this partial defense of the realist's position. Is it not obvious, the phenomenalist asks, that perceptual mental acts must have perceptual objects? But if every perceptual act must intend a perceptual object, then the relevant perceptual act in an hallucinatory situation cannot be an exception. Whenever there occurs a perceptual act in an hallucinatory situation, there must be a perceptual object which the act intends. Yet, we all agree that an hallucinatory situation does not contain such an object. How, then, can an hallucinatory perceptual situation contain a perceptual act, when it is agreed on all sides that it does not contain the corresponding perceptual object? How, for example, can a certain perceptual situation contain a mental act of seeing a pink rat, when the situation does not contain a pink rat? The realist's view must be false, no matter how plausible it may appear at first, because from the fact that hallucinatory perceptual situations do not contain perceptual objects, it follows that they cannot possibly contain perceptual mental acts. Contrary to all our convictions, one cannot *see* a pink rat in an hallucination, because there is no pink rat to be seen.[47]

This line of reasoning, though used against the realist, can easily be modified in such a way that it apparently refutes phenomenalism. Consider, for instance, the following "argument from hallucination" which is designed to show (a) that hallucinatory situations cannot possibly contain (the relevant) acts of sensing, and (b) that therefore phenomenalism must be wrong. According to the phenomenalist, a so-called perceptual object A consists of the (complex) sense-impression B. The so-called perception of A consists really of the sensing of B. Now, an hallucinatory percep-

---

but sense-impressions. The question is not what kinds of further acts a phenomenalist may admit, but whether or not he admits acts that intend entities other than sense-impressions. Notice also that our realistic analysis agrees with the fact that veridical and hallucinatory perceptual situations are phenomenally indistinguishable; both contain acts of perceiving.

[47] I think it is quite obvious that this argument does not rest on the kind of reasoning now often employed in this context. One argues these days that someone cannot be seeing the pink rat, because we do not say of him that he is seeing it, but rather that he thinks he is seeing it. I shall not say what I think of this argument. Suffice it to say that the phenomenalist quoted above argues quite differently from the intentionality of acts to the existence of their objects.

tual situation, in which someone perceives the perceptual object A, does not at all contain A, as we all agree. It follows, therefore, that the situation does not contain the sense-impression B, for the so-called perceptual object A is nothing but the sense-impression B. Since the situation cannot contain the sense-impression, it cannot contain a mental act of sensing B. But this means that the hallucinatory situation can contain neither the relevant sense-impression nor the relevant act of sensing. Hallucinatory perceptual situations, contrary to what the phenomenalist asserts, do not consist of certain acts of sensing and certain sense-impressions. Moreover, recalling the fact that veridical perceptual situations do not differ phenomenally from hallucinatory ones, we must conclude that not even veridical perceptual situations consist of certain acts of sensing sense-impressions. The "argument from hallucination" thus refutes phenomenalism!

Of course, the phenomenalist will immediately protest that this refutation rests on a misunderstanding of his position. And, of course, he has a point; I did not advance the argument in earnest. I merely mentioned it in order to give the phenomenalist an opportunity to explain his position in greater detail. Taking this opportunity, he explains that the so-called perceptual object A does not consist of a (complex) sense-impression B. Rather, it consists of a temporal series or family F of sense-impressions.[48] In veridical perception, only some of the sense-impressions that constitute F are sensed at a given moment. Hence, to say that the perceptual object A is present in a veridical perceptual situation, is to say, speaking precisely, that certain sense-impressions are sensed and that these sense-impressions belong to the family F which constitutes the perceptual object A. To say that the perceptual object A is not present in an hallucinatory situation, even though it is seen, is to say, again speaking precisely, that certain sense-impressions are sensed, but that these sense-impressions do not belong to F. According to this account, certain sense-impressions are sensed, irrespective of whether the situation is

[48] For the following view compare, for example, C. D. Broad, *The Mind and Its Place in Nature.*

veridical or hallucinatory. But sometimes the experienced sense-impressions belong as a matter of fact to a certain family, while at other times they do not. Let us call sense-impressions of the first kind *real* and those of the second kind *wild*. If the sensed sense-impressions are real, a real (so-called) perceptual object is present; if they are wild, no such object is present: the situation is merely hallucinatory.

There is no doubt that this version of phenomenalism is not refuted by our so-called argument from hallucination. But by the same token, it clearly shows that a certain version of realism cannot be refuted by the original argument from hallucination. For surely, to assume that a realist must hold that hallucinatory perceptual situations literally contain perceptual objects is as naïve as to hold that according to the phenomenalist all the sense-impressions which constitute a perceptual object must be present in an hallucinatory situation. A perceptual object, I claimed earlier, has spatio-temporal parts; these parts contain perceptual particulars. We may therefore say that a *family* of such particulars "constitutes" a perceptual object.[49] In veridical perception, certain perceptual particulars are presented, and these particulars belong to a certain family. To say that the perceptual object A is contained in the veridical perceptual situation is to say, more precisely, that certain perceptual particulars are presented and that these particulars belong to a certain family. An hallucinatory perceptual situation (also) contains perceptual particulars. But these particulars are not part of a family—they are "wild." Hence perceptual particulars are presented in all perceptual situations. But these particulars are different and must be distinguished from the sense-impressions which also occur in all perceptual situations. The perceptual particulars are perceived, while the "sensory" particulars are sensed (or experienced). However, percep-

[49] Recall, however, what I said about ontological analysis. In case of a veridical perception represented by 'this is a penny,' the particular represented by 'this' is actual rather than possible; and so is the particular, if the perception is not veridical. However, in the former case, there are also certain further particulars which form a family, while in the latter case these additional particulars do not form such a family.

tual particulars presented in veridical situations belong to certain families, while those presented in hallucinatory situations are wild.[50]

This analysis of perceptual situations in terms of perceptual particulars bears a marked resemblance to the phenomenalistic analysis in terms of sense-impressions. Both accounts rely on the notion of wild particulars. Both accounts "analyze" perceptual objects into families of particulars. However, our view agrees with the fact that the world contains perceptual objects as well as sense-impressions; the phenomenalistic position does not. Our view agrees with the fact that perceptual mental acts are quite different in kind from mere mental acts of sensing; the phenomenalistic view does not. Our view takes account of the fact that even hallucinatory situations contain mental acts of perception; phenomenalism does not. And so on. Why, we may therefore ask, have some philosophers time and again defended a position which so obviously and outrageously clashes with the facts? One mistaken step, I think, accounts for the greater part of their confusions.

Whatever it is that a person may be said to see when hallucinating, it is accessible to him alone and it exists only as long as his hallucination lasts.[51] From this fact, many philosophers concluded that the hallucinating person must see sense-impressions. I suppose that they implicitly assumed that anything as "private" and as "mind-dependent" as the object of an hallucinatory mental act must be a sense-impression. But obviously, if the hallucinating person sees sense-impressions, the stage is set for the rest of the phenomenalistic story. We must therefore resist this very first mistaken step. We must insist that what a person sees when hallucinating are perceptual particulars as distinguished from sense-impressions. It is true that the pink rat seen in an hallucination is not a "public" object; it is not seen by other people in the room. It is also true that the pink rat would not have existed unless the hallucination had occurred. But from these facts we must not

---

[50] Gustav Bergmann has recently propounded a similar realistic view. Compare his "Realistic Postscript" in *Logic and Reality*.

[51] Compare A. J. Ayer, *The Problem of Knowledge*, p. 98.

conclude, as the phenomenalist does, that hallucinatory perceptual acts intend sense-impressions. These facts are perfectly compatible with our view that hallucinatory perceptual situations contain wild *perceptual* particulars. The perceptual particulars presented in hallucinatory situations are "private" and "mind-dependent." This is but another way of saying that they are wild. Yet, these wild perceptual particulars are quite different and must be distinguished from the sensory particulars which also occur in hallucinatory situations. In our view, certain perceptual particulars, though quite distinct from sense-impressions, do not belong to perceptual objects: unlike perceptual particulars which are (spatio-temporal) parts of a perceptual object, these perceptual particulars are not publicly observable and are not mind-independent.

A crucial mistake of the phenomenalist thus consists in his assumption that certain "private" and "mind-dependent" particulars must be sense-impressions. This mistake, I think, arises partly because the phenomenalist implicitly identifies sense-impressions with private, mind-dependent entities. However, this identification then creates a tension within the phenomenalistic system. In order to refute realism, the phenomenalist uses the argument from hallucination. From the argument, he concludes that the objective constituents of hallucinatory situations must be sense-impressions. He arrives at this conclusion because he takes for granted that private, mind-dependent entities are sense-impressions. He takes this for granted because implicitly or explicitly he believes that there are two kinds of entities—namely, private, mind-dependent ones and public, mind-independent ones; and he also believes that these two kinds are sense-impressions and perceptual objects, respectively. But once the phenomenalistic argument from hallucination has been used to attack realism, the phenomenalist must reverse his stand and try to convince us that sense-impressions are really not at all private and mind-dependent. He tries to convince us of this because he wants us to believe that a perceptual object is nothing but a family of sense-impressions. Since we all believe that perceptual objects exist when not being perceived, the phenomenalist argues that sense-impressions can and do exist when not being sensed. The phenomenalist tries to have his cake and eat it too. But he turns out to be wrong on both counts: he is wrong when he thinks that the particulars presented in hallucinatory perceptual acts are sense-impressions just because they are private and mind-dependent; and he is wrong when he thinks that certain sense-impressions must be mind-independent just because they are presented in veridical perception. The particulars presented in hallucinatory perceptual situations are not sense-impressions, but perceptual particulars; and sense-impressions are always mind-dependent, even those which are sensed in veridical perceptual situations.

I said that both our account and the phenomenalistic analysis make use of the distinction between wild and real particulars. This distinction must not be confused with the one I introduced earlier between actual and possible entities. Both real and wild perceptual particulars are actual entities; both kinds of particulars exist. But an actual perceptual particular may or may not belong to a family of perceptual particulars. If it does, we say that it is a real perceptual particular and that it belongs to a real perceptual object. On the other hand, if it does not belong to such a family, we say that it is a wild perceptual particular and that it is not part of a real perceptual object. Real perceptual particulars are publicly observable and mind-independent; and conversely: publicly observable and mind-independent perceptual particulars are real. On the other hand, wild perceptual particulars are not publicly observable and are mind-dependent; and conversely: a perceptual particular which is not publicly observable and which is mind-dependent is a wild particular. Hence to say of a perceptual particular that it is not real is not to say of it that it does not exist. And to say of it that it does exist, is not to say that it is real.

Earlier I defended the thesis that all mental acts are propositional. But this means that perceptual mental acts never intend just perceptual particulars. They always intend states of affairs. This is why I have been speaking of perceptual particulars as being presented rather than perceived. I wish to say that the entity perceived is always a state of affairs. But such a state of affairs is always a complex entity which may contain perceptual particulars. If it does contain perceptual particulars, I say that these particulars are presented through a perceptual mental act which intends a perceptual state of affairs. Consider, for example, a perceptual act whose intention is represented by the sentence 'This is a pink rat.' Assuming that this mental act occurs during an hallucination, the sentence 'This is a pink rat' represents a possible rather than an actual state of affairs. The perceptual particular presented and represented by 'this' is a wild perceptual particular—that is, it is not part of a certain family which, if there were such a family, would constitute a real pink rat. But even though the state of affairs represented by 'this is a pink rat' does not exist, the perceptual particular presented through the perceptual mental act exists. The complete analysis of hallucinatory perceptual situations rests thus on two main ideas: the idea that there are wild perceptual particulars (in addition to sense-impressions and real perceptual particulars), and the idea that mental acts sometimes intend states of affairs which are not actual, but merely possible.

We already noted that the phenomenalist makes use of the first of these two ideas by distinguishing between wild and real sense-impressions. However, he must also solve the problem of nonexistent objects as it arises for states of affairs. His distinction between wild and real sense-impressions alone will not do. To see this clearly, we must realize that the description of his position which I have so far given is not complete. The phenomenalist, I said, holds that the objective constituents of hallucinatory and veridical perceptual situations are sense-impressions. He holds further that the sense-impressions sensed in hallucinatory situations are wild, while those sensed in veridical situations are real. But the list of subjective constituents of perceptual situations cannot be exhausted by acts of sensing. Some kind of propositional mental act must also occur in every perceptual situation. Most phenomenalists hold that there occurs also a judgment, or a belief, or an expectation. For the phenomenalist does admit that a hallucinating person sees, say, a pink rat and does not merely see (sense) certain momentary sense-impressions. In other words, the phenomenalist admits that the notion of a perceptual object—that is, the notion of a whole family of sense-impressions—enters into the correct analysis of hallucinatory situations. He therefore holds that the hallucinating person does not just sense certain sense-impressions, but that he also believes (or judges, or expects) that the sense-impressions sensed belong to a certain family. Of course, this kind of belief (judgment, expectation) also occurs in veridical perceptual situations. But while the belief is true in veridical perceptual situations, it is false in nonveridical situations. In a veridical perceptual situation, the sensed sense-impressions do in fact belong to a certain family—they are in fact real. In the hallucinatory situation, on the other hand, the sensed sense-impressions happen not to belong to a family—they are in fact wild. In either case, though, the person believes that the sense-impressions which are experienced are real.

But this analysis leads to the familiar questions concerning what it is that a false belief intends. If the hallucinating person believes that the sense-impression S belongs to the family F, and if this belief is false, the act of believing must intend a state of affairs which does not exist (which is not actual, which is not the case). What does it mean to say *there are* such states of affairs? Can one hold that mental acts involve relations if one also holds that some intentions are not actual entities? These and other questions arise in the wake of the phenomenalistic analysis. They are not peculiar to our realistic approach. They arise whenever it is held that perceptual situations contain some kind of judgment or belief. And even though philosophers customarily distinguish between "presentations" and "judgments"—that is, between mental acts that present "things" and mental acts that intend states of affairs—they also as a rule insist that perceptual situations contain not only "presentations," but also some kind of propositional mental act.

So far I have only discussed hallucinatory perceptual situations. But philosophers usually distinguish between two kinds of delusive perceptual situations, hallucinations and illusions. I shall therefore add a few words about so-called illusions. I can be rather brief. An illusion differs from an hallucinatory situation in that the former contains real perceptual particulars, while the latter contains wild ones. However, the real perceptual particular presented in the illusionary mental act is either perceived as having properties which it in fact does not have, or it is perceived as belonging to a perceptual object (as belonging to a certain family) to which it in fact does not belong. For example, assume that someone (mistakenly) perceives that the perceptual object O has the property F, when in fact O does not have F. The content of his perceptual act would be expressed by the sentence 'This is F.' Now, the perceptual particular represented by 'This' is not wild but real, for it belongs to a certain perceptual object O. But this real particular happens not to have the property F. Hence, the sentence 'This is F' represents merely a possible state of affairs. Or assume that someone mistakes one perceptual object O for another perceptual object P. The illusionary perceptual mental act intends the state of affairs represented by the sentence 'This is a P.' In this case, as in the first one, the perceptual particular represented by 'This' is real and not wild; for it belongs to the perceptual object O. However, since it belongs to O and not to P, the sentence 'This is a P' is false. The illusionary perceptual act intends a possible rather than an actual state of affairs.

A few pages ago, I said that the correct ontological analysis of hallucinatory perceptual situations rests on two ideas: (1) the idea that there are wild as well as real perceptual particulars, and (2) the idea that mental acts can intend possible as well as actual states of affairs. We now see that the correct ontological analysis of illusionary perceptual situations rests only on the latter. To put it differently, the so-called argument from illusion does not refute realism; it merely shows that mental acts can intend possible states of affairs. This and only this is the conclusion philosophers should have drawn from the argument. And the so-called argument from hallucination does not refute realism; it merely shows that (in addition to possible and real states of affairs) there are wild perceptual particulars.

This concludes my defense of realism. Only a few words need to be added about the epistemological problem mentioned at the beginning of this section. In view of our previous discussion, the epistemological question can now be reformulated in the following way: How do we in fact determine (a) whether or not the intention of one of our perceptual mental acts is an actual rather than a possible state of affairs? and (b) whether the perceptual particular presented in a perceptual mental act is real rather than wild? The answer to both parts of the question is quite obvious. All we do and all we can possibly do is to check the various intentions of our mental acts against each other. We check one perception against another; we check our memories against perceptions and perceptions against memories; and so on. This is the obvious answer. Nor do the details matter, for on this point we share the general view of the phenomenalist. However, it is one thing to point out that this is in fact the only method we have in order to find out whether or not a perceptual situation is veridical; it is something else again to argue about the reliability of the method. Some philosophers claim that we can never be *certain* that a given perceptual situation is veridical. Others argue that we can be certain and often are. But in so arguing, they often try to prove much more than the facts warrant. Quite clearly, the existence of a certain perceptual act which intends a certain state of affairs never *guarantees* that this state of affairs is an actual rather than a possible one. It does not *logically follow* from the fact that a given perceptual act intends the state of affairs p that this state of affairs obtains. The fact that this perceptual act occurs is *logically compatible* with the fact that p is merely a possible state of affairs. It is therefore always *possible* that the intention p is merely a possible state of affairs. And since it is always possible that p is a possible state of affairs, it is not *absolutely certain,* in any given case, that p must be an actual state of affairs. I trust that I need not fill in any further verbal bridges. The connection between "absolute certainty" and "logical necessity" is quite transparent. Nor need I once more stress that one can hold that our method of determining which of our perceptions is veridical is contextual without having to hold at the same time the absurd view that therefore truth itself is merely a contextual matter. Having tried diligently to refute the idealistic arguments against realism, I shall hardly be suspected of having succumbed to the idealistic view that truth is relative.

INDEX

Abstraction: of universals, 66, 99–103; and concepts, 70; and sensory intuition, 70, 102–3; in Frege, 99–100; and common natures, 100–101; and perfect particulars, 101; analytic, 101–2; generalizing, 101–2; and mental acts, 102; extensive, 210

Ach, N., 7n, 10n

Acquaintance: with sense-impressions, 29–30; with substance, 58; and Brentano, 58; and perception, 61, 180; with universals, 66, 76, 215; and sensory intuition, 67, 69, 76; with exemplification, 78; through judgment, 79; and localization, 81; with particulars, 207–10, 214–16; principle of, 207–10, 215; direct, 208; and intentions, 208; and phenomenalism, 208

Acts, mental: 3–5, 12–13, 19, 22, 28, 39–59, 80, 216; and awareness, 3–4, 14–15, 17, 21; and seeing, 12; and objects, 15, 37–38; inspection of, 20, 22; as propositional, 25n, 30n, 78n, 82, 111; and intentions, 28, 219–20; and judgment, 30; and belief, 30; and relations, 39, 42, 46–47; in Brentano, 51–59; and universals, 71; and Frege, 98; and abstrac-

tion, 102; and thoughts, 107; and contents, 110–12; and truth, 113–14; and meaning, 135; and sensing, 226, 229

Alexander, S., 41n

Allaire, E. B., 45n, 61n, 187n, 204n

Analysis: ontological, 62; part-whole, 67; of acts, 110; categorial, 211–12; spatial, 211–12; temporal, 212–13; and equivalence, 213; of states of affairs, 213; of perceptual situations, 220–35

Analyticity: and sameness of meaning, 123–24, 126; explicated, 123n

Appearing terminology, 35–37

Aristotelians, 186–87

Aristotle, 14n, 17n

Arnauld, A., 183n

Attention: and inspection, 6, 19, 22–23; and observation, 6; and conscious states, 19; and perceptual objects, 19; nature of, 23; and sense-impressions, 31; and abstraction, 101; and contents, 123

Attributes: in Brentano, 57, 59; vs. universals, 57, 74; and mental substance, 58; and localization, 74; and perfect particulars, 74; and sensory intuition, 74